THE ALCOHOLIC MARRIAGE

THE ALCOHOLIC MARRIAGE:
Alternative Perspectives

Thomas J. Paolino, Jr., M.D.
Chief, Upper East Unit
Butler Hospital
and Assistant Professor of Psychiatry
Department of Psychiatry and Human Behavior
Brown University Medical School
Providence, Rhode Island

Barbara S. McCrady, Ph.D.
Chief, Problem Drinkers Program, Upper East Unit
Butler Hospital
and Assistant Professor of Psychiatry
Department of Psychiatry and Human Behavior
Brown University Medical School
Providence, Rhode Island

GRUNE & STRATTON
A Subsidiary of Harcourt Brace Jovanovich, Publishers
New York   San Francisco   London

Library of Congress Cataloging in Publication Data

Paolino, Thomas J, 1940-
    The alcoholic marriage.

    Includes bibliographies and index.
    1. Alcoholics—Family relationships.
    2. Alcoholics—Psychology. 3. Alcoholism—
    Treatment. 4. Alcoholism. I. McCrady,
    Barbara S., joint author. II. Title.
    HV5132.P36   362.8'2   77-14954
    ISBN 0-8089-1024-8

Grune & Stratton, Inc.
111 Fifth Avenue
New York, New York 10003

Distributed in the United Kingdom by
Academic Press, Inc. (London) Ltd.
24/48 Oval Road, London NW 1

Library of Congress Catalog Number 77-14954
International Standard Book Number 0-8089-1024-8
Printed in the United States of America

The introductory quote on page xi is taken from
Freud's *Introductory Lectures on Psychoanalysis* (1916–1917).
Volume 16, page 243, standard edition, published
in 1963 by the Hogarth Press in London.

For Anne and Denny
with deepest love

Contents

viii

Acknowledgments

While only the authors' names appear on the cover, the input and support from many people are essential to the production of a book. We want to acknowledge our debt to and our appreciation of the people who have helped us develop and produce our text.

Mr. Frank Delmonico, who is the Director of Administration at Butler Hospital, Stanley M. Aronson, M.D., the Dean of Medicine at Brown University Medical School, and Ben W. Feather, M.D., Ph.D., the former Chairman of the Brown University Department of Psychiatry and former Executive Director of Butler Hospital, have all had major roles in creating the working and scholarly environment at Butler Hospital and at Brown University Medical School which has provided us with the academic stimulation, time, and resources that have made this book possible.

Many of our colleagues and friends on the clinical and nonclinical staff at Butler Hospital, Brown University, and elsewhere have also provided advice, encouragement, and support throughout the writing of this book. We especially want to thank David Barlow, Ph.D., Edward Brown, M.D., Lawrence Erlbaum, Ruth Faris, M.S.W., Susan Furber, M.S.W., Tema Gouse, M.S.W., Barbara Lex, Ph.D., Richard Longabaugh, Ed.D., Paula Nannicelli, M.S.W., Robert Weiss, Ph.D., and our editors at Grune & Stratton for reviewing various parts of this manuscript and providing helpful and constructive feedback.

We also wish to thank our secretaries, Shawn McLaughlin, Katherine Dennis, and Deborah Robinson, who had the tedious and demanding task of typing the many drafts of this manuscript. Erika Schmidt, the librarian at Butler Hospital, helped us obtain a variety of literature that otherwise would have been inaccessible.

People to whom we would like to express our deepest gratitude, for reasons well known to them, are our spouses, Anne and Denny, our parents, Judge and Mrs. Thomas J. Paolino and Mr. and Mrs. James Sachs, our children, Pia, TJ, and Eric, and Rolf Arvidson, M.D.

We would also like to take this opportunity to publicly acknowledge the help that we have received from each other through honest editorial feedback, patient editing of numerous drafts, mutual support and encouragement, and sometimes some gentle nagging to help each other keep going and complete the manuscript.

The last but most important acknowledgment is to our alcoholic and nonalcoholic patients and their spouses: They inspired us to write this book by granting us the privilege to work with them in an attempt to help and understand them.

I do not wish to arouse convictions;
I wish to stimulate thought and to upset prejudices.
Sigmund Freud, 1917

1

General Considerations

The problem of alcoholism has always been particularly perplexing . . . whereas the social results of many other kinds of personality disturbances are only gradually apparent, the alcoholic is successful in involving his family and himself in a series of dramatic and distressing crises that demand immediate attention from the agency and community . . . why should these families of alcoholics hang together at all? What sort of people are these men and women who over and over are ready to fly apart and yet who remain inescapably bound? . . . so close is the interlocking between strengths and weaknesses that we should perhaps speak of the "alcoholic marriage," rather than the "alcoholic man". (Lewis, 1937, pp. 39, 44)

This book has five primary purposes, all of equal importance.

First, to present clearly *different* theoretical scientific perspectives of the alcoholic marriage. The single most influential and motivating force in writing this book was our concern that many mental health clinicians and researchers manifest profound sophistication in one perspective or school of thought, but simultaneously display only superficial familiarity with viewpoints alien from their own. If scientific truth about alcoholic marriage and human behavior in general is to be more than a matter of convention, convenience, or mutual consent among compatible observers, then serious students must possess a thorough knowledge of rival and alternative orientations.

Also, we believe that clinicians should operate out of some theoretical model or perspective of the alcoholic marriage. Any one or a combination of the four (psychoanalytic, sociological, behavioral, and systems theory) models discussed in this book is better than no theoretical model at all. Thus, a second goal of this book is to provide a choice of models which can be used alone or in combination with other perspectives to help clinicians organize their observations.

Although the only diagnostic category discussed is the alcoholic marriage, the third major goal of this book is for the reader not only to discover different perspectives about alcoholic marriages, but also to become acquainted with the different ways with which other forms of abnormal and normal human behavior can be conceptualized. This book is based on our firm conviction that:

A clash of doctrines is not a disaster–it is an opportunity . . . in the evolution of real knowledge it marks the first step in progress towards a victory. (Whitehead, quoted by Wallerstein, 1966, p. 222)

The fourth purpose of this book is to distinguish accurately the facts from the theories about alcoholic marriages, keeping in mind of course that the boundaries between facts and theories cannot always be absolutely defined.

Our final goal is to present the subject matter in an orderly style which illuminates historical perspectives on the evolution of thought and on the theoretical and empirical foundation on which the alcoholic marriage literature is based.

We define an alcoholic marriage as a marriage of a problem drinker to a nonproblem drinker. We are fully aware that there are many marriages in which both partners are problem drinkers; an in-depth review of these marriages, however, involves some different concepts and would detract us from the major goals of this book.

No book can totally avoid author bias, especially when the subject matter involves relatively new ideas still in a process of growth and not well tested empirically. We have written this book with the bias that all marital interaction is potentially comprehensible. Also, we favor a point of view best expressed as follows:

A person must have the help of at least one other person to become an alcoholic. He cannot become one by himself. Alcoholism cannot appear in a person apart from others, get worse without the help of others, or continue in isolation from other people . . . the alcoholic is virtually helpless, locked in by his illness. He cannot break the lock by himself, but neither can he keep the merry-go-round going unless others ride it with him and help him keep it going. (Kellerman, 1975, pp. 1 and 7)

We will focus our discourse on the wives[1] of alcoholics because the scientific literature on husbands is too sparse to warrant a comprehensive review (Bailey,

---

[1]Throughout this book we will frequently use the terms "spouse," "wife," or "husband," instead of the more cumbersome "spouse of the alcoholic," "wife of the alcoholic," "husband of the alcoholic." Any time the term spouse, wife, or husband does *not* refer to the nonalcholic member of the alcoholic marriage, then it will be clear to the reader from the context in which it is used.

1961; Corrigan, 1974; Fox, 1956; Lindbeck, 1972; Lisansky, 1957, 1958; Rimmer, 1974; Wood & Duffy, 1966). This sexual imbalance in the literature establishes restrictions of unknown severity; certainly, not all of the concepts discussed herein can be applied to both husbands and wives. For example, there is good evidence that female alcoholics are more likely than male alcoholics to manifest depressive episodes and suicide attempts (Schuckit, 1972); to have an alcoholic parent (Beckman, 1975); to marry a problem drinker (Kinsey, 1966; Lisansky, 1957, 1958; Schuckit, 1972); and to develop alcoholism in response to a definite and specific stressful life situation (Curlee, 1970; Lisansky, 1957, 1958; Wall, 1937); whereas male alcoholics are more likely to be "sociopathic" (Sugerman, Sheldon, & Roth, 1975; Winokur, Reich, Rimmer, & Pitts, 1970). It is hoped that husbands of alcoholics will be the subject of future conscientious research since reliable investigators report that the percentage of females among the American alcoholic population is somewhere between 15 and 50% i.e., 1.4–4.5 million people) (Block, 1964; Jellinek, 1960). There is, however, considerable conceptual overlap and blurring of sex differences; and in essence, we will present an overview of the literature of the alcoholic marriage and the nonalcoholic spouse, "on whom the alcoholic depends or from whom he[2] psychologically flees" (Clifford, 1960, p. 457).

Many alcohologists share our appreciation of the profound impact that partners of the alcoholic marriage have on each other's thoughts, feelings, and drinking behavior (Bailey, 1961, 1963a; Burton & Kaplan, 1968; Davis, Berenson, Steinglass, & David, 1974; Estes, 1974; Gliedman, 1957; Goldstein & Francis, 1969; Grant, 1929; Hersen, Miller, & Eisler, 1973; Kepner, 1964; Liberman, 1970; Mann, 1958; Miller, 1972; Miller & Hersen, unpublished manuscript; Steinglass, Weiner, & Mendelson, 1971; Sulzer, 1965; Ward & Faillace, 1970). All people living together and dependent on each other tend to influence each other, and it is not surprising that alcoholic marriages conform to this principle. It is important to emphasize that neither we nor the authors we cite believe that the nonalcoholic spouse should in any way be held to *blame* for the alcoholism. Influencing behavior is not tantamount to responsibility and confusion on this point often leads to unnecessarily bitter and destructive controversy.

Since the literature reported herein inadequately distinguished between "alcoholism," "alcohol abuse," "alcohol misuse," and "problem drinker," these terms are used interchangeably. The following definition applies to all of these: A problem drinker is someone whose drinking leads to the existence or imminence of a dysfunction as perceived by the drinker and/or significant

---

[2]The use of the word "he" does not, of course, imply that only men are alcoholics. The word "he" is used only for linguistic convenience.

others, including health professionals. This "dysfunction" may be in any one of several areas: (1) social, interpersonal, or vocational; (2) psychological, as manifested by impaired cognition and/or feeling state, including abnormal testing; and (3) physiological, including abnormal physical or laboratory findings associated with alcohol intake (Fowler & Longabaugh, 1975).

This definition is, of course, too loose for a researcher's purposes, but provides the flexibility needed for the clinician and encompasses the subjects of all periodicals and books discussed in this book.

THE PROBLEM OF ALCOHOLISM

An awareness of the magnitude of the destructiveness of alcoholism is necessary for full appreciation of our discussion of alcoholic marriages. There are an estimated 9 million men and women who are alcohol abusers in the United States today (Chafetz, 1971). This is 9% of the total drinking population 15 years of age or older (Cahalan, Cisin, & Crossley, 1969); however, it is critical to be aware of the fact that the effects of the misuse of alcohol extend far beyond the individual who misuses alcohol. For every alcohol misuser, it is estimated that five other persons suffer directly. This would mean that approximately 45 million Americans, more than 20% of the population, are negatively affected by the alcohol misuser. Although there are differences in the incidence of alcohol misuse in different age, ethnic, religious, occupational, and socioeconomic groups, alcoholism affects people in all walks of life.

Alcohol misuse can affect the individual's physical health, his ability to carry out his social roles, and his subjective state of well-being. The life span of the alcoholic can be reduced by as much as 10 to 12 years (Chafetz, 1971). Several studies have implicated excessive use of alcohol, especially when combined with smoking, in the development of cancers of the mouth, pharynx, larynx, esophagus, and liver (World Health Organization, 1964). Although it is difficult to separate the effects of smoking from the effects of heavy drinking, evidence suggests that alcohol and tobacco apparently have a potentiating effect in increasing the risk of developing cancers of these various systems (Rothman & Keller, 1972). A host of gastrointestinal, cardiac, skin, neurologic, muscular, hematologic, and metabolic diseases are related to the misuse of alcohol. Some of the most well known of these are Wernicke–Korsakoff syndrome, cirrhosis of the liver, esophageal varices, and alcoholic myopathy.

In addition to specific illnesses related to the misuse of alcohol, alcohol plays a major role in many forms of accidents and injuries. In one-half of all traffic fatalities, the victim has a significant blood-alcohol level (Chafetz, 1971). A study of 300 fatalities resulting from nonhighway accidents revealed that 58% of these people had been an alcohol abuser or alcoholic (Waller, 1972). It has been reported that 39% of persons injured in fights or assaults had blood alcohol levels at or above the .05 mg% level (Wechsler, Kasey, Thum, & Demone, 1969). Several studies have indicated that more than 50% of the offenders in criminal homicide cases had taken alcohol prior to committing the murder (Wolfgang, 1958). Also, one-third of suicide victims have a significant blood alcohol level (Robbins, Murphy, Wilkins, Gosner, & Kayes, 1959).

In addition to the many physical problems which the alcohol misuser experiences, he also has often lost or nearly lost many jobs, has been arrested more frequently than the general population, and has significant problems with spouses and relatives. The child of an alcoholic parent is more likely to become a problem drinker than the child of a nonalcoholic (Goodwin, 1971; Goodwin, Schulsinger, Hermansen, Guze, & Winokur, 1973). The important subject of the children of alcoholics is beyond the scope of this book; we refer the interested reader to the expansive discussion by Fox (1962) and the recent reviews by El-Guebaly & Offord (1977) and Ablon (1976). There is no way to measure the subjective suffering and pain which the individual alcohol misuser experiences as the result of his alcohol misuse nor can any statistic reflect the potential loss of the creativity of many of these people.

Finally, the economic effects of the alcohol abuse on society as a whole must be considered. A recent study (Berry, Boland, Larson, Hayler, Sillman, Fein, & Feinstein, 1974) estimated that in 1971 the annual cost to U.S. society for alcohol-related problems was over 25 billion dollars. These costs were broken down into several areas. The largest area, amounting to approximately 9.35 billion dollars, was the lost production of goods and services attributable to the reduced productivity of the problem drinker.

Health and medical costs incurred in the treatment for alcohol-related conditions were approximately 8.29 billion dollars per year. Included in these costs were expenditures for many types of health care, as well as for medical construction, training, and education. The third largest cost to society for alcohol misuse was 6.4 billion dollars related to motor vehicle accidents. Also included in the 25 billion dollars total cost were expenditures in the criminal justice system for crimes that were alcohol related, expenditures by the social welfare system, and the economic costs of fires that might be attributed to the misuse of alcohol.

MARRIAGE

A comprehensive discussion of marriage is not the primary task of this book. We should mention, however, that we believe a conjugal relationship to be the most rewarding and yet the most demanding of all interactions within our culture. Marriage is not simply a legal arrangement. Marriage is also a complex relationship involving emotional, interpersonal, familial, legal, vocational, physical, and spiritual dimensions that comprise the intricate fabric of human behavior (Hicks & Platt, 1970). Marriage is a voluntary, relatively permanent, exclusive, and goal-oriented relationship that is a source of great emotional security and a means for satisfying many human needs; but marriage is also an institutionalized relationship that engenders various degrees of bond or bondage and makes numerous demands on each spouse as a result of the mixing of four family systems: (1) the family of origin, (2) the family of procreation, and (3) the two in-law families. Also, a study of marital patterns can reveal valuable information about the psychodynamics of each marital partner which might not otherwise be so accessible. Ernest Jones' words on love apply equally to marriage:

No man's inner life, the core of his personality, can be comprehended without some knowledge of his attitude towards the basic emotion of love. Nothing reveals the essence of his personality so piercingly and completely as the gross, and subtle, variations of the emotional responses in this sphere, since few situations in life test so severely his mental harmony. (Jones, 1953, p. 98)

Statistical reports confirm the concept that the marital system is under much stress. Research indicates that 25% of married couples in the general population are unhappy with their marriage (Landis, 1963; Renne, 1970) and that 80% of married couples consider divorce at some time during their marriage (Elmore, 1974). There were 1,026,000 divorces among the general population in the United States in 1975 (U.S. Department of Health, Education, & Welfare, 1976). Although the marriage rate is decreasing, the divorce rate is steadily increasing and in 1974 the divorce rate was 50% of the marriage rate (U.S. Department of Health, Education, & Welfare, 1975). In addition, the number of children per capita not living with their biological parents as a result of divorce is progressively increasing (Plateris, 1970).

The demands on any marriage become especially severe when one or both partners have psychological weaknesses or are experiencing serious troubles. It is a tragic fact that alcohol misuse and a satisfying marriage are incompatible (Burgess & Cottrell, 1939; Dominian, 1972; Fox, 1956; Levinger, 1966; Straus, 1950; Terman, 1938). As we show in Appendix A alcoholics marry no less but divorce and separate more frequently than the general population. Because of the complex problems adherent in alcohol misuse, it can be said without fear of serious contradiction that every alcoholic's marriage is a tormented one (Al-Anon Family Group Headquarters, 1971). Also, the nonalcoholic spouse's presenting problems to the helping professionals are very frequently marital conflict rather than complaints about the partner's alcoholism (Cohen & Krause, 1971; Lewis, 1954). One study (Bailey, 1963b) has shown that at least 20% of applications to agencies for family service are associated with alcohol misuse. For these and other obvious reasons, a thorough understanding of the alcoholic marriage is a prerequisite for a comprehensive approach to the understanding, prevention, early detection, and treatment of the widespread and crippling disorder called alcoholism.

MODE OF PRESENTATION

Our book deals primarily with concepts rather than research design, although we have on occasion included a discussion of the specific methodological strengths and weaknesses of some studies. References are provided for many statements and we trust for all statements which elicit in our readers a desire to go beyond the ideas discussed herein.

The readers who might most benefit from this book are advanced clinicians and social agency people in the mental and community health fields where alcoholics and their spouses are so often encountered. We believe that an understanding of rival perspectives will help the clinician pick and choose those aspects of each perspective that can be most effectively applied by that specific therapist–patient combination in their particular settings. There are also other categories of readers for whom we have written this book, however. We expect that the formal (classroom) and informal students of normal and abnormal psychology will be attentive readers since we discuss a variety of theoretical concepts that may enlighten interested students of human behavior even if they do not clinically apply such knowledge. Furthermore, since we discuss most of the empirical research on alcoholic marriages, clinical researchers in both the alcoholism and nonalcoholism marriage field may be attracted readers. Finally, our book could be informative to alcohol abusers and their families, although such readers, if not formally schooled or trained in the area of human behavior, might struggle with some, but certainly not all, of the theoretical concepts discussed.

In writing each chapter, we have kept in mind that many of our readers might be well informed in one or more perspectives of human behavior but at the same time lack even the most fundamental or basic knowledge of the perspectives discussed in other chapters. This situation created a challenge for us to write each chapter so that it would not be oversimplified for readers proficient in that specific subject, nor too complex for those to whom the subject was new. We have tried to meet this challenge by using the alcoholic marriage literature to illustrate the perspective discussed while simultaneously presenting the various perspectives of human behavior as they relate to the literature. We have provided a mixture of generalities and specific examples so that each chapter will be of some educational value to each reader regardless of the reader's previous knowledge in that area. Even if the reader is quite familiar with a specific perspective of human behavior, we hope that the integration of the alcoholic marriage literature is instructive, especially since, to the best of our knowledge, there is no previous attempt to present the alcoholic marriage literature in this manner.

The format of this book is as follows: Chapters 2 and 3 contain an exposition of the disturbed personality hypothesis and the decompensation hypothesis, mutually relating psychoanalytically oriented concepts that dominated the early alcoholic marriage literature. We begin chapter 2 by discussing the psychoanalytic principles of the mind which form the foundation of the disturbed personality and decompensation principles. We provide the reader with a brief discussion of psychoanalytic perspectives of the mind so that the reader can fully appreciate the mentalistic approach of the psychoanalytic perspective in contrast to the sociological, behavioral, and systems theory approaches discussed in subsequent chapters which place little importance on the concepts of the individual mind (psychic apparatus).

Chapter 4 surveys the sociological stress theory perspective which is at variance with the psychoanalytic conceptualizations. After a brief description of the sociological perspective of marriage we discuss the pioneer alcoholic marriage research of Joan Jackson and some of the research subsequent to Jackson's introduction of the stress theory.

Chapter 5 discusses the relevant basic principles of learning, how these principles have been applied to the alcoholic marriage, and the status of research and concepts in the area of learning principles and alcoholic marriages.

Chapter 6 reviews the basic assumptions and principles of general systems theory. We then discuss how this general perspective has been applied to conceptualizing alcoholism and the alcoholic marriage. Specific research on communication approaches, transactional analysis, and general systems conceptions is reviewed.

Chapter 7 discusses the implications for treatment of the various findings about the alcoholic marriage. Specific emphasis is placed on the implications of the research findings reviewed in the preceding chapters for identifying client populations, issues to consider in assessment, and specific treatment techniques.

Appendix A contains an overview of statistical data on the percentage of alcoholics who never marry or marry then separate or divorce in comparison to the general population. There is also a discussion on statistics relating to date of marriage and onset of alcoholism. We believe that these demographic data are very relevant to this book but, so as not to detract from the alternative perspective format, we choose to place this discussion in an appendix.

Appendix B is a list and description with examples of the various "defense mechanisms" of the mind. Alcoholic marriage clinical material is used to provide examples. The defense mechanisms are important in order to understand the role of the psychoanalytic perspective in the alcoholic marriage literature.

Appendix C provides an expanded description of the concepts of one of the earliest and most influential systems theorists, Murray Bowen.

Appendix D provides an expansion of a description of many of the concepts of transactional analysis, which is described more briefly in the text of the systems theory chapter.

Of course, many, if not most, alcoholic marriage theorists do not sharply and perspicuously fall into one or the other of these perspectives, nor do the perspectives themselves always contain concepts that are alien to another point of view. However, the alcoholic marriage literature can be categorized in accordance with the chapters of this book, and we believe that this is a useful expository technique in reviewing the literature, as long as the reader bears in mind that various elements of each perspective unavoidably overlap to some degree.

REFERENCES

Al-Anon Family Group Headquarters, Inc. *The dilemma of the alcoholic marriage.* Cornwall, N.Y.: Cornwall Press, 1971.

Ablon, J. Family structure and behavior in alcoholism: A review of the literature. In B. Kissin & H. Begleiter (Eds.), *The biology of alcoholism* (Vol. 4). New York: Plenum Press, 1976, pp. 205–242.

Bailey, M. B. Alcoholism and marriage (a review of research and professional literature). *Quarterly Journal of Studies on Alcohol,* 1961, *22,* 81–97.

Bailey, M. B. Research on alcoholism and marriage. *Social Work Practice.* New York: Columbian Univ. Press, 1963, pp. 19–30. (a)

Bailey, M. B. The family agency's role in treating the wife of an alcoholic. *Social Casework,* 1963, *44,* 273–279. (b)

Beckman, L. J. Women alcoholics: A review of social and psychological studies. *Quarterly Journal of Studies on Alcohol,* 1975, *36,* 797–824.

Berry, R., Boland, J., Laxson, J., Hayler, D., Sillman, M., Fein, R., & Feinstein, P. *The economic costs of alcohol abuse and alcoholism—1971.* Prepared for the NIAAA under Contract #HSM-42-73-114, March 31, 1974.

Block, M. Latest on overdrinking. *U.S. News and World Report,* 1964, *56,* 50–56.

Burgess, E. W., & Cottrell, L. S. *Predicting Success or Failure in Marriage.* New York: Prestige Hall, 1939.

Burton, G., & Kaplan, H. M. Marriage counseling with alcoholics and their spouses—II. The correlation of excessive drinking behavior with family pathology and social deterioration. *British Journal of Addiction,* 1968, *63,* 161–170.

Cahalan, D., Cisin, I. H., & Crossley, H. M. *American drinking practices.* Rutgers Center of Alcohol Studies. New Brunswick, N.Y., 1969.

Chafetz, M. *First special report to the U.S. Congress on alcohol and health.* Department of Health, Education, & Welfare, Publication #(ADH)74-68, 1971.

Clifford, B. J. A study of the wives of rehabilitated and unrehabilitated alcoholics. *Social Casework,* 1960, *41,* 457–460.

Cohen, P. C., & Krause, M. D. *Casework with the wives of alcoholics.* New York: Family Service Association of America, 1971.

Corrigan, E. M. Women and problem drinking, Notes on beliefs and facts. *Addictive Diseases: An International Journal,* 1974, *1,* 215–222.

Curlee, J. A comparison of male and female patients at an alcoholism treatment center. *The Journal of Psychology,* 1970, *74,* 239–247.

Davis, D., Berenson, D., Steinglass, P., & Davis, S. The adaptive consequences of drinking. *Psychiatry,* 1974, *37,* 209–215.

Dominian, J. Marital pathology: A review. *Postgraduate Medical Journal,* 1972, *48,* 517–525.

El-Guebaly, N., & Offord, D. R. The offspring of alcoholics: A critical review. *The American Journal of Psychiatry,* April 1977, *134,* No. 4, 357–365.

Elmore, J. L. *Marriage: A sinister system,* The Carrier Clinic Letter, No. 35. Bell Mead, N.J.: Carrier Clinic, November 1974.

Estes, N. J. Counseling the wife of an alcoholic spouse. *American Journal of Nursing,* 1974, *74,* 1251–1255.

Fowler, R., & Longabaugh, R. L. The problem oriented record: Problem definition. *Archives of General Psychiatry,* 1975, *32,* 831–834.

Fox, R. The alcoholic spouse. In V. W. Eisenstein (Ed.), *Neurotic interaction in marriage* (chap. 15). New York: Basic Books, 1956.

Fox, R. Children in the alcoholic family. In W. C. Bier (Ed.), *Problems in addiction: Alcohol and drug addiction.* New York: Fordham Univ. Press, 1962, pp. 71–96.

Gliedman, L. H. Current and combined group treatment for chronic alcoholics and wives. *International Journal of Group Psychotherapy,* 1957, *7,* 414–424.

Goldstein, M. K., & Francis, B. *Behavior modification of husbands by wives.* Paper presented at the National Council on Family Relations Annual Meeting, Washington, D.C., 1969.

Goodwin, D. W. Is alcoholism hereditary: A review and critique. *Archives of General Psychiatry,* 1971, *25,* 545–549.

Goodwin, D. W., Schulsinger, F., Hermansen, L., Guze, S. B., & Winokur, G. Alcohol problems in adoptees raised apart from alcoholic biologic parents. *Archives of General Psychiatry,* 1973, *28,* 238–243.

Grant, J. M. Treatment of alcoholics. *Family,* 1929, *10,* 138–143.

Hersen, M., Miller, P. M., & Eisler, R. M. Interactions between alcoholics and their wives: A descriptive analysis of verbal and nonverbal behavior. *Quarterly Journal of Studies on Alcohol,* 1973, *34,* 516–520.

Hicks, M. W., & Platt, M. M. Marital happiness and stability: A review of the research in the sixties. *Journal of Marriage and Family,* 1970, *32,* 553–574.

Jellinek, E. M. *The disease concept of alcoholism.* New Haven: College and University Press, 1960.

Jones, J. *The life and work of Sigmund Freud* (Vol. 1). New York: Basic Books, 1953.

Kellerman, J. L. Alcoholism: A merry-go-round named denial. *New Hampshire Program on Alcohol and Drug Abuse Bulletin,* 1975, *25*(1), 1–12.

Kepner, E. K. Application of learning theory to the etiology and treatment of alcoholism. *Quarterly Journal of Studies on Alcohol,* 1964, *25,* 279–291.

Kinsey, B. A. *The female alcoholic: A social psychological study.* Springfield, Ill.: Charles C Thomas, 1966.

Landis, J. T. Social correlates of divorce or nondivorce among the unhappy married. *Marriage and Family Living,* 1963, *25,* 178–180.

Levinger, G. Sources of marital dissatisfaction among applicants for divorce. *American Journal of Orthopsychiatry* 1966, *36,* 803–807.

Lewis, M. L. The initial contact with wives of alcoholics. *Social Casework,* 1954, *35,* 8–14.

Lewis, M. S. Alcoholism and family: Case work. *The Family,* 1937, *18,* 39–44.

Liberman, R. Behavioral approaches to family and couple therapy. *American Journal of Orthopsychiatry,* 1970, *40*(1), 106–118.

Lindbeck, V. L.: The woman alcoholic: A review of the literature. *The International Journal of Addictions,* 1972, *7,* 567–580.

Lisansky, E. S. Alcoholism in women: Social and psychological concomitants. I. Social history data. *Quarterly Journal of Studies on Alcohol,* 1957, *18,* 583–623.

Lisansky, E. S. The woman alcoholic. *Annals of the American Academy of Political and Social Science,* 1958, *315,* 73–81.

Mann, M. *New primer on alcoholism.* New York: Holt, 1958.

Miller, P. M. The use of behavioral contracting in the treatment of alcoholism: A case report. *Behavior Therapy,* 1972, *3,* 593–596.

Miller, P. M., & Hersen, M. Modification of marital interaction patterns between an alcoholic and his wife (unpublished manuscript).

Plateris, A. A. *Increases in divorces U.S.—1967. Vital and health stastics.* Data from a National Statistics System, 1970, HEW Series 21, No. 20, pp. 1–18.

Renne, K. S. Correlates of dissatisfaction in marriage. *Journal of Marriage and the Family,* 1970, *32,* 54–67.

Rimmer, J. Psychiatric illness in husbands of alcoholics. *Quarterly Journal of Studies on Alcohol,* 1974, *35,* 281–283.

Robbins, E., Murphy, G., Wilkinson, R., Gosner, S., & Kayes, J. Some clinical considerations in the prevention of suicide based on a study of 134 successful suicides. *American Journal of Public Health,* 1959, *49,* 888.

Rothman, K., & Keller, A. The effect of joint exposure to alcohol and tobacco on risk of cancer of the mouth and pharnyx. *Journal of Chronic Diseases,* 1972, *25,* 711–716.

Schuckit, M. The alcoholic woman: A literature review. *Psychiatry in Medicine,* 1972, *3,* 37–43.

Steinglass, P., Weiner, S., & Mendelson, J. A systems approach to alcoholism. A model and its clinical application. *Archives of General Psychiatry,* May 1971, *24,* 401–408.

Straus, R. Excessive drinking and its relationship to marriage. *Marriage and Family Living,* 1950, *12,* 79–82.

Sugerman, A., Sheldon, J., & Roth, C. Defense mechanisms in men and women alcoholics. *Journal of Studies on Alcohol,* 1975, *36,* 421–424.

Sulzer, E. S. Behavior modification in adult psychiatric patients. In Ullman & Krasner (Eds.), *Case studies in behavior modification,* New York: Holt, Rinehart & Winston, Inc., 1965, pp. 196–200.

Terman, L. M. *Psychological factors in marital happiness.* New York: McGraw-Hill, 1938.

U.S. Department of Health, Education, & Welfare, National Center for Health Statistics. Annual summary for the United States, 1974. *Monthly Vital Statistics Report,* May 30, 1975, *23*(13).

U.S. Department of Health, Education & Welfare, National Center for Health Statistics. *Monthly Vital Statistics Report,* March 4, 1976, *24*(12).

Wall, J. H. A study of alcoholism in women. *American Journal of Psychiatry,* 1937, *93,* 943–953.

Waller, J. A. *The roles of alcohol and problem drinking, drugs and medical impairment.* Report to the Department of Health, Education, & Welfare, Environmental Control Administration, 1972.

Wallerstein, R. S. The current state of psychotherapy. Theory, practice, research. *Journal of the American Psychoanalytic Association,* 1966, *14*(1), 183–225.

Ward, R. F., & Faillace, L. A. The alcoholic and his helpers. *Quarterly Journal of Studies on Alcohol,* 1970, *31,* 684–691.

Wechsler, H., Kasey, E. H., Thum, D., & Demone, H. W. Alcohol level and home accidents. *Public Health Reports,* 1969, *84,* 1043–1050.

Winokur, G., Reich, T., Rimmer, J., & Pitts, F. N., Jr., Alcoholism: III. Diagnosis and familial psychiatric illness in 259 alcoholic probanes. *Archives of General Psychiatry,* 1970, *23,* 104–117.

Wolfgang, M. E. *Patterns in criminal homicide.* Philadelphia: Univ. of Pennsylvania Press, 1958.

Wood, H. P., & Duffy, D. L. Psychological factors in alcoholic women. *American Journal of Psychiatry,* 1966, *123,* 341–345.

World Health Organization. Cancer agents that surround us. *World Health,* 1964, *9,* 16–17.

2

Psychoanalytic Concepts
and the Disturbed
Personality Hypothesis

The disturbed personality hypothesis (DPH) was the first attempt to conceptualize the alcoholic marriage (Bailey, 1961; Edwards, Harvey, & Whitehead, 1973).

The DPH focuses on the mind of the spouse and proposes that, to a greater or lesser extent, the spouse of an alcoholic is characteristically a barely compensated, interpersonally restricted, insecure, outwardly dominant, but deeply dependent excessively anxious, sexually inadequate, guilt ridden, and abnormally angry woman with pathogenic childhood experiences.

PSYCHOANALYTIC PERSPECTIVES OF THE MIND
UPON WHICH THE DISTURBED PERSONALITY
HYPOTHESIS IS BASED

Before discussing the DPH literature [and its related decompensation hypothesis (DH) literature] in detail, it is necessary for the reader to have some understanding of the psychoanalytic view of the mind. Only after grasping these basic concepts will the reader understand the origin of the DPH.

Throughout this book we will be using such terms as "mind," "mind oriented," "mentalistic," and "psychic apparatus." All of these terms refer to the following definition of "mind": The mind is a characterization of mental processes that function in specific and identifiable ways. This mind is, of course, an anthropomorphism and does not concretely exist. The mind is, instead, an expedient and satisfactory shorthand for discussing the various abstract groups of psychic processes that fit accepted definitions based on specific common features which are relatively permanent, repetitive, and predictable (DeWald, 1972). The mind is theoretical, like the idea of atoms, since it is never directly perceived; however (according to the psychoanalytic perspective), the mind can be a concept of experiential value since it offers a logical interpretation of thoughts, feelings, and behavior that are manifested, for example, by the partners of an alcoholic marriage and that are otherwise incomprehensible.

Obviously, a thorough exposition of the psychoanalytic perspective of the mind is beyond the scope of this book. We believe, however, that a brief discussion of psychoanalytic mentalistic concepts is especially warranted, since to the best of our knowledge there has never been a published attempt to discuss the psychoanalytic principles as they relate to alcoholic marriage literature. Also, and equally important, the reader must understand the meaning of the psychoanalytic *mind-oriented* approach to the alcoholic marriage so that he can grasp the differences between this perspective and the views of the sociologists, behaviorists, and systems theorists discussed in chapters 4, 5, and 6. These latter theorists place relatively little emphasis on the psychic apparatus, but rather focus on the overt behavior of individuals or groups.

A restriction we will impose is a limitation on our discussion to "classical" Freudian thinking. Just as with all perspectives of human behavior, psychoanalytic theory does *not* consist of adherents in uniform agreement with each other's views. Many of Freud's closest followers have disagreed with certain parts of his theories of the mind but remain in enough agreement to be considered "Freudians." Other theorists, although fundamentally psychoanalytically oriented, have disagreed with many of Freud's basic concepts to the degree that they are loosely categorized as "neo-Freudian." Although it is tempting to discuss the various "Freudian" and "neo-Freudian" perspectives of the mind, such digressions would complicate this chapter by diminishing its uniformity and weakening the conceptual linkage which we will develop between psychoanalytic theory and the DPH. Therefore, all the ideas expressed in our discussion of the psychoanalytic perspectives of the mind are from Freud's writings or from authors writing to clarify Freud's ideas. If the reader wants to learn more about the other psychoanalytic schools of thought, we recommend the exhaustive reviews by Ellenberger (1970) and Munroe (1955).

The reader must remember that the concepts of the mind presented in this section are separated for the purposes of presentation, since in actuality all psychic processes are to various degrees constantly and simultaneously operating. Thus part of our task in this chapter is to explain the relevant psychoanalytic concepts which form the conceptual foundation for the disturbed personality hypothesis and its derivative the decompensation hypothesis. Our purpose is not to prove or disprove the psychoanalytic concepts in themselves but rather to show how they have been used by DPH proponents to support their hypothesis. The reader must keep in mind throughout this chapter that although the psychoanalytic principles are foundations from which the DPH theory evolved, the DPH literature is usually not *directly* associated with the principles themselves. It is only through a series of deductions that we have associated the DPH with psychoanalytic principles. *Although, as we will show, the DPH is founded on psychoanalytic principles and perspectives of the mind, the proponents of the DPH are not trained psychoanalysts nor scholars of psychoanalytic theory.* Rather, the DPH proponents are usually Freudian-*oriented* therapists who report their impressionistic accounts of clinic, social work agency, and private practice contacts and who rarely acknowledge their conceptual linkage to Freudian psychoanalytic theory. For many years, these well-meaning and conscientious clinicians have made a major contribution and have had a widespread influence on the thought and conduct of the people treating alcoholics and their spouses. Without exception, however, the DPH proponents are *not* major contributors to the psychoanalytic literature itself.

Freud's ideas about the mind, what it is, and how it works, began with a focus on the anatomy and physiology of the brain (Freud, 1950 [1895]) and extended to the spheres of psychopathology, psychology, and philosophy over an incredibly productive 44 years of writing. Freud's changing ideas about the mind do not sharply succeed themselves; however, his theories of the mind do roughly fall out into two basic categories, the *topographical* and the *structural,* that can be differentiated chronologically and conceptually. We believe that the bipartite division of Freud's concepts of the mind is a useful format to follow in our attempt to show the psychoanalytic principles underlying the DPH and so we will present each view separately. We expect our readers to remember, however, that the various elements of the two "distinct" views of the mind to some degree overlap and parallel each other and that many aspects of one view are not incompatible with the other.

The Topographical Perspective of the Mind

The "topographical" perspective of the mind is, by definition, that psychoanalytic conceptualization which describes the mind in spatial terms to provide an image of where certain parts of the mind exist with respect to other parts of the psychic apparatus. To assign a psychic topography to a mental event is to indicate "within what system or between what systems" (Freud, 1915a, p. 173) the mental event occurs. The topographical perspective of the mind concentrates on the concept that ". . . our psychical mechanism has come into being by a process of stratification" (Freud, 1950 [1892–1899], Letter 52, p. 223), and was derived in part from Hughlings Jackson's spatial perception of the nervous system as a group of psychical processes superimposed upon each other in a hierarchical order (Rapaport, 1960). As will be seen later, the concept of "stratification" is associated with accessibility to consciousness, a concept of major relevance to the DPH.

The topographical aspect of the mind is sometimes called depth psychology. It was in this spatial sense that Freud's first use of the word "unconscious" appeared (Breuer & Freud, 1895, p. 76). Thus, Freud's earliest assumption of the existence of unconscious mental processes was associated with a topographical exposition. As is discussed later, the concept unconscious has had a profound role in the creation and longevity of the DPH.

Since the topographical perspective of the mind was introduced in *The Interpretation of Dreams* (Freud, 1900), it is often erroneously assumed that the topographical concepts were derived mostly from Freud's investigation of dreams. Actually, it was Freud's psychological studies of the neurotic symptoms that led to the topographical theories (Arlow & Brenner, 1964):

> *Every time we come upon a symptom we can infer that there are certain definite unconscious processes in the patient which contain the sense of the symptom. But it is also necessary for that sense to be unconscious in order that the symptom can come about. Symptoms are never constructed from conscious processes; as soon as the unconscious processes concerned have become conscious, the symptom must disappear. Here you will at once perceive a means of approach to therapy, a way of making symptoms disappear. (Freud, 1917 [1916–1917], p. 279)*
>
> *By carrying what is unconscious on into what is conscious, we lift the repressions, we remove the preconditions for the formation of symptoms, we transform the pathogenic conflict into a normal one for which it must be possible somehow to find a solution. (Freud, 1917 [1916–1917], p. 435)*

In contrast to the topographical perspective, Freud's structural perspective of the mind conceptualizes the mind as consisting of abstract "structures" (thus the word "structural") which are not stratified in accordance with their relationship to consciousness. The structural perspective is discussed in more detail in a subsequent section in this chapter.

The topographical perspective proposes that the mind consists of the psychical system: perception *(Pcpt)*, memory *(Mnem)*, unconscious *(Ucs)*, preconscious *(Pcs)*, and conscious *(Cs)*, which are essentially defined and placed by their relationship to the state of consciousness (see Figure 2-1). The arrows in Figure 2-1 indicate that the mind has a sense of direction and that psychic excitations usually travel from the sensory to the motor end. Thus, psychic movements begin with internal or external perceptual stimuli of the mind and terminate in a discharge of motor activity. The direction of psychic energy is reversed in dreams and other mental states. This reversal of energy flow is termed "regression" and it usually refers to a current of excitation flowing away

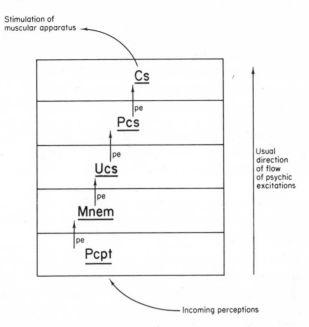

Figure 2.1   Schematic drawing of Freud's topographical perspective of the mind. The usual direction is the "progressive" direction as opposed to its opposite, "regressive" direction. The abbreviation "pe" stands for "psychic excitations." [Modified after Freud (1900). *The interpretation of dreams.* London: Hogarth Press, 1953, Chapter VII.]

from the direction of motor outflow. The direction of flow of psychic energy is, of course, of critical importance. For example, hallucinations and dreams result from a reversal of flow such that the stimulus of the perceptual system comes *from* the memory system.

The system preconscious is closest to consciousness and is a critical system in stimulating volitional movements of the system conscious. This transition from the system preconscious to the system conscious can result by a mere increase in intensity of the excitation or in increased attention by the system conscious.

In these earlier writings, (Freud 1900, especially chapter 7) Freud favored the idea of dividing the mind into the repressed and repressing. The system preconscious is the repressing system and has the *exclusive* role of preventing transmission of mental energy from the sensory end to the motor end of the psychic apparatus; accordingly, the system preconscious is located between the memory and conscious systems of the psychic apparatus, essentially functioning as a screen between the two poles of the mind. If repression fails, the psychic elements (i.e., the sexual wishes) in the system unconscious become accessible to the system conscious.

The system unconscious "has no access to consciousness *except via* the preconscious [italics in the original]" (Freud 1900, p. 514). In contrast to the system preconscious, the system unconscious is much less inclined to transmit to the next highest psychic layer. The system unconscious contains only sexual instincts (see the section on the id) and these drives conflict with realistic concerns of the system preconscious.

The system conscious is that part of the mind that provides us with awareness of both the external and internal world. Also, the system conscious is the site from which emerge the psychical innervations and stimulations of the motor system. Thus, the system conscious controls access to motility.

Relationship between the Topographical Perspective and the DPH

Since this book is about alcoholic marriages, the next logical question concerns the relationship between Freud's topographical perspective of the mind and the alcoholic marriage concepts and literature. The answer to this lies in the concept of the unconscious and its subtle but crucial role in the establishment of the DPH. The DPH claims that the spouses have an unconscious need to be married to an alcoholic and that this "need" is a neurotic symptom. The DPH proponents do not specifically associate their theories of the alcoholic marriage to the topographical perspective; nevertheless, the conceptual connection between the DPH and the topographical theory of the mind does exist. The connection is that the alcoholic marriage is viewed by the DPH proponents as a manifestation of conflicts between the preconscious (repressing) parts of the mind and the unconscious thoughts and feelings. The DPH proponents propose that an alcoholic marriage is a symptom and this "symptom" is a substitute for some thoughts and/or feelings that are repressed. The DPH concept that a symptom is a substitute for something repressed has been derived from the topographical perspective of the mind. Even though the topographical perspective was eventually abandoned by psychoanalysts in favor of the structural perspective (see the following section), the conceptual relationship between symptoms and repression remains the same for both perspectives of the mind as that relationship relates to the DPH.

The influence of the topographical perspective will be more clearly seen when we discuss the DPH and its derivative, the decompensation hypothesis (DH), literature in more detail (see pages 32 and 62). At that time the reader will see that the DPH and DH proponents label the spouse as neurotic and strongly assert that she is motivated by neurotic *unconscious* mental processes that determine most, if not all, of what she thinks, does, or feels. The proponents of the DPH and DH take advantage of Freud's focus on the role of the unconscious by proposing that apparent discontinuities of the alcoholic marriage are due to *unconscious* intrapsychic conflicts. For example, the spouse often complains that being married to an alcoholic is something foreign to her whole being and quite unconnected with the rest of her mental life, and yet she remains married despite the psychic and physical pain inflicted on her. The psychoanalytic principle of the unconscious states that there are causal connections by which her behavior is understandable which are, however, repressed into the layers of the mind that are inaccessible to consciousness. The spouse's need to be married to an alcoholic is kept unconscious but nonetheless quite powerful in its effect on marital and drinking behavior.

Our readers might justifiably wonder why we are connecting the role of the unconscious to the topographical theory when, in fact, the powerful effect of unconscious mental processes is something that is discussed in most theories of human behavior. In response to this concern, we remind our readers that the *existence* of unconscious *mental* processes is so widely accepted today that many contemporary students of the mind and human behavior too easily forget that in Freud's earlier days the existence of unconscious *mental* processes was not assumed by many of Freud's colleagues and was vehemently argued against by others. Beginning with his topographical theories, Freud (e.g., 1900, 1915a) spent a vast amount of energy endorsing the concept unconscious and upholding its legitimacy in the face of opposition. Eventually, the existence of unconscious psychic processes was accepted by essentially all students of human behavior, although of course the sociologists, behaviorists, and systems theorists (discussed in chapters 4–6) place relatively little importance on its practical value in treating emotional disorders or in conceptualizing the alcoholic marriage. Although the role of the unconscious is critical to structural as well as to other theories of the mind and human behavior, the *origin* of the concept unconscious historically lies with the topographical theory. Thus, it is the topographical theory of the mind that deserves credit for providing the DPH and DH proponents with a concept by which they attempt to explain their clinical observations of the alcoholic marriage.

The Structural Perspective of the Mind

Whereas the topographical theory of the mind gave rise to the concept unconscious, the remaining basic principles of the DPH are derived from its successor, the *structural* perspective of the mind.

The decisive reason for Freud's rejection of the topographical theory was that it did not adequately explain his clinical observations of mental conflict (Arlow & Brenner, 1964). After proposing the topographical functional anatomy of the mind, Freud observed that some repressive forces were *inaccessible* to consciousness and thus must be in the system unconscious, not the system preconscious as the topographical theory claimed. Freud came to this conclusion following repeated observations of patients' various ways of resisting an awareness of unconscious material while the patients showed no awareness of the resistive activity. Hard work by Freud and the patient might or might not have made the repressive forces accessible to consciousness. The critical point to be made at this juncture is that according to the topographical theory of the mind, psychic forces responsible for repression are *only* in the system preconscious and thus accessible to consciousness; anything that is inaccessible to consciousness is by definition a sexual wish (or a psychic representation of a sexual wish) in the system unconscious. Thus, Freud was faced with a contradiction between his topographical theory and his clinical observations as an analyst. He had no other alternative but to reject his theory that the functional anatomy of the mind could be partitioned in accordance with whether or not the psychic component was accessible to consciousness.

Another of Freud's clinical observations was that some people have a need to suffer. Freud observed in his analytic patients that this need was often quite inaccessible to consciousness and therefore should be in the system unconscious. This conclusion, however, conflicted with the topographical thesis that *only sexual* impulses are in the system unconscious (Arlow & Brenner, 1964).

As our readers will see in the discussion of the "nonempirical DPH proponents" (see page 32), these authors report that more than sexual conflicts are operating unconsciously in the spouse and are engendering and supporting the alcoholic marriage. Thus, these DPH proponents would agree with Freud that the clinical data contradict the topographical theory. DPH proponents would argue that "intrapsychic conflicts," the foundation of all alcoholic marriages, are not merely conflicts between sexual instincts (see page 22) and anti-instinctual elements of the mind, although sexual conflicts play an important role in the alcoholic marriage. There are other elements in conflict, such as sado-masochistic conflicts, and these conflicts also engender and support the alcoholic marriage. According to the topographical theory, these nonsexual conflicts should be in the system preconscious. Clinical experience reveals their inaccessibility to consciousness, however, thus putting them in the system unconscious and rendering the topographical theory an inadequate explanation of mental conflict.

These theoretical conflicts led Freud (1923) to offer what he considered to be a more acceptable alternative to the topographical theory of the mind, namely the "structural" perspective, whereby the mind consists of three major structures: the id, ego, and superego. The id is totally and directly associated with the instincts (see page 22 for a definition of instinct); the ego governs the instincts; and the superego is that part of the ego that deals with morality, conscience, guilt, and self-criticism. This division of the mind is in accordance with what Freud considered to be the two categories of intrapsychic conflicts: (1)

the conflicts between the instincts with their related thoughts and feelings on the one hand and the defensive (ego) and moral (superego) anti-instinctual forces on the other hand; (2) the conflicts between the defensive ego and the moral superego.

The conceptual focus on psychic structures is one of the major ways in which the psychoanalytic perspective of human behavior differs from the sociological, behavioral, and systems theories. As will be seen in chapters 4, 5, and 6, these latter three theories focus on the interpersonal, intergroup, and intragroup behavior with little interest in the structures and the conflicts of these structures within the mind.

Under normal circumstances, the id is always unconscious, but the ego and superego consist of components that are unconscious, preconscious, and conscious (cf. Figure 2-2). Thus, the accessibility to consciousness is no longer a criterion for dividing the mind, as it was with the topographical theory. The words "conscious," "preconscious," "unconscious" are now used only in the descriptive sense although, of course, they are still of critical importance. In the structural theory, the only difference between "preconscious" and "conscious" is the qualitative state of accessibility to consciousness, and there is no such thing as a "system preconscious" or "system unconscious" possessing exclusive functions as in the topographical theory.

The structural perspective of the mind is the view held by contemporary psychoanalysts. Certain concepts of the topographical perspective, however, are quite compatible with, and in fact have been incorporated into, the structural theory. For example, both theories (1) attempt to isolate and identify groups of mental processes which have specific functions (i.e., are mentalistic); (2) assume that all symptoms and much normal behavior result from intrapsychic conflict; (3) emphasize the importance of repression, regression, and the conflict between instincts and anti-instinctual forces; (4) presuppose the validity of strict psychic determinism (see page 32), and the existence of unconscious psychic processes; (5) assume that psychic energy is acquired from instinctual drives; and (6) agree that the major function of the mind is to regulate the energy

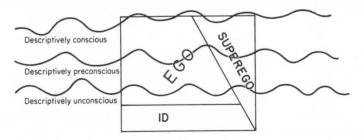

Figure 2.2   Freud's structural model of the mind. Straight lines indicate the boundaries of the psychic macrostructures. Wavy lines indicate a descriptive sense that attributes the specific quality of conscious, preconscious, or unconscious to the macrostructures.

within it and to facilitate discharge of that energy in the organism's best interest. For a more detailed description of the similarities and differences between the topographic and structural psychoanalytic perspectives of the mind, we refer our readers to Arlow and Brenner (1964).

An in-depth description of id, ego, and superego is not the purpose of this chapter. Rather, our purpose is to expose to our readers the conceptual relationships between the psychoanalytic concepts and the DPH. Thus, not only will our descriptions of the id, ego, and superego be brief but we will limit ourselves to those concepts that are most relevant to the DPH.

Id

The id is similar to what Freud called system unconscious in his topographical perspective of the mind. To the id and the system unconscious belong the instincts and the repressed psychic elements.

Familiarity with the psychoanalytic concept of "instinct" is necessary for any discussion of the relationship between the id and the DPH. The psychoanalytic concept of instinct is at times difficult for the uninitiated to grasp since it is a borderline concept between the psychical and the organic. The instinct is an abstract concept of psychic energy that is repressed by mental processes and influences human thoughts, feelings, and action at all times by means of a forceful and continuous stimulation of the mind. A term that can be used interchangeably with instinct is "need." By thinking of an instinct as a need, we facilitate understanding of the satisfaction that is always required of the "instinct." All instincts have the same purpose, namely to achieve complete satisfaction. The satisfaction is achieved by reduction of the source of the instinct's excitation. Although Freud changed his theories about the anatomy of the mind, the mental apparatus always remained a group of systems for the discharge and regulation of psychic energy, the source of the energy being the "instinct" (Bibring, 1941; Freud, 1915b).

Freud referred to the psychic energy concept as an abstraction only because he could not tangibly prove the existence of "energy" or "organic forces." The concept was developed, however, as if the energy were a tangible substance, such as a chemical or a hormone, and Freud believed that eventually scientists would more directly prove the existence of these organic substances.

Although an instinct is a stimulus of the mind, it differs strikingly from the concepts of external physiological or psychological stimuli of the mind which are discussed in the learning theory chapter of this book. The psychoanalytic instinctual stimulus of the mind arises from within the organism, is constant, and is unavoidable, whereas the external (learning theory) stimulus is intermittent and can be disposed of or avoided by evasive bodily actions. In essence, the psychoanalytic concept of instinct is that the "instinct" represents the requirements of the body on the mind as a result of the body–mind attachment.

"Component instincts" are identified by further categorizations of the primal instincts. Some of the component sexual instincts that are relevant to the alcoholic marriage and which are discussed in this book are the oral, anal, genital, and sadistic sexual instincts.

The instincts and their associated thoughts and feelings are actually energized by a psychic energy that is a combination of the two primal instincts of aggression and sexuality. The two kinds of energy are never totally separate but rather merge to various degrees: "(the instincts) are themselves compounded of fusions of two primal forces (Eros and Destructiveness) [Freud's parentheses] in varying proportions" (Freud, 1940 [1938], p. 197).

The concept of a fusion of the two primal instincts results from Freud's observations in psychoanalysis that there is a certain amount of sexual gratification in all acts of aggression no matter how ruthless such action might appear to be; likewise, there is always some aggressive energy involved in the sexual events no matter how loving or affectionate such events appear to the usual observer (as will be seen on page 33, some of the DPH adherents emphasize the sexual gratification experienced by the wife when the alcoholic physically and mentally abuses her).

To summarize, the mind is impelled to action by means of instinctual forces (drives or instincts). These instincts are forceful, continuous stimuli of the mind that engender sexual (loving) or aggressive (destructive) action. The instincts and the psychic (drive) energy that impel them are conceptualized as internal psychical phenomena originating from the vital layer of the mind; this layer of the mind is called the id.

The instincts are represented by thoughts or feelings that affect the human being at all times. The external environment serves only as a mediator. The instincts possess a biological basis and have an inherently (genetically) determined direction. Of course, Freud does not ignore the importance of the external environment. In fact, he makes his position quite clear on the question of whether or not a symptom should be considered as due to the environment or the biological constitution of the person. Freud believed that it made no more sense to ask this question than to ask whether or not a baby is conceived and born as a result of its father or its mother (Freud, 1917 [1916–1917]). Freud did believe, however, that the *existence* of instincts and of psychic energy was in no way a function of psychological adjustment to the world outside of the self (Munroe, 1955, p. 108). Also, Freud always related the pathogenic role of factors external to the mind, to the intrapsychic function of the instinct within the mind of the individual person. The role of the environment or of people in the environment external to the mind cannot in itself cause a symptom without a frustration of the intrapsychic instinctual drives:

The meaning of psychical conflict can be adequately expressed in another way by saying that for an external [italics in the original] *frustration to become pathogenic an* internal *[italics in the original] frustration must be added to it. (Freud, 1917 [1916–1917], p. 350)*

During the long period of infancy, childhood, and adolescence, the instincts pass through critical periods of development, usually called oral, anal, phallic, latency, and genital psychosexual stages. In order for normal psychosexual development to occur, intrapsychic conflicts must be resolved during the course of critical interactions between the instincts, other intrapsychic processes, and external environmental events. If these conflicts are resolved and an optimal amount of gratification is achieved at each stage, then there is normal flow of psychic energy from object to object[1] or from one means of gratification to another. If the intrapsychic conflicts are not resolved, then a "fixation" (psychological bondage) might occur at a specific stage or mode of development. The "fixation" is essentially an abnormal lack of transfer of psychic energy to subsequent psychosexual stages and may be very significant or relatively minor, depending on a variety of circumstances and individual traits. For example, a person may experience emotional deprivation during the breast feeding period of his infancy. This person may then remain "fixated" at the oral stage. This fixation may manifest itself in "oral" activities that cause serious problems, such as alcoholism or excessive dependency on an alcoholic spouse (see the pro-DPH report of Gaertner, 1939; Lewis, 1954; and Price, 1945, discussed on pages 33–39); or the fixation may manifest itself in slight overdrinking, overeating, or oversmoking; or the fixation may be unnoticeable.

Relationship between the concept id and the DPH.   Now that our readers have some understanding of Freud's concepts in general of the id and its component drives, we will discuss the relationship between these specific psychoanalytic concepts and the DPH. Later in this chapter we will discuss some of the DPH literature in more detail. It is hoped that our readers will recognize in that discussion specific examples of the generalizations we make in this section.

---

[1]The concept "object" is a critical component of Freud's dual instinct theory. There are three aspects of the instinct: *source, aim,* and *object.* The source is an organic process, somewhere in the body, that has as its mental stimulus an "instinct." It is unknown whether the somatic source is of a chemical or mechanical nature, but it is a *biological* and not a psychological procedure. The source determines the instinct but we identify the instinct by its psychological component, the *aim,* rather than the biological source, although sometimes this source can be assumed from the aim. The aim of every instinct is the need to achieve satisfaction by eliminating or decreasing the excitation at the site of the instinct's source. Although all instincts have the identical ultimate aim, different instincts have various ways of achieving the aim. The *object* is the person or thing by which or through which the instinct attempts its aim. The object is not necessarily biologically related to the instinct and is certainly the most variable of the three major characteristics of an instinct. The object may be in the external environment or be a segment of the person's own anatomy.

A basic conceptual presupposition of the concept of the id is that the id and its psychic energy are predominately self-directed. Also, as already mentioned, the instincts have a biological basis and their *existence* is entirely determined by internal, genetic sources. Thus, the id's orientation is centered on the mind of the individual. When things and people in the external environment are considered in relationship to the id, it is always in regard to how the external environment meets the intrapsychic instinctual needs within the mind of the individual. This orientation is precisely what is seen in the disturbed personality hypothesis. The DPH focuses on intrapsychic processes of the spouse, usually assumed to be pathological, with relatively little attention paid to the overt interpersonal, intragroup, and intergroup behavior.

The concept of fixation at psychosexual states is also one of the concepts from which the DPH has evolved. The theory of psychosexual development focuses on the periods up to around age six and asserts that the personality is essentially determined during this time. In one of his very last writings, published posthumously, Freud reasserts this concept:

> It seems that neuroses are acquired only [italics ours] in early childhood (up to age of six), even though their symptoms may not make their appearance till much later. The childhood neurosis may become manifest for a short time or may even be overlooked. In every [italics ours] case the later neurotic illness links up with the prelude in childhood. (Freud, 1940 [1938], p. 184)[2]

Obviously then, according to psychoanalytic theory, the spouse of an alcoholic has developed her personality (and her neurosis) *before* being married. *The DPH proponents have adopted this concept by proposing that the nonalcoholic's choice to marry an alcoholic or potential alcoholic is based on the nonalcoholic's intrapsychic psychopathology which antedates marriage since it basically developed as a result of "fixation" during psychosexual development.* Such an orientation would hardly be consistent with the stress, learning, and systems theories discussed in chapters 4, 5, and 6. These latter three theories assert that the current environment is just, if not more, important than the past environment and that current psychic and behavioral manifestations shown by the spouse certainly do not have to be necessarily a result of some *past* fixation or pathogenic experience.

---

[2]It is of interest to note that in the very next sentence of this passage Freud alludes to a stress theory (see chapter 4) approach, although he does not, of course, label it as such, and he is careful to remain within the developmental psychoanalytic perspective, referring only to the stresses of childhood:

> It is possible that what are known as traumatic neuroses (due to excessive fright or severe somatic shocks, such as railway collisions, burial under falls of earth, and so on) are an exception to this: their relations to determinants in childhood have hitherto eluded investigation. (Freud, 1940 [1938], p. 184)

The Ego

The ego represents what may be called reason and common sense, in contrast to the id, which contains the passions. (Freud, 1923, p. 25)

The ego is a differentiated part of the id, a figurative layer of the id that develops under the influence of stimuli from the external environment (Hartmann, 1939). Discussion of the innumerable ways that the ego serves its masters is beyond the purpose of our presentation on how the ego relates to the DPH. Thus, we will discuss the ego only as it is associated with "defense mechanisms" since of all the concepts associated with the ego, it is the concept of defense mechanisms that has most profoundly influenced the DPH.

Defense mechanisms. "Defense mechanism" is the name given to the mental process by which the ego wards off anxiety and other psychic dangers and attempts to resolve unconsciously the intrapsychic conflicts that result from mutually incompatible instinctual drives, external realities, and internal demands and prohibitions (Sjöbäck, 1973; Vaillant, 1971).

Intrapsychic conflicts often result from unconscious thoughts and feelings or instinctual desires threatening to erupt into consciousness. It is this threat that thereby engenders anxiety ("signal anxiety") which in turn precipitates defense mechanisms.

Although Freud always underestimated the value of defense mechanisms, he certainly insisted on the need for categorization of defenses and emphasized the possibility that certain sets of defense mechanisms determine specific mental illnesses (Freud, 1926 [1925]).

In 1936, Freud again emphasized the work that had to be done on the defense mechanisms:

There are extraordinarily large numbers of methods (or mechanisms, as we say) [parentheses in the original] used by our ego in the discharge of its defensive functions . . . my daughter, the child analyst, is writing a book (upon them). Freud 1936, quoted by Vaillant, 1971, p. 108)

Of course, it was only after Anna Freud's magnum opus *(The Ego and the Mechanisms of Defense,* 1936) that there was an extensive description of defense mechanisms. Anna Freud made the point that defense mechanisms utilize a great variety of activities, for example, fantasies and intellectual processes (and according to DPH and DH proponents, marriage to an alcoholic). Also, Anna Freud emphasized the idea that defense mechanisms do not operate only against instinctual wishes, but against any situation, thought, or feeling associated with anxiety (such as the variety of anxiety-producing situations that are associated with the marriage of nonalcoholic to an alcoholic).

Freud chose the word "mechanism" to indicate his conviction that mental events manifest themselves in a way that allows organized scientific investigation (Laplanche & Pontalis, 1967, p. 109). The attempt to investigate defense mechanisms is made somewhat less difficult by categorizing the various intentions or "purposes" of the defense mechanisms. Vaillant's excellent paper (1971) offers four categories of purposes of defense mechanisms (although the categories are Vaillant's, the alcoholic marriage examples are ours): (1) to maintain affects within acceptable limits during situations when the person's affective status is subject to sudden and major changes, for example, a response to the loss of a parent or the dissolution of a marriage due to alcoholism; (2) to maintain psychic equilibrium by avoiding or delaying acute expansion of biological drives, for example, sexual feelings during adolescence ("instinctual anxiety") or during the disinhibiting influence of alcohol; (3) to gain some "time out" in order to integrate sudden alterations in self-image, for example, adolescence, menarche, or a wife's realization that she cannot keep her husband sober; (4) to master intrapsychic conflicts with critical people such as an alcoholic spouse whom the person cannot psychologically avoid ("object anxiety").

Certain aspects of the many complexities of defense mechanisms should be made clear before a more specific discussion of the ego as it relates to the DPH. A defense mechanism can be considered "maladaptive" if it exacerbates a conflict or if it leads toward unnecessary regression. On the other hand, a defense mechanism can be considered "coping" or "adaptive" if it leads toward the resolution of conflict and toward minimizing regression. Also, maladaptive defense mechanisms interfere with realistic wish gratifications, whereas adaptive mechanisms increase the probability of realistic satisfactions (Vaillant, 1971). As discussed later (see page 33), the DPH proponents focus on the *maladaptiveness* of the spouse's defense mechanisms and the "stress theorists" (chapter 4) focus on coping behavior but do not associate the coping to psychoanalytic mentalistic concepts.

The ego mechanisms of defense always change, to some degree, the cognitive ability to perceive the realities of both the intrapsychic and the external world. The degree to which the alterations in perception are adaptive, consistent with reality, and in accordance with that specific society's definition of "normal" is what determines the degree of "normalcy" attached to that perception. As discussed on page 42, some researchers have proposed that spouses of alcoholics perceive their husbands in a characteristic way that distinguishes these spouses from wives of nonalcoholics. The psychoanalytically oriented DPH adherents would attribute these differences in perception at least partly to ego mechanisms of defense.

Another point that is critical in our discussion of the relationships of the concept of defense mechanisms to the DPH is that a specific defense mechanism almost never functions in isolation. Instead, the various defense mechanisms combine and collaborate with each other to form a personality profile that best suits the ego's function. *We use terms such as "symptoms,"* "personality," "traits," "neurosis," "psychosis," "character disorder," and "alcoholism" to refer to mosaics of defense mechanisms which have combined into certain recognizable behavior patterns. [See Whalen's description (page 37) of categories of wives of alcoholics based essentially on the wives most predominant defense mechanisms.]

The number of defense mechanisms that a psychoanalyst can describe is probably limited only by the restraints on the describer's boldness, creativity, and imagination. Defense mechanisms are dynamic and frequently blend into associated defense mechanisms, thus making it at times impossible to separate them descriptively. To avoid trying to describe mutually exclusive defense mechanisms just because of overlap in exactness, complexity, and uncertainty of these concepts, however, would be to "throw out the clinical baby with the scientifically imperfect bath water" (Vaillant, 1971, p. 112). Thus, psychoanalysts attempt to define separate defense mechanisms. The nonempirical DPH proponents have applied these definitions to their descriptions of the spouse of the alcoholic. Some of the defense mechanisms commonly attributed to the spouses by the nonempirical pro-DPH theorists are compensation, conversion, denial (disavowal), displacement, distortion, idealization, identification, incorporation, isolation, projection, rationalization, reaction formation, repression, sublimation, and symbolization. It is beyond the scope of this book to provide an in-depth description of the various, commonly mentioned defense mechanisms. For the interested reader, however, we have in Appendix B briefly defined with alcoholic marriage examples those defense mechanisms listed in the preceding sentence. For readers who are interested in a more extensive grasp of the psychoanalytic definitions we refer to Vaillant (1971), Anna Freud (1936), Sjöbäck (1973), Moore and Fine (1968), Laplanche and Pontalis (1967), and Hendrick (1958).

Relationship between the concept ego and the DPH.   As with the concepts of the topographical perspective and the id already discussed, the obvious question to be answered in this book concerns the relationship between the concept of the ego and the DPH. The answer is, of course, very complicated and centers around the role of defense mechanisms as conceptualized in the pro-DPH literature.

The DPH proponents apply the psychoanalytic concept of defense mechanisms by first assuming that for most, if not for all people, being married to an alcoholic is in itself a symptom, and thus the marriage is a manifestation and conglomeration of defense mechanisms. Or to put it another way, the spouse is struggling with unresolved conflicts and the ego unconsciously attempts to find an acceptable compromise by engendering and maintaining an alcoholic marriage. The alcoholic marriage, therefore, serves as a means to prevent unacceptable unconscious mental phenomena within the *nonalcoholic spouse* from reaching painful awareness. For example, being appropriately angry at a sadistic alcoholic husband is one way for the wife to keep unconscious her irrational anger at all men and to defend herself against the anxiety of becoming aware of this irrational anger.

According to the DPH proponents, there are many specific ways that numerous defense mechanisms operate to maintain the alcoholic marriage. In fact, the DPH proponents invariably list a variety of "traits" or characteristics of the alcoholic's spouse. These traits are in one way or another combinations of defense mechanisms. The ego, then, is mainly relevant to the DPH as the repository of the defense mechanisms underlying the nonalcoholic spouse's investment in the alcoholic marriage.

The Superego

The superego is the name given to that group of psychic functions that involve the formation of moral or ethical prohibitions and demands, conscience, ideals, goals, self-observation, and self-punishment (masochism). Some parts of the superego resemble the ego in that they are mature and logical. Other parts of the superego resemble the id in that they are primitive and illogical.

The term "superego" was first introduced by Freud with the publication of *The Ego and the Id* (Freud, 1923). Freud asserted that the superego is a specialized division of the ego which has the unique capacity to dominate the ego. This domination of the ego may be manifest in various ways. The superego, guided by its moral principles, may govern the anti-instinctual activity of the ego. In this role, the superego creates concordance with the ego as both structures team up against the id.

Another role of the superego may be less harmonious or even in discordance with the ego. For example, the superego might be critical or give rise to a sense of guilt within the ego. In extreme pathological cases, the superego's criticism of the ego results in unyielding ruthlessness and unbridled self-destructiveness as can be seen in severely depressed, sado-masochistic, or obsessive compulsive patients.

We see how . . . one part of the ego [the superego] sets itself over against the other, judges it critically, and, as it were, takes it as its object. . . . We shall really find grounds for distinguishing this agency from the rest of the ego. (Freud, 1917 [1915], p. 247)

Development.   A brief discussion of the development of the superego is relevant to this chapter since, as will be seen later, the developmental concepts of the superego are closely associated with the DPH proponent's view of the wife of an alcoholic. It is frequently said by psychoanalysts that the superego is the heir to the Oedipus complex and develops only after the abandonment of the Oedipus complex. By "Oedipus complex" Freud means the child's wish to do away with the parent of the same sex and have the parent of the opposite sex all to himself/herself (Freud, 1925). The superego develops as a consequence of the Oedipus complex by the following process: Powerful psychic conflicts develop through the phallic Oedipal phase of psychosexual development. One way to cope with these conflicts is by the defense mechanisms of *identification* and *internalization* of parental figures, especially the moral or ethical aspects of the parental objects. Usually, the major source of identification that forms the nucleus of the superego is the parent of the same sex who is the rival of the Oedipal child. For example, the Oedipal boy wishes to do away with his father and claim his mother. These forbidden wishes engender in the child fears that father will castrate and/or abandon him. By *identifying* with father, the little boy is able to internalize that aspect of the father which the child most fears. Thus, by making the feared aspect a part of himself, the child is able to better control his fears and implement a defense against them. Also, the identification serves another function. By identifying with the father, the little boy satisfies the wish to share in the father's sexual omnipotence and proceeds with further development of his own masculine identity.

The process of formation of the superego differs in boys and girls. In boys, the castration fears lead to a repression of the Oedipal triangular complex and a "severe superego is set up as its heir" (Freud, 1933 [1932], p. 129). On the other hand, the castration fear in girls reinforces the Oedipus complex rather than destroys it:

> What happens with a girl is almost the opposite [of boys]. The castration complex prepares for the Oedipus complex instead of destroying it . . . . Girls remain in it [the Oedipus complex] for an indeterminate length of time; they demolish it late and, even so, incompletely. In these circumstances, the formation of the superego must suffer; it cannot attain the strength and independence which give it its cultural significance . . . . (Freud, 1933 [1932], p. 129)

In essence then, according to Freud, females have superegos that are incompletely developed and less resistant to external influences. In other words, the part of the mind responsible for conscience, guilt, morals, etc., is less flexible, more intolerant, and less adaptable in females than in males. (This aspect of Freudian theory on sexuality is obviously not well received by most women and in fact is one of the reasons why feminist movements are very critical of Freud.) An elaboration of Freud's theories on the differences between males and females is beyond the scope of this book and we refer the interested reader to Freud's writings on this subject (e.g., Freud; 1905, 1906, 1923, 1925, 1933 [1932]), and the many expository reviews (e.g., Jones, 1953b). In the following section of this chapter we discuss the relevance to the DPH of the implied male supremacy aspects of psychoanalytic theory.

Whether we are considering boys or girls, the superego begins to exert its influence around the phallic psychosexual stage (ages 5–6) and it is responsible for the person's continued sense of morality, conscience, etc. In essence, through identification and internalization of parental figures, the superego continues the same functions that were performed by the parents; that is, in the early years of life the parents observed the ego (child), issued commands, made judgments, and delivered punishments. Gradually starting around the age of five, however, the superego takes over this function for the rest of the individual's life. The nature and extent of superego development, then, will naturally have profound implications for future life choices, for example, the choice of a marriage partner.

Relationship between the concept superego and the DPH. There are three broad categories of superego functioning that are indirectly related to the DPH. The first category is that of the role of *internalization* and *identification* (functions of the superego as well as the ego) as that role relates to the woman's choice of a husband. Implied throughout the DPH literature is the attitude by DPH adherents that wives choose alcoholics as husbands because of processes of identification and internalization of their own parents, and because of value systems that result from these childhood experiences. Some pro-DPH authors even suggest that wives of alcoholics tend to have fathers who are alcoholics and thus choose an alcoholic for a husband in the unconscious hope of prolonging (symbolically) the original father–daughter relationship (see our discussion of Gaertner, 1939, on page 34).

The second category of superego function as it relates to the DPH is the role that masochism and guilt play in the lives of women who marry alcoholics. As is nicely exemplified by Whalen (1953) (see page 37) and Gaertner (1939) (see page 34) almost all of the pro-DPH subjective periodicals and books suggest that wives of alcoholics suffer from guilt that antedates marriage and creates masochistic needs that are satisfied by abuse from the alcoholic husband. These DPH proponents have borrowed the psychoanalytic concepts of masochism and incorporated these concepts into various explanations of the psychodynamics of an alcoholic marriage.

The third category of relevance between the superego and the DPH involves the issue of sexual distinctions in morality and dependency. Freud believed that diminished productive energy and decreased constructive adventurousness occur in all people as a result of society's restrictive sexual morality which is taken on as a function of the superego. Females, considered more sexually restricted than males, would suffer more from the restrictive morality and thus would be more likely to be less accomplished, less intelligent, less agressive, and more passive than males. The supposed passivity and inferiority of females is not due to biological determinants, but to cultural prohibitions. Thus, females are categorized as morally restrictive and passive people. Almost all pro-DPH literature presupposes that "dominant" traits in the wife are "abnormal." If the wife is the most "dominant" or "aggressive" member of the family, then there is a tendency for these clinicians and authors to label the woman "abnormal," whereas the label of aberrancy is not attached to a *male* spouse who wants to control or dominate his wife.[3] We propose that the Freudian concepts of superego are the origins of the specific tendency among pro-DPH and pro-DH authors and clinicians to label dominant females as neurotic (see page 45 for a further discussion on the dominant–dependency issue).

Psychic Determinism

There is another concept that should be included in our discussion of the application of psychoanalytic principles to alcoholic marriage literature: the concept of strict psychic determinism. The principle of psychic determinism (or psychic causality) is that a mental event is never a random phenomenon. That is, nothing happens by chance and every psychic event is determined by a preceding chain of mental events. As with the physical world, the mental world is incapable of random causation and discontinuity. Therefore, chance is nonexistent and every psychic symptom, whatever its nature, is the result of other mental or physical problems all operating within the totality of natural law. Determinism is therefore in direct opposition to the doctrine of "free will."

The concept of determinism is a synthesis and abstraction of a multitude of observations and can be applied to schools of thought other than psychoanalytic theory. Determinism is also fundamental to the stress, learning, and systems theories as would be logically expected since "scientific investigation would indeed be pointless if the order it strove to ascertain did not exist" (Jones, 1953a, p. 365).

At this point of our discussion the point of emphasis is the psychoanalytically oriented alcohologists' *application* of the psychic determinism concept to the alcoholic marriage. Specifically, these authors have applied psychic determinism to elaborate on the basic theme that just as there is a psychic reason for the alcoholic to misuse alcohol, so is there a mental process that leads the spouse to marry an alcoholic and/or be unable to leave him, and/or contribute to his alcohol misuse. In other words, the concept of psychic determinism has been adopted by the DPH proponents to support their view that spouses of alcoholics did not marry an alcoholic by chance and they have a vested interest in the *alcoholic* part of the alcoholic marriage.

DPH PROPONENTS

We have up to now, presented a sketch of psychoanalytic concepts of the mind and in general have shown how the disturbed personality hypothesis evolved from psychonalytic mentalistic concepts. Now it is time for us to present some of

---

[3]We are indebted to Ms. Kathy Kogan for this idea.

the specific literature which introduced and support the DPH. We again emphasize as we did in the beginning of this chapter, that the DPH (and DH) literature is derived from, but should not be considered, psychoanalytic literature. *Likewise, the various research projects that support or challenge the DPH (and DH) are investigating the various theories about alcoholic marriages, and not the underlying psychoanalytic principles.*

We divide the pro-DPH literature into two categories: nonempirical[4] support and empirical support, and will present some of the research that challenges the validity of the DPH. We should mention at this time that the decompensation hypotheses (DH), discussed in chapter 3, is actually an extension of the DPH, but for the purpose of clarity of presentation we have saved our discussion of the decompensation hypotheses for a separate chapter.

DPH Proponents: Nonempirical Support

The reader will remember that at the beginning of this chapter we described the DPH as a mind-oriented theory that a spouse of an alcoholic is to various degrees "characteristically a barely compensated, interpersonally restricted, insecure, outwardly dominant, but deeply dependent, excessively anxious, sexually inadequate, guilt ridden, and abnormally angry woman with pathogenic childhood experiences" (see page 13). There are numerous papers in the professional journals and books written by responsible and well-intentioned authors who are essentially DPH proponents. The following is a long but far from complete list of such authors: Baker (1945), Baldwin (1947), Bergler (1946), Blinder and Kirschenbaum (1967), Boggs (1943–1944), Bullock and Mudd (1959), Clifford (1960), Ewing and Fox (1968), Forizs, (1954), Fox (1956), Futterman (1953), Gaertner (1939), Igersheimer (1959), Kalashian (1959), Karlen (1965), Lewis (1937, 1954), Loescher (1970), Pattison, Courlas, Patti, Mann, and Mullen (1965), Pixley and Stiefel (1963), Price (1945), and Whalen (1953).

It is not necessary to describe in detail what each of these and other pro-DPH nonempirical support authors have said. Rather, for the sake of conciseness, we have selected four reports (Gaertner, 1939; Lewis, 1954; Price, 1945; Whalen, 1953) which essentially are representative of the nonempirical pro-DPH body of literature. As we have already mentioned, it is our hope, and one of the goals of this book, that the reader will recognize in the forthcoming discussion, some of the specifics that support the generalizations regarding the psychoanalytic concepts of the mind, especially those generalizations we made when discussing the relationships between the concepts of the topographical

---

[4]We are using the term "nonempirical" to mean not based on experimental systematic and controlled observation, as opposed to the "empirical" reports of the DPH proponents discussed on page 39.

perspective, id, ego, superego, psychic determinism, and the DPH. Also, we want to emphasize that the value of these pro-DPH nonempirical authors' ideas must be perceived within a historical context. What currently might seem like a simplistic idea about alcoholic marriages might, at the time or place that the article was published, have been a progressive, constructive, and enlightening idea when compared to the knowledge and interest about alcoholic marriages at that time or place.

Gaertner (1939) was one of the first to write about wives of alcoholics. Gaertner presents her psychoanalytically oriented subjective impressions and conclusions after an in-depth study of 15 alcoholic marriages. The couples studied were casework cleints at the Institute of Family Service of the Charity Organization Society of New York City.

Gaertner's major thesis about the alcoholic was that he is strongly sadomasochistic and fixated at the oral psychosexual stage, utilizing primitive defense mechanisms, especially denial and projection:

The primitive ego mechanism of projection is activated by a strong tendency to regress to a narcissistic stage of ego organization. (Gaertner, 1939, p. 12)

Gaertner (1939) believed that:

Alcoholism is a necessary defense which has been erected against impulses which the ego cannot recognize [i.e., unconscious]; it would be both unkind and foolish to tear down this defense unless resolution of the basic conflicts made its use unnecessary. (p. 42)

After a long psychoanalytic description of the way in which the mind of an alcoholic works, with emphasis on the unconscious and the role of fixations, defense mechanisms, unresolved Oedipus complexes, and the sexuality of sadomasochism, Gaertner turned her discussion toward the wives.

Twelve (out of 15) of the wives came from "broken homes." During infancy and childhood, 10 of the women lost one or both parents by death, and 2 by divorce. Gaertner (1939) asserted that these losses in infancy or childhood resulted in the child experiencing "acute libidinal deprivation" (p. 10). For those wives who lost one or both parents during "the oral stage of development" (p. 10), Gaertner proposed that they were never able to cope adequately with the loss of love (in other words, they employed maladaptive defense mechanisms):

In the case of those suffering early oral deprivation, the unconscious seems unwilling to relinquish the hope that stimulation of the oral zone may produce the mysterious pleasure so suddenly withdrawn. (Gaertner, 1939, p. 11)

Thus, one of Gaertner's major theses was that the spouses experienced pathogenic childhood experiences that rendered them an "abnormal group of people":

In the psychosexual development of the child no point is so vital as an adequate solution of the Oedipus situation. Upon it hinges the capacity of an individual to adjust to the object world. The reaction patterns which the child utilizes to work out the difficult relationships with his parents become the pattern for all his future human relationships. Undoubtedly, the individuals studied were under a severe handicap in that the great majority of them were prevented from working out the Oedipus situation by the death of a parent at a crucial time. (Gaertner, 1939, p. 13)

Gaertner then goes on to suggest that the wife is an aggressive woman specifically selected by the alcoholic to meet his masochistic needs:

A masochistic attitude seems to open the door to alcoholism. Many people who become terrified at the idea of not being their own masters often have a sneaking desire to be mastered. In a weak man such a characteristic may drag him into marriage with an aggressive woman. . . . (Gaertner, 1939, p. 28)

Gaertner pointed out that the wives superficially complained about their husbands, usually saying that they would not divorce their husband "for the sake of the children." However, at a deeper (unconscious) level, they were described as having an intrapsychic need to stay married to the alcoholic despite the pain, inconvenience, and in some cases, threat to their lives. The following quote nicely summarizes Gaertner's ideas on these issues and also again exemplifies the superego's identification and internalization of parental figures (see page 29) so that the wife chooses a husband similar to her alcoholic father:

But the women stay with their husbands, regardless. They purport to hate their husbands, but when real rapport has been established with the case worker admit that they really love the men. These wives say that they are ashamed of [sic] their neighbors, yet they themselves are the first to confide their hard lot. Examination of the cases shows that no fewer than eight of the women knew before marriage that their fiances were heavy drinkers. Several of these women had even been gravely warned by members of the community who knew the prospective husbands, or by the relatives. Two of the wives had alcoholic fathers and one had been brought up in the home of an alcoholic uncle so, presumably, had a first-hand acquaintance with the behavior of an intoxicated man. One wonders if, in the case of these three women, they never quite detached themselves form their first heterosexual love, and so married men similar to the father-person. (Gaertner, 1939, pp. 32–33)

Just as she did with her explanation of the behavior of the alcoholic, Gaertner focused on sexual aspects in her descriptions of the wives. Gaertner (1939) felt that the wives were "undersexed . . . had no great desire to marry, and do not much enjoy sexual intercourse" (p. 33). Gaertner gives specific examples in an attempt to support these conclusions. One woman thought sex was "dirty"; another got "nauseous" at the thought of sex or the sight of semen; one woman claimed to know nothing about sex until after marriage and would never had married had she known what it was like; and all 15 of the women claimed to have never been enthusiastic about sex, marriage, or pregnancy.

Gaertner also concluded that these women have a need to dominate their husbands. To support this conclusion, Gaertner (1939) reported that 6 of the women were the major source of family income, most of the 15 assumed full responsibility for financial affairs, and all of the women "seemed to resent the fact that small children keep them from working" (p. 34). It is important for our readers to bear in mind that Gaertner focused on intrapsychic (mentalistic) variables within the wife, placing relatively little importance on the actual or hypothesized stress of living with the alcoholic (see sociological theory, chapter 4) or the other environmental variables considered by the learning (chapter 5) and systems (chapter 6) theories.

Gaertner developed the idea that not only the alcoholic, but the wife also is sadomasochistic:

[the spouses] elected to play the martyr role, and the reason that they stay with their husbands is that fundamentally it satisfies them to do so. A normal woman would not tolerate such a situation; these women need the role and so suffer it, gaining destructive satisfaction. (Gaertner, 1939, p. 35)

To support this conclusion, Gaertner (1939) gave some specific examples. One 36-year-old wife said that she had abandoned any hope of happiness for herself and now lives only for her children. Another woman said that people tell her she is too unselfish and her life would have been much different "if I hadn't done everything I should as a wife and mother" (p. 35). Still another wife postponed medical care for herself by saying "I can do without, I always do for everyone else first" (p. 36).

Gaertner offers an explanation of why masochism is characteristically present in these women. Masochism is a manifestation of an abnormally functioning superego. The wives have a basic impulse to gain pleasure from pain. Initially the mind of such a woman seeks people in the environment to satisfy this wish. However, the superego creates guilt and moral prohibition for such thoughts and so the mind must engender "a secondary turning of the sadistic impulses against one's self" (Gaertner, 1939, p. 36). This turning against self not only serves the superego by preventing the prohibited act, but the unconscious turning against the self is also a way that the superego punishes the ego and fulfills an unconscious need for punishment. Thus, as mentioned in our section on the general description of the mind (see page 29), the superego is responsible for the guilt, masochism, and self-retribution so commonly seen in wives of alcoholics (according to the DPH).

Although, as already stated, wives are considered abnormally dominant (as the result of intrapsychic forces), the dominance is not unambivalent and this conflict is resolved in part by masochism:

> *Still, while the wife enjoys playing the martyr role, she is ambivalent in her reactions. That she craves the response she can muster through masochism indicates that she is really not such a self-sufficient person as she may at first appear. She, too, may never have outgrown the dependency needs of childhood, and yet has placed herself in a position where all responsibility is hers. It is the function of the caseworker to sustain her, and this may constitute the only treatment possible. Again, if the caseworker can help the wife release [make conscious] some of the pent-up hostility aimed at the husband, he will be spared at least a little of the nagging and ridicule which emphasize his inadequacy as the head of the family and are part of the pattern driving him to drink. The wife can satisfy some of her masochistic desires through posing to the worker as a martyr, and, therefore will have less need to provoke her husband to sadistic behavior toward her. (Gaertner, 1939, p. 43)*

In conclusion, Gaertner's exposition is an excellent example of the kind of thinking that introduced, promoted, and sustained the DPH. The three other typical pro-DPH nonempirical reports are now discussed in less detail.

Whalen (1953) believed that "certain types of women are attracted to the alcoholic man and marry him hoping to find an answer to deep, unconscious needs of her own" (p. 641).

Based on subjective impressions, Whalen described the four categories of wives:

1. "Suffering Susan" whose need to punish herself (masochism) dominates her personality and leads her to marry an alcoholic, who will provide her with the misery she requires.
2. "Controlling Catherine" who unconsciously defends against her distrust of men by marrying a weak alcoholic whom she can control, thereby minimizing the risk of being hurt by him.
3. "Wavering Winifred" who unconsciously defends against her profoundly low self-esteem by marrying an inadequate man so that she will feel needed and important despite her ambivalence (wavering) about the price she must pay to satisfy this need to be wanted.
4. "Punitive Polly," usually a professional woman, who must compete with, defeat, and punish men. This explains her choice of an alcoholic for a husband.

Whalen's report is an excellent example of a specific application of the psychoanalytic concept of defense mechanisms (see page 26). For example,

"Punitive Polly" excessively utilizes the defense mechanisms of *denial* and *rationalization.* According to psychoanalytic theory, "denial" is a primitive mechanism "in which the *ego* avoids becoming aware of some painful aspect of *reality"* (Moore & Fine, 1968, p. 31).

Rationalization is a more highly developed and mature defense mechanism that is "the intellectual distortion by which the individual explains an unconsciously motivated act or symptom" (Hendrick, 1958, p. 8).

Although Whalen does not delineate the psychoanalytic concepts, her description makes it quite clear that "Punitive Polly" has an unconscious need to punish and defeat all men. The wish to be punitive is consciously quite unacceptable to "Punitive Polly" and so she utilizes *denial* of the wish and supports the *denial* by marrying an alcoholic who will abuse her so that she can *rationalize* whatever awareness or potential awareness she might have of her punitive needs.

In retrospect, Whalen's concepts seem naive and bear little resemblance to the realities of personality profiles. Whalen's simplistic theoretical approach should not detract from the overall importance of her report, however. The separation of spouses into four categories was one of the first scientific reviews that gave serious professional attention to the variability among wives of alcoholics.

Lewis (1954) described wives of alcoholics as insecure women who are confused about their own sexual identity. Lewis said that they choose an alcoholic husband who will not only be dependent on them but also will behave in a way that will enable the wives to utilize the defense mechanism of *rationalization* in order to cope with their aggressive need to be punitive.

In referring to professional experience with 50 wives, Lewis gave the following summary of guilt and the implied function of the superego discussed on page 29:

It seemed to us that there was a remarkable consistency both in the pathological personality patterns and in the background experiences of these women . . . these patterns of behavior reflected in a notable degree, difficulties in two general areas–dependency and sexual immaturity . . . their anxiety about their own sexuality might have been part of the reason for the attraction to weak men . . . some of the women had had actual childhood experiences in which their aggressive impulses might seem to have injured someone . . . marriage to a weak, or already castrated, man might seem to offer an escape from tension . . . . There were also many instances of implied masturbation anxiety . . . guilt over masturbation could explain, in part, their ready acceptance of the punishment implicit in a marriage to an alcoholic. These examples of deepseated dependency problems and sexual anxieties in our group seemed to indicate that the emotional problems of these women were often great since they had been trying, for some time, to find relief of tension. (Lewis, 1954, pp. 11–13)

Lewis went on to cite from her sample examples of obesity, vomiting, choking when troubled, and preoccupation with breastfeeding, food, and drinks as evidence of unresolved oral and dependency needs: "literally hungry for love and acceptance" (Lewis, 1954, p. 12).

Price (1945) interviewed 29 wives and formulated the subjective impressions that the wife of an alcoholic is an insecure, anxious, hostile, and basically dependent woman who accepts no responsibility for her husband's drinking and who feels "unloved, resentful, and aggressive" (p. 623) toward her husband because the alcohol precludes satisfaction of her abnormal dependency needs. Price also reported the wife's interference with husband's treatment: "unconsciously and perhaps even consciously, she fought treatment of her spouse as one more way she could keep him inadequate" (p. 623).

DPH Proponents—Empirical Support

Before we begin to examine empirical studies relevant to the DPH, it is appropriate to consider for a moment what forms of empirical data could provide clear support or refutation for the DPH. In essence, we are raising the question: What are appropriate ways to measure the psychoanalytic concepts discussed in the beginning of the chapter? Freud himself would agree that to test any theory completely, deductions must be derived which can be subjected to rigid empirical test through the study of observable behavior.[5] One of the most significant difficulties with psychoanalytic theory is that no one single set of deductions from actual behavior adequately represents the theory. For example, the concept of fixation at the anal stage of development leads to two contradictory predictions about a person's behavior. On the one hand, an anally fixated individual may be described as rigid, uncompromising, moralistic, and excessively clean and neat. An unusually messy person, however, might also be regarded as fixated at the anal stage. Clearly, testing the relationship between anal fixation and overt behavior can lead to confusing and contradictory results.

One attempt to test psychoanalytic theory empirically has been through projective tests. Projective tests, such as the Rorschach and Thematic

---

[5]Freud frequently mentioned that Jean-Martin Charcot (1835–1893) was one of his most revered and influential teachers. Freud often included in his writings his favorite of Charcot's principles:

Theory is all very well but it does not prevent the facts from existing. (Charcot quoted by Freud in Freud, 1886, preface and footnotes to the translations of Charcot's Tuesday Lectures, 1892–1894, Standard Edition, Volume 1, p. 139, London: Hogarth Press, 1966)

Apperception Test (TAT), are based on the notion that, given an ambiguous stimulus, a person will project his own conflicts and impulses onto that stimulus, and therefore reveal these unconscious aspects of his personality to the astute examiner. Although the validity of the projective hypothesis has been questioned repeatedly (Megargee, 1966), it is notable that none of the studies of the spouse's personality have involved projective measures.

The measures most frequently used to test the DPH have been general indices of psychopathology, primarily the Minnesota Multiphasic Personality Inventory (MMPI). The MMPI, a 565-item true–false test, was originally designed to aid in psychiatric diagnosis (Dahlstrom & Welsh, 1960; Hathaway & McKinley, 1951). Different patterns of scores on the MMPI were validated against various criterion populations of psychiatric patients. Therefore, the MMPI is best considered as a general measure of psychological disturbance, rather than a measure of unconscious conflicts. Hence, using the MMPI to test the DPH is a somewhat questionable procedure. In fact, one could almost argue that wives of alcoholics should look quite healthy on the MMPI if the DPH and DH are correct, since their psychic apparatus is in equilibrium while their spouses are actively drinking. In other words, if being married to an alcoholic is the mind's way of resolving intrapsychic conflicts, then spouses should not be experiencing excessive anxiety or other symptoms and therefore should not look seriously disturbed.

With these extreme cautions in mind, we now review the empirical literature designed to test the DPH.

General Indices of Disturbance

The MMPI has been used to study both the alcoholic (Button, 1956; Rosen, 1960) and his wife (Kogan, Fordyce, & Jackson, 1963; Paige, LaPointe, & Krueger, 1971; Rae & Forbes, 1966).

Paige et al. (1971) administered the MMPI to 25 alcoholics and their wives. They concluded that "the neurotic tendencies in each (alcoholic and spouse) make for the discordance in their marriage. That is, they are not responsible (do not have the capacity) to satisfy each other's needs in an adaptive way" (p. 71).

The Paige study had methodological weaknesses. For example, the 25 wives were selected from a group of 323 wives whose alcoholic husbands were receiving treatment. Also, only spouses who had volunteered and were married and living with their husbands were tested, resulting in possible selection bias. Paige and co-workers originally selected 50 wives for testing. These investigators do not indicate why these specific 50 wives were selected, but do state that half of the 50 refused testing. Furthermore, no control groups were used, so the findings could be secondary to factors other than being married to an alcoholic. Another major criticism of this study is the ambiguity that surrounds the basis from which these workers draw their conclusions. Apparently, they base their conclusions on the scores of 40 MMPI subscales reportedly measuring specific psychological characteristics. The 13 regular MMPI scales were within normal range (no T scores above 70), however, and it is unclear what data justified their conclusions.

Rae and Forbes (1966) reported another empirical study which favors the DPH, but which is also subject to methodological criticism. These authors reported that 11 out of 25 wives had "abnormal Psychopathic Deviate scores representing a fundamental personality trait" (p. 199). Examination of the data, however, reveals that although 11 wives had a Pd subscale T score above 60, the *mean* T score for the 11 wives as well as for the total sample, fell within the normal range (no T scores above 70). Thus, their data do not appear to support their conclusions.

Rae and Forbes also studied only a small sample of wives of *hospitalized* alcoholics, and used no controls. The most significant contribution is that these workers attacked the unitary concept of the personality of the alcoholic's wife by showing that the wives could be separated into at least two MMPI profile subgroups.

Kogan et al. (1963) have presented perhaps the most methodologically sound empirical pro-DPH investigation, although even this study has some methodological problems. MMPI scores of 50 wives of actively drinking alcoholics were compared to 50 wives of nonalcoholics matched for age and socioeconomic variables. Five quantitative MMPI measures were calculated:

1. Welsh's Anxiety Index (AI) (Welsh, 1952).
2. Gough's psychotic triad (Gough, 1947) which is the Paranoid (Pa), Psychasthenic (Pt), and Schizophrenic (Sc) scores on the MMPI with greater than 69 as severe, 60–69 as mild, 56–59 as questionable, and less than 56 as normal.
3. Modlin's three measures of personality impairment (Modlin, 1947). (1) The mean scores of the MMPI subscales Hypochondriasis (Hs), Depression (D), and Hysteria (Hy), categorized as being severe if greater than 69, mild if between 60 and 69, and normal if less than 60. (2) AV: The mean score for eight MMPI subscales [excluding Masculinity (Mf) since it has questionable validity in female subjects]; scores are categorized the same as (1). (3) The number of T scores greater than 70. More than two is severe, one or two is mild, none is normal.

Kogan and co-workers did a median test of the distribution of AI scores for the two groups and demonstrated that wives of alcoholics had higher scores (*p* <.01); however, the T-score range for the two groups was 26–29 (spouses) and 21–118 (control group). Also, the authors did not report the frequency of distribution of the AI score for the two groups. Two (AV and T scores greater than 70) out of the three Modlin scales and also the Psychotic Triad scores were more abnormal in the spouse of the alcoholic (*p* <.02). The two experimental groups, however, showed no significant differences for the A measure. Also, over half of the wives of alcoholics tested normal on Modlin measures scores and normal on Psychotic Triad scores.

In the section on empirical evidence against the DPH, we will discuss the studies of Ballard (1959), Corder, Hendricks, and Corder (1964), and Rae and Drewery (1972), who also used the MMPI to study alcoholics' wives under more controlled conditions and observed quite different results than those of Paige et al. (1971), Rae and Forbes (1966), and Kogan et al. (1963).

Interpersonal Perception Studies

Interpersonal perception studies report the observations of subjects as perceived by, or as they perceive, significant others. Although interpersonal perception studies do not necessarily focus on "disturbances" within an individual spouse, the research does report on whether or not there is something unique about spouses of alcoholics, and so we have chosen to include discussion of these concepts in this section of our book. There is also an implication or presupposition throughout most interpersonal perception literature that intrapsychic factors strongly influence and sometimes distort interpersonal perceptions. Therefore, we feel justified in discussing the interpersonal perception literature in the DPH chapter. We should add at the outset that critics have pointed out the major possibilities of confounding variables associated with the analysis of interpersonal perception protocols (Cronbach, 1955; Orford, 1975; Wright, 1968).

Mitchell (1959) was one of the earliest researchers to attempt an understanding of interpersonal sensitivity and communication within the alcoholic marriage. Mitchell administered the Marriage Adjustment Schedule No. 1A to 28 couples in which the husband was an alcoholic. Each subject was asked to describe himself/herself and his/her spouse with respect to 17 personality traits (Preston, Peltz, Mudd, & Froscher, 1952) used in previous studies of marriage partners.

The paired responses were compared to those of a control group of 28 couples with serious marital problems other than drinking, thereby holding constant the experience of a stressful marriage. The control group was matched to the experimental group in duration of marriage, education, age, and religion.

Mitchell found that the traits of control and willingness to accept responsibility were significantly more conflicting issues in the alcoholic marriage group compared to controls. Mitchell concludes from his data that wives of alcoholics are dominant, nagging, aggressive, demanding, and dependent.

It is not clear how Mitchell draws these conclusions since, as will be seen on page 48, Mitchell provides strong evidence invalidating the DPH. The lack of a control group not experiencing marital conflict is also a serious methodological fault. It could be that Mitchell believed that both groups were "disturbed" although the two groups "perceived" each other quite differently in some ways.

Drewery and Rae (1969) administered the interpersonal perception technique (Drewery, 1969) to 22 alcoholic marriage and 26 nonpsychiatric married couples matched for occupation and socioeconomic status. A striking difference was reported in the way the two groups differed in the concordance of the spouse's description of her or his partner. The control wife's description of her husband was very similar to her husband's self-description, whereas the alcoholic's wife's description of her husband was very dissimilar to her husband's self-description. This finding suggests that wives and husbands in alcoholic marriages tend not to share a common perception of the husband. Nonempirical pro-DPH adherents such as Gaertner (see page 34) would explain this phenomenon as at least partially due to psychological fixations and neurotic bondages to the father of childhood so that perceptions of the husband are distorted. As will be seen on page 48, Mitchell reports that this specific interpersonal perceptional interaction (which Mitchell calls "Sensitivity to Partner") does not distinguish his experimental group from his control group.

Other investigators explored the DPH through controlled experimentation with interpersonal perception techniques. Kogan and Jackson (1963) administered Leary's (1957) Interpersonal Checklist (ICL) to 40 wives and to a control group of 40 wives of nonalcoholics. The ICL consists of 128 adjectives or phrases which describe self, ideal self, spouse, and ideal spouse, in terms of eight evenly divided subsections or *variables:* Managerial–Autocratic; Competitive–Exploitive; Blunt–Aggressive; Skeptical–Distrustful, Modest–Self-effacing; Docile–Dependent; Cooperative–Overconventional; Responsible–Overgenerous (Kogan & Jackson, 1961; LaForge & Suczek, 1955; Leary, 1957).

Each of the 40 alcoholics' wives completed the ICL twice: describing the husband when "drunk" and when sober, while the control wives were asked to describe themselves and their husbands "when things are going smoothly in our family" and "when things are not going smoothly in our family."

Scores on three variables of self-perception significantly differentiated the responses of the experimental group and those of the control group. Following an interpretation of their results, Kogan and Jackson (1963) concluded that the experimental wives were *more* likely to see themselves as (1) adhering to the stereotyped, feminine role; (2) being submissive; (3) being passive (Kogan and Jackson do not specifically define "passive" or "submissive"). See the following section.

A consistency exists between the findings of Kogan and Jackson (1963) and Drewery and Rae (1969) who also showed significantly higher stereotyped femininity in the wives as compared to control wives of nonalcoholic marriages. The Kogan and Jackson as well as the Drewery and Rae studies subscribe to the Parson and Bales (1956) conception of masculine and feminine roles in most marriages in which the male role is essentially administrative and instrumental, whereas the female role is to relieve emotional pain and support the rest of the family members:

The husband is expected to be a "good provider" to be able to secure to the couple a "good position" in the community. The wife, on the other hand, is expected to develop skills and human relationships which are essential to making the home harmonious and pleasant. (Parson & Bales, 1956, p. 163)

Kogan and Jackson (1963) also found significant differences between the two groups of subjects in the way that the wives perceived their husbands. The authors interpreted their results as evidence that wives of the alcoholics were significantly *more* likely to see their husbands whether drunk or sober as (1) possessing fewer socially desirable traits; (2) displaying less emotional warmth; and (3) being suspicious, gloomy, and resentful.

Kogan and Jackson (1964) asked 46 wives of alcoholics to perceive themselves and their husbands during times "when my husband is sober" and "when my husband is drunk." The experimental group in this study consisted of 40 wives of the previous sample (Kogan & Jackson, 1963) plus 6 additional wives.

Reportedly, 50% of the wives of the alcoholics perceived their husbands as "atypical" whether or not the husband was intoxicated (see page 49 for contradictory results from another study). Of the 23 wives who viewed their husbands as atypical, 13 did not see themselves as normal. Four of the 46 wives saw themselves as "atypical" only when their husbands were intoxicated. The self-perception of "typical" or "atypical" in 80% of the experimental wives was unrelated to whether or not the husband was drunk. This was a major finding. In less precise terms, Kogan and Jackson (1964) concluded that the wives of the alcoholics saw themselves as having emotional difficulties regardless of whether the husbands were drunk or sober. This observation was also made by Gliedman, Nash, and Webb (1956), who reported the subjective impression that "the wives tended to be dissatisfied with themselves as persons regardless of whether the husbands were sober or intoxicated" (p. 91).

A recent study in London observed that the wives' perception of the alcoholic when sober changed very little over a 1-year period during which time the alcoholic's drinking habits changed markedly (Orford, Oppenheimer, Egert, Hensman, & Guthrie, 1976).

At first glance it would appear that these reports (Kogan & Jackson, 1963, 1964; Gliedman et al., 1956; Orford et al., 1976) support the DPH, which suggests that the alcoholic's drinking is not the primary problem in the marital conflict and that the psychological difficulties in the nonalcoholic spouse would not be significantly changed by the alcoholic's abstinence. It is because of this apparent conclusion that we have placed these studies in the empirical *support* section of the DPH chapter. The sociological perspective proponents (see chapter 4) would criticize these reports for not considering the secondary problems engendered by alcoholism and existing during both intoxication and sobriety. For example, if a chronic money shortage has resulted from prolonged alcoholism, then it would make little difference how the wife perceives herself or her husband when drunk as compared to when he is sober, since the financial problems remain stable as the alcoholic's current state of sobriety fluctuates.

Dependency–Dominance Studies

"Dependence" or "dominance" of a spouse as perceived by herself or her partner is another parameter that has been studied in alcoholic marriage populations. Although dependence and dominance are not necessarily "disturbances" or "symptoms," we have included these studies in this empirical support subsection of our DPH discussion since the dependency and dominance as defined by these interpersonal perception studies are closer to disturbances than "nondisturbances." Also, as mentioned on page 24, some nonempirical pro-DPH proponents have directly associated dependence to the psychoanalytic concept of fixation at the oral psychosexual stage.

Kogan and Jackson (1963) (see page 43) reported a significantly greater frequency of passivity in the wives of alcoholics compared to those in the control group. In this study, the trait of passivity is a self-perception, whereas in many of the earlier studies (e.g., Gaertner, 1939; Lewis, 1937; Price, 1945) (see page 33) the trait of excessive dominance or dependence was subjectively assigned to the wife by other people.

Kogan and Jackson's (1963) finding of dependency among wives seems to conflict with other investigators' (see pages 42 and 50) findings of significant dominance among wives of alcoholics. Elucidation of these discrepancies requires expanded research. It is very interesting to note, however, that various investigators define dominance and dependency from different perspectives. For example, a researcher might assess dependency–dominance by examining roles within the family (see Lemert's study, page 50), or the researchers might choose to evaluate directly the monadic subjective feeling states of the subject and use this information as the basis of the assessment, as was done by Kogan and Jackson (1963) (see page 43).

At this point we caution our readers not to interpret the findings of similarities within the group of alcoholic spouses as necessarily supporting the DPH, since the similarities could be as much the result of common life situations as of common personality profiles (Cohen & Krause, 1971; Kogan & Jackson, 1963). This concept is expanded upon in subsequent chapters of this book.

Mitchell (1959) (see page 42) found that the alcoholic tended to perceive more dominance in his spouse than his spouse perceived in herself. This observation was also reported by Gunther and Brilliant (1967) in their analysis of data gathered from administering the Interpersonal Checklist (LaForge & Suczek, 1955) to 40 alcoholics and their spouses. Other reports (Drewery & Rae, 1969; Duhamel, 1971; McCrady, 1975) also support this finding.

The discrepancy between partners in their perception of dominance was not found to be characteristic of other conflicting marriages (Mitchell, 1959), or of normal marriages (Drewery & Rae, 1969). These findings could be interpreted in three ways.

1. One could conclude that the spouses of alcoholics are characteriologically dominant people but for one reason or another, they do not show it on paper and pencil test results; that trait is discovered only by the recorded observations of other observors such as the marital partner. This conclusion focuses on the intrapsychic variables within the spouse.

2. One could conclude that the perceived dominance is mostly the result of the wife assuming the roles of father and husband which the alcoholic has vacated and without which the family unit would disintegrate. Since this "dominant" role is relatively new and hopefully temporary, the wife still perceives herself in a less dominant role than she is actually taking. This supposition focuses on the stress of the situation rather than intrapsychic conflict and is partly supported by a recent study of Orford et al. (1970). These authors reported that 53% of 100 alcoholic husbands and their wives have established a pattern of wife-dominated decision making and family responsibility, even though the couples ideally subscribed to the more traditional male-dominated family unit.

3. One could also entertain the interesting possibility that the alcoholic's description of his spouse is the result of his perceptual distortion based on his intrapsychic and environmental need to have someone dominate him. The latter argument might be supported by Kogan and Jackson (1963) who found that wives described themselves as more passive than the self-description of wives of nonalcoholics. It is interesting, however, that Kogan and Jackson's findings could also be explained in several ways; for example, one could argue that the wife is unambivalently passive, or one could claim that the wife must repress her dominant traits because of her conflicted need for her husband to take care of her.

Of course, speculation of this sort proves nothing, but it does serve to suggest a variety of hypotheses testable by the clinical researcher and suggestive of the psychoanalytic, sociological, behavioral, and systems theory perspectives discussed in this book. The existence of at least three alternative explanations of the discrepancy between partners in dominance perception is an excellent example of the complex behavioral and intrapsychic variables responsible for "personality traits."

EMPIRICAL EVIDENCE AGAINST THE DPH

Many alcohologists and other students of human behavior have challenged the DPH. In fact, a large part of the remainder of this book offers conceptual and empirical evidence that essentially should put the DPH (and the related decompensation hypothesis) to rest forever. Since we have previously discussed some empirical general indices of disturbance, interpersonal perceptions, and dependency–dominance studies supporting the DPH, we will now present empirical studies with similar research protocols that do *not* support the DPH. Other evidence against the DPH will be found in the appropriate chapters.

General Indices of Disturbance Studies

Ballard (1959) administered the MMPI to the same experimental and control subjects used by Mitchell (1959) (see page 42). Ballard found that the alcoholic husbands were significantly more disturbed than the control husbands, but the wives showed no more psychopathology than the wives of nonalcoholics. There was even some evidence that the wives were better adjusted (had more adaptive defense mechanisms) than the control wives in spite of the burden of having to live with a problem drinker. Ballard also reported no distinguishing personality traits (symptoms) between the two groups.

The lack of psychopathology among wives of alcoholics was also reported by Corder and co-workers (1964) who administered the MMPI to 43 wives of alcoholics and 30 wives of nonalcoholics matched for age, income, and educational level. The mean value for each MMPI scale was within the normal range for both groups.

Other general indices of disturbance have yielded data not supporting the DPH. For example, in a study in which the Psychological Screening Inventory (Lanyon, 1970, 1973) was administered to 40 spouses of hospitalized alcoholics, it was shown that the spouses' scores were well within the normal range (Paolino, McCrady, Diamond, & Longabaugh, 1976).

Rae and Drewery (1972) have shown how very closely researchers must assess the group of spouses before making generalizations about these people. Rae and Drewery studied 33 hospitalized male alcoholics by administering the interpersonal perception technique (Drewery, 1969). The spouses of 51 nonpsychiatric control couples were also tested. The MMPI was given to all subjects and then the spouses of the alcoholics were divided into a Pd (Psychopathic Deviate) group and a NPd (nonpsychopathic Deviate) group, according to the characteristics shown in the Pd scale. It was found that the NPd marriages involving a NPd wife were very similar to the control marriages in their scores on the interpersonal perception technique, whereas the marriages involving a Pd wife were "grossly deviant" (Rae & Drewery, 1972, p. 61). It was also concluded that there was significant confusion in the "social sexual roles" and "dependence–independence" areas within the Pd marriage, whereas the NPd group was very similar to the control group. However, Rae and Drewery did not specifically define what they meant by "social sexual roles" and "dependence–independence" and so these conclusions leave readers with the same ambiguity as do other studies measuring variables that are not specifically defined.

Interpersonal Perception

In the study discussed on page 42, Mitchell (1959) concluded that anger between marital partners was no more frequent in the alcoholic marriage group than in the troubled non-alcoholic marriage group.

Mitchell also compared the relative magnitude of three marital interpersonal components:

1. Sensitivity to Partner—the degree to which the mate's description of partner is the same as the partner's self-description. This component is sometimes referred to as "empathy."
2. Assumed Similarity—the degree to which a spouse projects his/her own personality traits onto the marital partner.
3. Partner Likeness—the degree to which marital partners are alike.

With the husband as a point of reference, these components are symbolized by Mitchell in the operational scheme depicted in Figure 2-3. Mitchell showed a statistically significant resemblance between the two groups of subjects (alcoholic marriage and control group) in the magnitude of *Sensitivity to Partner,* and *Assumed Similarity.*

Mitchell also reported that when the wives of *both* groups scored low on Sensitivity to Partner, they scored high on Assumed Similarity. The patterns of interaction were not specific for alcoholic marriages, an observation that suggests there is nothing unique about the interaction within an alcoholic marriage.

Of course, a similarity in "interaction" does not prove that wives of alcoholics are not a "disturbed" group. The reader must remember, however, that the DPH not only claims that spouses of problem drinkers are a "disturbed group"; the DPH proponents also claim that the spouses of alcoholics have in common certain characteristics of the mind and patterns of interaction *which make them distinguishable from other people.* Thus, an interpersonal perception test showing spouses of alcoholics to be *similar* to spouses of nonalcoholics is helpful in completely assessing the validity of the DPH. As noted on page 42, Mitchell seems both to support and challenge the DPH. The lasting value of Mitchell's work is that his research was a pivotal study in casting doubt on the validity of the DPH, since he clearly showed that certain personality traits and interpersonal components are characteristic of troubled marriages and not specific to the alcoholic marriage.

Kogan et al. (1963) (see page 41) also closely analyzed their data for patterns

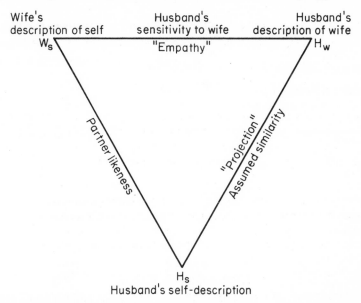

Figure 2.3 Operational schematic for the measurement of understanding of partner and assumed similarity. (Modified by permission of author and publisher, from: Mitchell H. E. Interpersonal percepton theory applied to conflicted marriages in which alcohol is and is not a problem. *American Journal of Orthopsychiatry*, 1959, *29*, 547–559. Copyright © 1959 the American Orthopsychiatric Association, Inc. Reproduced by permission.)

of personality function. Their conclusion was that in comparison to the control group the wives "failed to reveal patterns of personality functioning occurring either with high frequency or with significantly greater frequency" (p. 232).

It should be noted that recent research contradicts Kogan and Jackson's (1964) (see page 44) finding that the wife's perception of the alcoholic is relatively stable whether the husband is drunk or sober. There are reports clearly showing that between drinking episodes, some spouses perceive their alcoholic partners in positive terms, such as kind, dependable, alert, and good-natured, despite the chronic problems engendered by alcoholism. When the alcoholic is *drunk*, however, these same spouses perceive their marital partners in strongly negative terms, such as hostile, belligerent, selfish, and suspicious (Tamerin, Tolor, DeWolfe, Packer, & Neumann, 1973).

Dependency–Dominance Studies

In evaluating the quality and quantity of dependence problems, Lemert (1960) divided 141 wives into two groups: 76 wives whose husbands' alcoholism antedated marriage (Group 1) and 55 wives whose husbands developed drinking problems after marriage (Group 2). The results were that 36% of Group 1 were considered to be dominant wives as compared to 15% of Group 2.

This study is included in the section on empirical evidence against the DPH since the results challenge the DPH notion of conceptualizing "alcoholic marriages" as one group of people. Furthermore, Lemert, by example, points out the importance of defining the personality traits that the research is trying to evaluate. Lemert defines the husband's dependency in any marriage as the existence of one or more of the following: (1) wives dominating the family; (2) economic dependency on parents; (3) abnormal emotional relationship with parents or spouse.

Although we disagree with this specific definition of dependency, we are in agreement with Lemert that most research studies inadequately specify the dependency that they are measuring. We challenge the whole idea of determining the presence or absence of dependency in the marriage of alcoholics without specific definition of what is being measured. What is being labeled "dependency" by one researcher or family might not be called dependency by another group of researchers or subjects.

Family task performance and decision making are extraordinarily complicated behavior in all families, including those without serious troubles (Olson & Rabunsky, 1972; Orford, 1975; Turk & Bell, 1972). One family member might be responsible for deciding on action, whereas a second member appoints the person who is to perform the task, and a third person chooses the time for action. Furthermore, these roles are exchanged from task to task. For example, Orford et al. (1976) in their study of 100 male alcoholics and their spouses report that the husbands were slightly overinvolved in social and sexual decision making but underinvolved in family tasks. Thus generalizations from reports assessing "dominance," "dependency," "assertion," "aggression," etc., can and have led to confusing results, since different researchers are using identical terms for different behaviors.

The literature on the dependence issue within the individual alcoholic is as mixed as that on the alcoholic marriage. Although it is generally considered by the public that alcoholics are "dependent" individuals, a thorough review of the literature (McCrady, 1975) has shown that studies which use subtle measures of dominance, such as the MMPI or CPI, have found that problem drinkers characterize themselves as "dependent," whereas those studies using checklists found that problem drinkers do not describe themselves as different than "normal" controls.

 It is our opinion that the most logical conclusions from the research on dominance and dependence in alcoholic marriages is that there is a strong indication that "dominance–dependence" conflicts exist in alcoholic marriages to a significant degree although the definitions of dependence are unclear and it is unknown to what degree these patterns are antecedents or consequences (see chapter 6) of alcoholism. Thus the existence of dominance–dependence conflicts in the marriage still, by itself, reveals little about the personalities of the partners before marriage. More positive statements regarding the existence of dependence–independence conflicts in alcoholic marriages and further illumination of these conflicts cannot come from past investigations.

We remain critical of the tendency for past dependency–dominant alcoholic marriage researchers to focus on those marriages in which the husband is an alcoholic. Almost all the pro-DPH and pro-DH literature rests on the supposed investments which the nonalcoholic's wife has as a woman, being married to a man who is dependent on her through his alcoholism. The wife's desire to control her husband is, in our opinion, frequently labeled "pathological" not so much because it is a manifestation of a mental aberration or a maladaptive coping mechanism, but because the wife's behavior is a reversal of the culturally prescribed roles. (See page 31 for the relationship of this idea to the superego.) We propose that the strength of the DPH and DH would weaken if those alcoholic marriages in which the alcoholic is the *female* were scrutinized. Such investigations would no longer be uncovering *culturally* "abnormal" behavior since it is usually culturally expected (and hence not "pathological") for a husband to wish to "dominate" his wife, and he probably would not need to marry an alcoholic woman in order to do so. The postulated fabric of unconscious desires of the DPH and DH therefore becomes a weak construct in explaining the marriage between an alcoholic woman and a nonalcoholic man.

SIMILARITIES TO STUDIES OF THE ALCOHOLIC

The evolution of thought regarding one "personality type" among those who marry alcoholics parallels the early development of conceptualizations of one "alcoholic personality." The underlying assumption of these early studies on the alcoholic was that alcoholism was *caused* by a particular personality structure (Sutherland, Schroeder, & Tordella, 1950). Sutherland et al. (1950) and Syme (1957) carefully reviewed all research studies which tried to determine a consistent set of traits characteristic of the alcoholic.

The studies reviewed generally had one of two criteria for the diagnosis of alcoholism: membership in Alcoholics Anonymous or hospitalization because of alcoholism. These early studies employed either projective tests, such as the Rorschach, Thematic Apperception Test (TAT), or Rosenzweig Picture-Frustration Study, or nonprojective personality inventories, such as the MMPI. Projective tests were considered the most likely research vehicles with which to identify unconscious themes common among alcoholics. Nonprojective personality inventories measured aspects of personality more accessible to conscious awareness.

Although the majority of these early studies found few reliable differences between alcoholics and controls, some consistent differences were reported. Consistent findings on the Rorschach were interpreted to suggest that the alcoholic's ambition surpassed his ability, that alcoholics were highly "suggestible," and that alcoholics were slightly extroverted (Sutherland et al., 1950). Sutherland and co-workers concluded, however, that "no satisfactory evidence has been discovered that justifies the conclusion that persons of one type are more likely to become alcoholics than persons of another type" (p. 559). Reviewing an additional 7 years of literature, Syme (1957) reached the same conclusion, as did Lisansky (1967) in a review of another 10 years of research. This consistent finding of no one personality pattern characteristic of alcoholics is quite similar to the findings of no one personality type among the spouses of alcoholics.

The consistency in results is paralleled by the consistency in methodological problems characteristic of both sets of research. First, sample sizes were relatively small in most studies. In addition, samples were biased because they encompassed mainly state hospital or Veterans Administration (VA) Hospital subjects. As Bailey (1967) cogently pointed out, this is a special subsection of the population of alcoholics. These individuals usually have more severe and chronic problems, have fewer family and community ties, and are often unemployed. They are not representative of the whole population of alcoholics. This bias was quite similar to the bias toward only studying spouses who had sought treatment because of their own discomfort, or who came to the attention of treatment personnel or researchers because of their spouse's hospitalization.

A fourth and most significant flaw in the early studies of alcoholics or their spouses was the common assumption that researchers were seeking one personality pattern. Skinner, Jackson, and Hoffman (1974) note that if there are *several* distinctive personality types among alcoholics and their spouses, studies looking for characteristics across subtypes could easily account for negative results, for the differences would be averaged out among the various groups.

Recent studies of the alcoholic personality have become more sophisticated both in methodology and in the research questions being asked. Four recent studies have delineated several subtypes among alcoholics (Goldstein & Linden, 1969; Partington & Johnson, 1969; Skinner, et al., 1974; Whitelock, Overall, & Patrick, 1971). These studies were carefully executed, used large sample sizes ranging from 136 to 513 subjects, and employed multivariant statistics. In addition, each research group replicated their work by dividing their samples into two or three subsamples. Some of the findings have also been replicated across researchers (Skinner et al., 1974; Whitelock et al., 1971). These studies have isolated four to eight personality constellations associated with alcoholism. The same personality types have been isolated through the use of the MMPI and the Differential Personality Inventory. Three subtypes identified across all studies include:

1. A group characterized by low frustration tolerance, poor control over anger, antisocial acts, and lack of concern over others' evaluations. This group generally has made up 20 to 40% of the sample.
2. A group experiencing acute anxiety and depression, difficult marital relationships, and a special concern with their physical health.
3. Individuals who feel little need for treatment, and are generally uncooperative.

The identification of several personality patterns among alcoholics is reminiscent of Whalen's (see page 37) early attempt to describe several types of wives of alcoholics. Unfortunately, the early descriptive work was not extended in recent years through the types of sophisticated methodology characteristic of the alcoholic personality research in the 1970s. The one noteable exception to this statement is the work of Rae and Forbes (1966) (see Appendix A, page 173) and Rae (1972) which attempted to look at interactive MMPI patterns of alcoholics and their spouses, and found distinctive characteristics in marriages between alcoholics and spouses who were both high on the psychopathic deviate (Pd) scale of the MMPI, couples who were both low on this scale, and couples in which one was high and the other low. This recognition of variability suggests an increased sophistication in personality research on wives of alcoholics, which could be extended in the following years. It should be noted, however, that finding consistent personality patterns does not a priori suggest that support will be found for the DPH. Future research may indeed show one subgroup among wives of alcoholics which shows significant personality disturbances, and other subgroups with very different characteristics.

DISCUSSION AND SUMMARY

We have proposed that the proponents of the disturbed personality hypothesis have formulated their theories from basic psychoanalytic topographic and structural concepts of the mind that involve the unconscious, id, ego, and superego as well as the secondary ideas that have evolved from these fundamental concepts. The DPH proponents focus on descriptions and investigations into the mind of the spouse. These investigators adapt a one-sided monadic perspective in that they regard the behavior of the spouse as an expression mostly of the spouse's intrapsychic variables. Although a great deal is postulated about the impact of the nonalcoholic member of the marital pair, the DPH authors say very little about the alcoholic's impact on the nonalcoholic member. Although not explicitly stated, the DPH proponents have adopted the Freudian theory that the personality structure (i.e., the psychic apparatus) is essentially completed by around 6 years of age (the end of the "phallic" psychosexual period); all later experiences are considered to be strongly influenced by earlier life periods. Thus, the spouse's personality is essentially determined before marriage to the alcoholic.

Most of the DPH authors report clinical impressions based on accumulations of case histories. Case histories have limited power toward valid generalizations, and frequently illustrate the unusual rather than the usual instance. It is our strong opinion that no collection of clinical experience can possibly *prove* a psychological theory. Case histories must be validated by solid, well-controlled clinical research. Clinical observations and impressions should be presented as illustrations of theory and not as proofs thereof. It is a sad fact that wives of alcoholics have been stigmatized as a result of well-intentioned authors not following this dictum.

Although the DPH literature is of little predictive clinical value, DPH proponents have had a valuable role in the conceptualization of the alcoholic marriage. DPH theorists were among the first to propose that the spouse is not necessarily a helpless victim of circumstance. They were also the first to introduce the concept that the psychopathology of alcohol misuse is not solely confined within the person of the alcoholic and that the spouse might play a part in the onset and maintenance of the alcoholic's drinking problem.

The critics of the DPH were instrumental in bringing about a shift in focus so that the "personality" of the spouse of an alcoholic was no longer seen as a constant variable existing in isolation, but rather "personality" was conceptualized as a dependent variable changing in response to intrapsychic, sociocultural, and interpersonal factors. These critics of the DPH literature have proved that many factors go into the choice of an alcoholic mate and that drinking patterns are only one of a complex system of psychological, environmental, and sociocultural variables responsible for the marital misery which follows.

Thus the experimental data so far do not support the theory that spouses of alcoholics are a disturbed group. To say that these spouses are psychologically disturbed only grossly oversimplifies the concept of an alcoholic marriage. *In essence, there is ample evidence that the only common denominator among spouses of alcoholics is that they have married alcoholics.*

Although the DPH is founded on specific psychoanalytic principles, the DPH proponents have not used instruments to test the validity of these operational concepts. For example, we have discussed in this chapter empirical investigations that analyze the results of administering the MMPI, Interpersonal Checklist, the Marriage Adjustment Schedule, and the Lanyon Psychological Screening Inventory. These reports conclude by supporting or not supporting the DPH despite the fact that these instruments do not provide and were not designed to provide significant information about the role of the id, ego, and superego at their various conscious, preconscious, and unconscious levels.

Again we want to emphasize that although the DPH proponents have made significant and constructive contributions to the alcoholic marriage literature, the DPH proponents are not, nor do they claim to be, scholars of psychoanalytic theory, despite the fact that the DPH is based on psychoanalytic principles. *We also want to emphasize that although there is no strong empirical evidence validating the DPH, this by no means invalidates the profound psychoanalytic principles of the mind from which the DPH evolved. The necessity and legitimacy of the psychoanalytic concepts of the conscious, preconscious, and unconscious aspects of the id, ego, and superego must stand or fall on their own and must not be incriminated by association with deduced oversimplified and dubious hypotheses such as the DPH.*

Reductionism, a concept relevant to our discussion, "means that a perfectly sound idea is being applied too generally, with neglect or exclusion of concomitantly operating systems-of-events (Munroe, 1955, p. 22). We think that it is quite safe to say that reductionism accurately describes the evolution of the DPH from the psychoanalytic theories of the mind.

Just as the invalidation of the DPH does not negate the validity of psychoanalytic theory, so does it not negate the possibility that assortative mating occurs among alcoholic marriages. The literature on marriages in the general population has been reviewed by several authors and the bulk of the evidence supports the hypothesis that most people in the general population adhere to a principle of homogamous assortative mating (like marries like) (Orford, 1975). Rigorous research must expand to a wider scope of sociocultural and personality variables in an attempt to understand what, if any, common denominators are involved in alcoholic marriages. Assumptions about complementary mate choice among alcoholic marriages have been grossly oversimplified in the same manner that these concepts have been oversimplified among other diagnostic categories such as spouses of opiate addicts (Taylor, Wilber, & Osnos, 1966) and spouses of compulsive gamblers (Boyd & Bolen, 1970). We predict (in agreement with Orford, 1975) that the mating patterns for alcoholic marriages will be demonstrated by future research to be similar to those of the general population in that spouse similarity will be significantly greater for race, age, religion, education, social class, and interests than for personality profiles (at least as measured by current personality test instruments).

REFERENCES

Arlow, J. A., & Brenner, C. Psychoanalytic concepts and the structural theory. *Journal of the American Psychoanalytic Association*, Monograph Series No. 3. New York: International Univ. Press, 1964.

Bailey, M. B. Alcoholism and marriage (A review of research and professional literature). *Quarterly Journal of Studies on Alcohol*, 1961, *22*, 81–97.

Bailey, M. B. Psychophysiological impairment in wives of alcoholics as related to their husbands drinking and sobriety. In R. Fox (Ed.), *Alcoholism, behavioral research, therapeutic approaches*. New York: Springer, 1967.

Baker, S. M. Social casework with inebriates. Alcohol Science & Society, New Haven, *Quarterly Journal of Studies on Alcohol*, 1945, Lecture 27.

Baldwin, D. S. Effectiveness of casework in marital discord with alcoholism. *Smith College Studies on Social Work*, 1947, *18*, 69–122.

Ballard, R. The interaction between marital conflict and alcoholism as seen through MMPI's of marriage partners. *American Journal of Orthopsychiatry*, 1959, *29*(3), 528–546.

Bergler, E. *Unhappy marriage and divorce: A study of neurotic choice of marriage partners*. New York: International Univ. Press, 1946, pp. 144–146, 149, 150, 160.

Bibring, E. The development and problems of the theory of the instincts. *International Journal of Psychoanalysis*, 1941, *22*, 102–131.

Blinder, M. G., & Kirschenbaum, M. The technique of married couple group therapy. *Archives of General Psychiatry*, 1967, *17*, 44–52.

Boggs, M. H. The role of social work in the treatment of inebriates. *Quarterly Journal of Studies on Alcohol*, 1943–44, *4*, 557–567.

Boyd, W. H., & Bolen, D. W. The compulsive gambler and spouse in group psychotherapy. *International Journal on Group Psychotherapy*, 1970, *20*, 77–90.

Breuer, J., & Freud, S. (1895) *Studies on hysteria* (standard ed., Vol. 2). London: Hogarth Press, 1955, pp. 1–307.

Bullock, S. C., & Mudd, E. H. The interaction of alcoholic husbands and their nonalcoholic wives during counseling. *American Journal of Orthopsychiatry*, 1959, *29*, 519–527.

Button, A. D. A study of alcoholics with the MMPI. *Quarterly Journal of Studies on Alcohol*, 1956, *17*, 263–281.

Clifford, B. J. A study of the wives of rehabilitated and unrehabilitated alcoholics. *Social Casework*, 1960, *41*, 457–460.

Cohen, P. E., & Krause, M. S. *Casework with the wives of alcoholics*. New York: Family Service Assoc. of America, 1971.

Corder, B. F., Hendricks, A., & Corder, R. F. An MMPI study of a group of wives of alcoholics. *Quarterly Journal of Studies on Alcohol*, 1964, *25*, 551–554.

Cronbach, L. J. Processes affecting scores on "Understanding of Others" and "Assumed Similarity." *Psychological Bulletin*, 1955, *52*, 177–193.

Dahlstrom, W. G., & Welsh, G. S. *An MMPI handbook.* Minneapolis: Univ. of Minnesota Press, 1960.

DeWald, P. A. *Psychoanalytic process.* New York: Basic Books, 1972.

Drewery, J. An interpersonal perception technique. *British Journal of Psychiatry,* 1969, *42,* 171–181.

Drewery J., & Rae, J. B. A group comparison of alcoholic and nonalcoholic marriages using the interpersonal perception technique. *British Journal of Medical Psychology,* 1969, *115,* 287–300.

Duhamel, T. R. The interpersonal perceptions, interaction and marital adjustment of hospitalized alcoholic males and their wives. *Dissertation Abstracts International,* 1971 (10B), 6254.

Edwards, P., Harvey, C., & Whitehead, P. C. Wives of alcoholics: A critical review and analysis. *Quarterly Journal of Studies on Alcohol,* 1973, *34,* 112–132.

Ellenberger, H. *The discovery of the unconscious: the history and evolution of dynamic psychiatry.* New York: Basic Books, 1970.

Ewing, J. A., & Fox, R. E. Family therapy of alcoholism. *Current Psychiatric Therapies,* 1968, *8,* 86–91.

Forizs, L. A closer look at the alcoholic. *North Carolina Medical Journal,* 1954, *15,* 81–84.

Fox, R. The alcoholic spouse. In V. W. Eisenstein (Ed.), *Neurotic interaction in marriage* (chap. 15). New York: Basic Books, 1956.

Freud, A. (1936). *The ego and the mechanisms of defense.* New York: International Univ. Press, 1966.

Freud, S. (1900). *The interpretation of dreams* (standard ed., Vols. 4 and 5). London: Hogarth Press, 1953, pp. 1–626.

Freud, S. (1905). *Three essays on the theory of sexuality* (standard ed., Vol. 7). London: Hogarth Press, 1953, pp. 1–244.

Freud, S. (1906). *My views on the part played by sexuality in the etiology of neurosis (1906 [1905])* (standard ed., Vol. 7). London: Hogart Press, 1953, pp. 269–281.

Freud, S. (1915a). *The unconscious* (standard ed., Vol. 14). London: Hogarth Press, 1957, pp. 159–209.

Freud, S. (1915b). *Instincts and their vicissitudes* (standard ed., Vol. 14). London: Hogarth Press, 1957, pp. 109–141.

Freud, S. (1917 [1915]). *Mourning and melancholia* (standard ed., Vol. 14). London: Hogarth Press, 1957, pp. 237–259.

Freud, S. (1917 [1916–1917]). *Introductory lectures on psychoanalysis* (standard ed., Vol. 16). London: Hogarth Press, 1963, Chapter 22.

Freud, S. (1923). *The ego and the id* (standard ed., Vol. 19). London: Hogarth Press, 1961, pp. 1–60.

Freud, S. (1925). *Some psychical consequences of the anatomical distinction between the sexes* (standard ed., Vol. 19). London: Hogarth Press, 1961, pp. 241–251.

Freud, S. (1926 [1925]). *Inhibitions, symptoms and anxiety* (standard ed., Vol. 20). London: Hogarth Press, 1959, pp. 75–173.

Freud, S. (1933 [1932]). *New introductory lectures* (standard ed., Vol. 22). London: Hogarth Press, 1964, pp. 1–183.

Freud, S. (1936). *A disturbance of memory on the acropolis* (standard ed., Vol. 22). London: Hogarth Press, 1964, pp. 239–251.

Freud, S. (1940 [1938]). *An outline of psychoanalysis* (standard ed., Vol. 23). London: Hogarth Press, 1964, pp. 139–209.

Freud, S. (1950 [1895]). *Project for a scientific psychology* (standard ed., Vol. 1). London: Hogarth Press, 1966, pp. 281–388.

Freud, S. (1950 [1892–1899]). *Letter No. 52, Extracts from the Fliess Papers* (standard ed., Vol. 1). London: Hogarth Press, 1966, pp. 173–281.

Futterman, S. Personality trends in wives of alcoholics. *Journal of Psychiatric Social Work,* 1953, 37–41.

Gaertner, M. L. *The alcoholic marriage. A study of 15 case records and pertinent psychoanalytic writings.* Thesis, New York School of Social Work, 1939.

Gliedman, L. H., Nash, H. T., & Webb, W. L. Group psychotherapy of male alcoholics and their wives. *Diseases of the Nervous System,* 1956, *17,* 90–93.

Goldstein, S. G., & Linden, J. D. Multivariate classification of alcoholics by means of the MMPI. *Journal of Abnormal Psychology,* 1969, *74,* 661–669.

Gough, H. G. Diagnostic patterns on the MMPI. *Journal of Clinical Psychology,* 1947, *2,* 23–37.

Gynther, M. D., & Brilliant, P. J. Marital status, readmission to hospital, and intrapersonal and interpersonal perceptions of alcoholics. *Quarterly Journal of Studies on Alcohol,* 1967, *28,* 52–58.

Hartmann, E. (1939). *Ego psychology and the problem of adaptation.* New York: International Univ. Press, 1958.

Hathaway, S. R., & McKinley, J. C. *The manual for the Minnesota Multiphasic Personality Inventory.* New York: Psychological Corp., 1951.

Hendrick, I. *Facts and theories of psychoanalysis* (3rd ed.). New York: Alfred A. Knopf, 1958.

Igersheimer, W. W. Group psychotherapy for nonalcoholic wives of alcoholics. *Quarterly Journal of Studies on Alcohol,* 1959, *20,* 77–85.

Jones, E. *The life and work of Sigmund Freud* (Vol. 1). New York: Basic Books, 1953. (a)

Jones, E. The libido theory. In *The life and work of Sigmund Freud* (Vol. 2). New York: Basic Books, 1953. (b)

Kalashian, M. M. Working with the wives of alcoholics in an outpatient clinic setting. *Marriage and Family Living,* 1959, *21,* 130–133.

Karlen, H. Alcoholism in conflicted marriages. *American Journal of Orthopsychiatry,* 1965, *35,* 326–327.

Kogan, K. L., Fordyce, W. E., & Jackson, J. K. Personality disturbance in wives of alcoholics. *Quarterly Journal of Studies on Alcohol,* 1963, *24* (2), 227–238.

Kogan, K. L., & Jackson, J. K. Some role perceptions of wives of alcoholics. *Psychological Reports,* 1961, *9,* 119–124.

Kogan, K. L., & Jackson, J. K. Role perception in wives of alcoholics and nonalcoholics. *Quarterly Journal of Studies on Alcohol,* 1963, *24,* 627–639.

Kogan, K. L., & Jackson, J. K. Personality adjustment and childhood experiences. *Journal of Health and Human Behavior,* 1964, *5,* 50–54.

LaForge, R., & Suczek, R. G. The interpersonal dimension of personality: III. An interpersonal checklist. *Journal of Personality,* 1955, *24,* 95–112.

Lanyon, R. I. Development and validation of a psychological screening inventory. *Journal of Consulting and Clinical Psychology, Psychology Monograph 35,* 1970, *35,* (1), P. 2, 1–24.

Lanyon, R. I. *Psychological screening inventory manual.* Research Psychologists Press, New York: Goshen, 1973.

Laplanche, J., & Pontalis, J. B. *The language of psychoanalysis.* New York: Norton, 1967.

Leary, T. *Interpersonal diagnosis of personality.* New York: Ronald Press, 1957.

Lemert, E. M. The occurrence and sequence of events in the adjustment of families to alcoholism. *Quarterly Journal of Studies on Alcohol,* 1960; *21,* 679–697.

Lewis, M. L. *The initial contact with wives of alcoholics. Social Casework,* 1954, *35,* 8–14.

Lewis, M. S. Alcoholism and family casework. *Family,* 1937, *18,* 39–44.

Lisansky, E. Clinical research in alcoholism in the use of psychological tests: A reevaluation. In R. Fox (Ed.), *Alcoholism: Behavioral research, therapeutic approaches.* New York: Springer, 1967, pp. 3–15.

Loescher, D. A. Time limited group therapy for alcoholic marriages. *Medical Ecology and Clinical Research,* 1970, *3,* 30–32.

McCrady, B. S. *Psychological functioning in the alcohol misuser: An integrative model.* Ph.D. Dissertation, 1975.

Megargee, E. I. *Research in Clinical Assessment.* New York: Harper, 1966.

Mitchell, H. E. Interpersonal perception theory applied to conflicted marriage in which alcoholism is and is not a problem. *American Journal of Orthopsychiatry,* 1959, *29,* 547–559.

Modlin, H. C. A study of the MMPI in clinical practice with notes on the Cornell Index. *American Journal of Psychiatry,* 1947, *103,* 758–769.

Moore, B. E., & Fine, B. D. *A glossary of psychoanalytic terms and concepts* (2nd ed.). New York: American Psychoanalytic Assoc., 1968, p. 31.

Munroe, R. L. *Schools of psychoanalytic thought: an exposition, critique and attempt at integration.* New York: Dryden Press, 1955.

Olson, D. H. & Rabunsky, C. Validity of four measures of family power. *Journal of Marriage and Family,* 1972, *34,* 224–234.

Orford, J. Alcoholism and marriage: The argument against specialism. *Quarterly Journal of Studies on Alcohol,* 1975, *11,* 1537–1560.

Orford, J., Oppenheimer, E., Egert, S., Hensman, C., & Guthrie S. The cohesiveness of alcoholism-complicated marriages and its influence on treatment outcome. *British Journal of Psychiatry,* 1976, *128,* 318–339.

Paige, P. E., LaPointe, W., & Krueger, A. The marital dyad as a diagnostic and treatment variable in alcohol addiction. *Psychology,* 1971, *8,* 64–73.

Paolino, T. J., McCrady, B. S., Diamond, S., & Longabaugh, R. Psychological disturbances in spouses of alcoholics: An empirical assessment. *Journal of Studies on Alcohol,* 1976, *37*(11), 1600–1608.

Parson, S. T., & Bales, R. F. *Families, socialization and interaction process.* Glencoe, Ill.: Free Press, 1956.

Partington, J. T., & Johnson, S. G. Personality types among alcoholics. *Quarterly Journal of Studies on Alcohol,* 1969, *30,* 21–34.

Pattison, E. M., Courlas, P. G., Patti, R., Mann, B., & Mullen, D. Diagnostic-therapeutic intake groups for wives of alcoholics. *Quarterly Journal of Studies on Alcohol,* 1965, *26,* 605–616.

Pixley, J. M., & Stiefel, J. R. Group therapy for wives of alcoholics. *Quarterly Journal of Studies on Alcohol,* 1963, *24,* 304–314.

Preston, M., Mudd, E. H., Peltz, W. L., & Froscher, H. B. Impressions of personality as a function of marital conflict. *Journal of Abnormal Psychology,* 1952, *47,* 326–336.

Price, G. M. A study of the wives of 20 alcoholics. *Quarterly Journal of Studies on Alcohol,* 1945, *5,* 620–627.

Rae, J. B. The influence of the wives on the treatment outcome of alcoholics: A follow-up study of two years. *British Journal of Psychiatry,* 1972, *120,* 601–613.

Rae, J. B., & Drewery, J. Interpersonal patterns in alcoholic marriages. *British Journal of Psychiatry,* 1972, *120,* 613–621.

Rae, J. B., & Forbes, A. R. Clinical and psychometric characteristics of the wives of alcoholics. *British Journal of Psychiatry,* 1966, *112,* 197–200.

Rapaport, D. The structure of psychoanalytic theory: A systematizing attempt. *Psychological Issues,* 1960, *2,* Monograph No. 6. New York: International Univ. Press.

Rosen, A. A comparative study of alcoholic and psychiatric patients with the MMPI. *Quarterly Journal of Studies on Alcohol,* 1960, *21,* 253-265.

Sjöbäck, H. *The psychoanalytic theory of defensive processes.* New York: Halsted Press, 1973.

Skinner, H. A., Jackson, D. N., & Hoffman, N. H. Alcoholic personality types: Identification and correlates. *Journal of Abnormal Psychology,* 1974, *83,* 685–666.

Sutherland, E. H., Schroeder, H. G., & Tordella, C. L. Personality traits in the alcoholic: A critique of existing studies. *Quarterly Journal of Studies on Alcohol,* 1950, *11,* 547–561.

Syme, L. Personality characteristics and the alcoholic: A critique of current studies. *Quarterly Journal of Studies on Alcohol,* 1957, *18,* 288–302.

Tamerin, J. S., Tolor, A., DeWolfe, J., Packer, L., & Neumann, C. P. Spouses' perception of their alcoholic partners: A retrospective view of alcoholics by themselves and their spouses. *Proceedings of the Third Annual Alcoholism Conference of the NIAAA,* June 1973, pp. 33–49.

Taylor, S. D., Wilbur, M. & Osnos, R. The wives of drug addicts. *American Journal of Psychiatry,* 1966, *123,* 585–591.

Turk, J. L., & Bell, M. W. Measuring power in families. *Journal of Marriage and the Family,* 1972, *34,* 215–222.

Vaillant, G. Theoretical hierarchy of adaptive ego mechanisms. *Archives of General Psychiatry,* 1971, *24,* 107–118.

Welsh, G. S. An anxiety index and an internalization ratio for the MMPI. *Journal of Consulting Psychology,* 1952, *16,* 65–72.

Whalen, T. Wives of alcoholics: Four types observed in a family service agency. *Quarterly Journal of Studies on Alcohol,* 1953, *14,* 632–641.

Whitelock, P. R., Overall, J. E., & Patrick, J. H. Personality patterns and alcohol abuse in a state hospital population. *Journal of Abnormal Psychology,* 1971, *78,* 9–16.

Wright, P. H. Need similarity, need complimentarity, and the place of personality and interpersonal attraction. *Journal of Experimental Research in Psychiatry,* 1968, *3,* 126–135.

3

The Decompensation
Hypothesis

WHAT IS THE DECOMPENSATION HYPOTHESIS AND WHO SUPPORTS IT?

The *decompensation hypothesis* is a logical extension of the disturbed personality hypothesis as an effort to explain the psychodynamics of the alcoholic marriage. The decompensation hypothesis represents a controversial school of thought which incorporates the psychoanalytic perspectives of the mind discussed in chapter 2. The DH explains the alcoholic's excessive drinking as *necessary* to preserve the marital relationship. According to the logic of this theoretical model, the alcoholic's excessive drinking is in some way satisfying an unconscious need of the nonalcoholic spouse and thereby functioning to keep the psychic apparatus of the nonalcoholic spouse in psychological equilibrium. We remind our readers that like the DPH, the decompensation hypothesis is a mentalistic approach, i.e., it focuses on the mind rather than on the interpersonal, intergroup, and intragroup aspects of the sociological, behavioral, and systems theories discussed in chapters 4, 5, and 6.

PROPONENTS OF THE DECOMPENSATION HYPOTHESIS

There are a considerable number of clinical reports supporting the decompensation hypothesis. Boggs (1944), in summarizing his clinical impressions, claimed that the wife:

. . . knocks the prop from under him at all turns, seemingly needing to keep him ineffectual so that she feels relatively strong and has external justification for hostile feelings. Thus she keeps the lid on her own inadequacies and conflicts . . . . (p. 562)

The psychoanalyst Futterman (1953) gives examples of psychotic and neurotic depression and phobias developing in wives following the husband's sobriety:

in many instances the wife of an alcoholic . . . seems to encourage the husband's alcoholism to satisfy her own psychological needs . . . she chooses as her foil a dependent, weak male with whom she can unconsciously contrast herself and upon whom she can project her own weaknesses, thereby denying their existence in herself. When this symbiotic relationship is disturbed by an improvement on the part of the husband, the wife decompensates. (p. 40,41)

Rhetoric such as this was supported by the subjective impressions of deSaugy (1962), following work with 100 couples, and by Mally (1965), following 6 years of experience in an alcoholism outpatient clinic.

Gliedman (1957) contacted 45 couples of alcoholic marriages and offered them treatment. Only nine couples responded to this offer, a major reason for their positive response being the wife's insistence that her husband get treatment for his drinking problem. The fact that the primary motivation for treatment of these nine couples came from the wife is noteworthy, since Gliedman reported that even though the wives were responsible for the husbands' seeking therapy, two of these nine spouses still "experienced a nervous breakdown when their husbands stopped drinking" (p. 419). (One could, of course, argue the opposite side and point out that seven of the wives did not decompensate.)

Kalashian (1959) subjectively noted not only psychological symptoms but also somatic disorders occurring in the nonalcoholic spouse following the husband's sobriety.

Browne and Adler (1959) discussed four cases of the spouses of alcoholics developing psychological decompensation following the alcoholic spouse's sobriety. These cases are especially interesting since the nonalcoholic spouses developed "oral" symptoms, such as gastrointestinal disorders, obesity, and even alcoholism itself. At least two of the spouses were "protected from becoming obese and alcoholic so long as their mates continued drinking. When this stops, then their own urges become pressing and must be satisfied more directly . . . . Thus, alcoholism tends to preserve such marriages" (pp. 6,7).

While studying 58 wives of alcoholics, Rae (1972) noted that 4 out of the 58 had to be hospitalized for psychiatric reasons following the husband's cessation of drinking.

Kohl (1962) shared his observations of four spouses of alcoholics who experienced severe emotional decompensation following the alcoholic's improvement or clinical recovery. Kohl was studying psychiatric inpatients in general and noted that 35 spouses of *nonalcoholic* psychiatric inpatients also decompensated following the patient's improvement. Kohl gathered these data from his subjective observations of an unspecified number of patients admitted to the Payne Whitney Psychiatric Clinic from 1950 to 1960. Kohl presents no control group nor does he report the number of patients "observed" whose spouses did not decompensate.

Igersheimer (1959) reported on 5 months of 1½ hour per week psycho-analytically oriented group psychotherapy with six selected wives of alcoholics. In three of these six women, marked anxiety occurred at times when their husbands were "doing better." No objective measures were used and the conclusions were based on subjective clinical impressions.

Martensen-Larsen (1956) has described his experience in Denmark as a psychotherapist in group psychotherapy for wives of alcoholics. Commenting on changes that take place following the husband's sobriety, he says:

> Making them (the wives) see how they consider and treat their husbands as children provokes anxiety, which we (therapists our parenthesis) have to deal with after the lines set up by Futterman who warns against nervous breakdown. At the time that we are succeeding in reestablishing their husbands, we may find in the wives the host's parasitic dependence on the parasite. (p. 36)

Mitchell and Mudd (1957) attempted to interview 33 alcoholic marriage couples in a series of 19 1- to 3-hour interviews for each partner. Only seven couples failed to complete the interviewing series and in at least four of these seven cases, the nonalcoholic spouse was responsible for the broken contact with the interviewer. Commenting on subjective impressions of all 33 couples, Mitchell and Mudd (1957) noted that a frequently expressed opinion by the counselors in this study was that "the wives' adjustment deteriorated as the drinking husband's situation improved" (p. 654). Again, no objective data are offered.

Deniker, deSaugy, and Ropert (1964) observed 100 alcoholics and their spouses and compared their findings to a control group of "normal" spouses. Deniker et al. concluded that the wife of the alcoholic "maintains her husband's alcoholism and. . . the rigidity of her defense system [defense mechanisms] makes it very difficult for her to modify her behavior" (p. 381). The instruments used were "extensive questionnaires" (p. 376). Deniker and co-workers do not indicate either the content or the empirical validity or reliability of these instruments.

MacDonald (1956) was the first to attempt a more objective study of the decompensation hypothesis. MacDonald studied 18 women committed to state mental hospitals who were also wives of alcoholics and found that for 11 of the 18 cases, the decompensation was associated with the decrease in the husband's drinking. Although these women had severe personality disorders, they had never decompensated during the mental stress engendered by the husband's alcoholism. In only one case out of the 18, was the decompensation related to an *increase* in the husband's drinking. In three cases, the onset of severe psychiatric disturbance coincided "almost exactly" (p. 283) with the onset of the husband's abstinence.

MacDonald's data are most interesting but must not be taken too seriously since the investigation is methodologically unsound. There are no control groups, there is a strong selection factor, and the sample is too small for significant statistical evaluation. Furthermore, the time relationship between the onset of the husband's alcoholism and the onset of the spouse's emotional decompensation is unclear. Although MacDonald (1956) uses the term "almost exactly" for three cases, he offers no specific time sequence for these cases. Of the three case histories that he presents in which abstinence is "associated with" (p. 283) emotional decompensation, two of them report husband's abstinence to have occurred 2 years before the wife's hospital admission and in the third case the time sequence is unclear "(the alcoholic) cut down (drinking) considerably . . . at the time of her (hospitalized patient) admission" (p. 284). MacDonald concludes his paper with the following admonition:

> *It is emphasized that this report is in the nature of a preliminary study only in that further large scale investigations, with appropriate statistical analysis, are necessary before valid conclusions can be drawn. (p. 286)*

Unfortunately, many subsequent authors did not follow MacDonald's obvious exhortation and his paper is frequently quoted as strong evidence of the validity of the decompensation hypothesis.

OPPOSITION TO THE DECOMPENSATION HYPOTHESIS

Many alcohologists have strongly disavowed the decompensation hypothesis. These critics would naturally also disagree with the DPH notion that alcoholic marriages can be adequately understood by unconscious determinants and concepts that focus on the psychopathology of the individual spouse.

One argument is that the cases seen in the therapists' offices, clinics, and social agencies do not represent the general population of alcoholics. The married couples consisting of a recovered alcoholic and a spouse who did *not* decompensate following the alcoholic's abstinence are not likely to be seeking therapy and, therefore, do not come to the attention of the people who write and teach about alcoholic marriages.

Jackson (1962) (see page 73) strongly argued against the validity of the decompensation hypotheses: "only one of the wives seen by the writer [Jackson] over an 8-year period showed an increase in disturbance of more than a temporary nature when the husband's alcoholism became inactive and apparently permanently so. On the contrary, the wives adjustment typically appears to have improved in most respects" (p. 481).

Burton and Kaplan (1968) studied 47 married couples in which one member was an alcoholic. The couples were in weekly group therapy for an average of 30 sessions over a 1-year period. Sound methodological pretreatment and follow-up data were obtained in evaluating not only the amount of drinking but also family pathology and social deterioration. The interval between the last therapy session and the follow-up interview ranged from 9 to 77 months (mean was 39 months). The subjects were evaluated by a Marriage Adjustment Schedule (copyrighted by Burton and Kaplan) of 22 possible areas of marital disharmony, including sex, children, personal habits, work, relatives, recreation, and financial matters. The couples were given these questionnaires before therapy and then at the follow-up interview. Each spouse was to check whether the amount of disagreement in each area was "none," "a little," "some," or "considerable." At follow-up, 75% of the couples indicated fewer marital problems and 56% of the alcoholics either significantly decreased drinking or achieved abstinence. There was no evidence supporting the decompensation hypothesis and there was strong evidence that "improvement in the area of marital conflict is associated with improvement in drinking behavior" (Burton & Kaplan, 1968, p. 169).

Other investigators agree with Burton and Kaplan that the marital relationship and mental health of the marital pair improved following decreased alcohol misuse (Cohen & Krause, 1971; Emrick, 1974; Finlay, 1966, Gallant, Rich, Bey, & Terranova, 1970; Gerard & Saenger, 1966; Gliedman, Rosenthal, Frank, & Nash, 1956; Loescher, 1970; Orford Oppenheimer, Egert, Hensman, & Guthrie, 1976; Paolino & McCrady, 1976; Smith, 1969).

Haberman (1964) administered the Index of Psychophysiological Disturbance to 156 wives of alcoholics. The Index is 22 questions associated with psychophysiological disturbance, such as gastrointestinal dysfunction, headaches, depression, memory loss, and weakness. This questionnaire was developed from the Midtown Community Mental Health Survey and has been shown to be a valid and reliable instrument (Langner, 1962; Haberman, 1963). The wives were selected from a large sample because they could clearly contrast by recall the difference between periods of abstinence and periods of heavy drinking. The results were that 85% of the wives showed less symptoms during the husband's abstinent period. Since there was exclusion from the study of all respondents who could not clearly contrast by recall the difference between abstinence and drinking, a significant selection factor existed and compromised the validity of Haberman's results.

Several investigators have reported that the nonalcoholic spouse's threat of divorce or insistence on the alcoholic receiving therapy have been significantly effective in getting the patient into treatment and in reducing the alcoholic's uncontrolled drinking (Clifford, 1960; Cohen & Krause, 1971; Ewing, Long, & Wetzel, 1961; Finlay, 1966; Gallant et al., 1970; Gerard & Saenger, 1966; Gliedman et al., 1956; Jackson & Kogan, 1963; James & Goldman, 1971). These findings are obviously inconsistent with the decompensation hypothesis and the disturbed personality hypothesis.

SUMMARY AND DISCUSSION

The literature is conflicting and at first glance tends to obscure more than clarify. Some alcohologists claim a high probability that the spouse of the alcoholic decompensates when the alcoholic is not misusing alcohol. Others, equally knowledgable, argue that the spouse will experience less psychological symptoms when the alcoholic achieves sobriety. To complicate the matter further, Kogan and Jackson (1964) found that 80% of 46 wives saw their own personalities as being unchanged whether or not the husband drank excessively. Kogan and Jackson concluded that according to this study, the husband's drinking was not a primary issue in the marital relationships, which therefore would not be significantly improved or worsened by abstinence.

The role of the unconscious determinants has to be studied under sophisticated rigorously controlled clinical research conditions in order to be thoroughly and scientifically understood. This is very difficult, however, because of the perhaps unresolvable methodological problems in the research of psychoanalytic variables (Knight, 1941; Rapaport, 1960). Eysenck's (1959) statement about the Freudian model also applies to the decompensation hypothesis:

What the Freudian model lacks above all is an intelligible, objectively testable modus operandi which can be experimentally studied in the laboratory, which can be precisely quantified and which can be subjected to formulation of strict scientific laws. (p. 71)

It is illogical to make the sweeping conclusion that a spouse has an unconscious need to be married to a problem drinker until it can be first proven that the spouse knew how to and could cure the alcoholism, but consciously or unconsciously would not or could not apply this remedy. There is not a definitive cure for alcoholism, however, and so there is one more strong argument against the proven validity of the decompensation hypothesis.

It can be safely said that the decompensation hypothesis is doomed to obsolescence since all publications supporting it are subject to severe methodological criticisms, whereas there are studies which have utilized relatively rigorous experimental designs in support of the opposing stress theory (see chapter 4). The subjective impressions of the decompensation hypothesis proponents should not be dismissed entirely, however. Instances of clinical lore are valuable as they offer a clustering of evidence which points out fruitful areas for further investigation; on the other hand, it is a mistake to make generalizations from a handful of subjective impressions.

Eysenck's (1959) words are again relevant:

It is unfortunate that insistence on empirical proof has not always accompanied the production of theories in the psychiatric field, much needless work and many heart-breaking failures could have been avoided if the simple medical practice of clinical trials with proper controls had always been followed in the consideration of such claims. (p. 62)

REFERENCES

Boggs, M. H. The role of social work in the treatment of inebriates. *Quarterly Journal of Studies on Alcohol,* 1944, *4,* 557–567.

Browne, W. J., & Adler, M. D. *The role of alcoholism in preserving the neurotic marriage.* Unpublished paper read at a meeting of the American Psychiatric Association, April 1959.

Burton, G., & Kaplan, H. M. Marriage counseling with alcoholics and their spouses—II The correlation of excessive drinking behavior with family pathology and social deterioration. *British Journal of Addiction,* 1968, *63,* 161–170.

Clifford, B. J. A study of the wives of rehabilitated and unrehabilitated alcoholics. *Social Casework,* 1960, *41,* 457–460.

Cohen, P. C., & Krause, M. D. *Casework with the wives of alcoholics.* New York: Family Service Assoc. of America, 1971.

Deniker, P., deSangy, D., & Ropert, M. The alcoholic and his wife. *Comprehensive Psychiatry,* 1964, *5,* 374–383.

deSaugy, D. L'alcoolique et sa femme; etude psycho-sociale et statistique sur led conditions de leur developpment individuel et de leur vie en commun. *Hygiene Mental,* 1962, *51,* 81–128, 145–201.

Emrick, C. D. A review of psychologically oriented treatment of alcoholism: I. The use and interrelationships of outcome criteria and drinking behavior following treatment. *Quarterly Journal of Studies on Alcohol,* 1974, *35,* 523–549.

Ewing, J. A., Long, V., & Wetzel, G. C. Concurrent group psychotherapy of alcoholic patients and their wives. *International Journal of Group Psychotherapy*, 1961, *2*, 329–338.

Eysenck, H. J. Learning behavior and behavior therapy. *Journal of Mental Science*, 1959, *105*, 61–75.

Finlay, D. G. Effect of role network pressure on an alcoholic's approach to treatment. *Social Work*, 1966, *11*, 71–77.

Futterman, S. Personality trends in wives of alcoholics. *Journal of Psychiatric Social Work*, 1953, 37–41.

Gallant, D. M., Rich, A., Bey, E., & Terranova, L. Group psychotherapy with married couples: A successful technique in New Orleans alcoholism clinic patients. *Journal of Louisiana Medical Society*, 1970, *122*, 41–44.

Gerard, D. L., & Saenger, G. Outpatient treatment of alcoholism: A study of outcome and its determinants. Toronto, Canada: Univ. of Toronto Press, 1966.

Gliedman, L. H. Current and combined group treatment for chronic alcoholics and wives. *International Journal on Group Psychotherapy*, 1957, *7*, 414–424.

Gliedman, L. H., Rosenthal, D., Frank, J. D., & Nash, H. T. Group therapy of alcoholics with concurrent group meetings of their wives. *Quarterly Journal of Studies on Alcohol*, 1956, *17*, 282–287, 655–670.

Haberman, P. W. The use of psychological test for recall of past situations. *Journal of Psychology*, 1963, *19*, 245–248.

Haberman, P. W. Psychological test score changes for wives of alcoholics during periods of drinking and sobriety. *Journal of Clinical Psychology*, 1964, *20*, 230–232.

Igersheimer, W. W. Group psychotherapy for nonalcoholic wives of alcoholics. *Quarterly Journal of Studies on Alcohol*, 1959, *20*, 77–85.

Jackson, J. K. Alcoholism and the family. In D. J. Pittman & C. R. Snyder (Eds.), *Society, culture and drinking patterns*. New York: Wiley, 1962, pp. 472–492.

Jackson, J. K., & Kogan, K. L. The search for solutions: Help-seeking patterns of families of active and inactive alcoholics. *Quarterly Journal of Studies on Alcohol*, 1963, *24*, 449–472.

James, J. E., & Goldman, M. Behavior trends of wives of alcoholics. *Quarterly Journal of Studies on Alcohol*, 1971, *32*, 373–381.

Kalashian, M. M. Working with the wives of alcoholics in an outpatient clinic setting. *Marriage and Family Living*, 1959, *21*, 130–133.

Knight, R. P. Evaluation of the results of psychoanalytic therapy. *American Journal of Psychiatry*, 1941, *98*, 434–446.

Kogan, K. L., & Jackson, J. K. Patterns of atypical perception of self and spouse in wives of alcoholics. *Quarterly Journal of Studies on Alcohol*, 1964, *25*, 555–557.

Kohl, R. N. Pathologic reactions of marital partners to improvement of patients. *American Journal of Psychiatry*, 1962, *118*, 1036–1041.

Langner, T. S. A twenty-two item screening score of psychiatric symptoms indicating impairment. *Journal of Health and Human Behavior*, 1962, *3*, 269–276.

Loescher, D. A. Time limited group therapy for alcoholic marriages. *Medical Ecology and Clinical Research,* 1970, *3,* 30–32.

MacDonald, D. E. Mental disorders in wives of alcoholics. *Quarterly Journal of Studies on Alcohol,* 1956, *17,* 282–287.

Mally, M. A. A study of family patterns in alcoholic marriages. *American Journal of Orthopsychiatry,* 1965, *35,* 325–326.

Martensen-Larsen, O. Group psychotherapy with alcoholics in private practice. *International Journal of Group Psychotherapy,* 1956, *6,* 28–37.

Mitchell, H. E., & Mudd, E. H. The development of a research methodology for achieving the cooperation of alcoholics and their nonalcoholic wives. *Quarterly Journal of Studies on Alcohol,* 1957, *18,* 649–657.

Orford, J., Oppenheimer, E., Egert, S., Hensman, C., & Guthrie, S. The cohesiveness of alcoholism-complicated marriages and its influence on treatment outcome. *British Journal of Psychiatry,* 1976, *128,* 318–339.

Paolino, T. J., & McCrady, B. S. Joint admission as a treatment modality for problem drinkers: A case report. *American Journal of Psychiatry,* February 1976, *133*(2), 222–224.

Rae, J. B. The influence of the wives on the treatment outcomes of alcoholics: A follow-up study of two years. *British Journal of Psychiatry,* 1972, *120,* 601–613.

Rapaport, D. The structure of psychoanalytic theory: A systematizing attempt. *Psychological Issues, Monograph 6,* 1960, 2.

Smith, C. G. Alcoholics: Their treatment and their wives. *British Journal of Psychiatry,* 1969, *115,* 1039–1042.

4

The Sociological Stress Theory

Before going on to discuss the stress theory literature, we hope to facilitate the readers' task by a brief description of the sociological approach to the alcoholic marriage since the sociological perspective is the conceptual foundation upon which the stress theory has developed.

In contrast to the mentalistic psychoanalytic perspective discussed in chapters 2 and 3, the sociological approach to the alcoholic marriage focuses on the structure, process, and functions of the family central unit. Sociologists concentrate on institutionalized regulations which control families and ways in which marriage partners behave in their cultural roles (Jackson, 1962). These workers attempt to clarify the interrelationships of social groups presupposing that any group of people is undoubtedly some thing more than the sum of the people who belong to it. This "some thing more" possessed by the group involves the group's own dynamics which warrant investigations as such.

The sociological perspective is more concerned with how the marital pair react under certain current social conditions and transition states. The sociological approach differs from the psychoanalytic perspective in that the former is less interested in childhood influences on adult life or in degrees of abnormality or normality among the psychic structures of the individual members of the marriage. If a group of wives of alcoholics show common neurotic personality traits, the sociologists look for similiar experiences of environmental stress in contrast to the psychoanalytically oriented clinician who will look for similiar intrapsychic conflicts and childhood problems. Another way to look at this is that whereas psychoanalytic theory focuses on the mind of the spouse, i.e., the basic intrapsychic realities and personality structure, the stress theory sociological scheme suggests that the clinical manifestations of the spouse are mostly the result of the variety of external factors such as cultural attitudes toward alcoholism and specific familial and environmental settings.

Since systems theory also focuses on the family as a social unit, our readers might wonder about the distinction between the "sociological" theory of this chapter and the "systems" approach discussed in chapter 6. The difference lies in the sociological approach to individual members of the family unit. Whereas systems theory focuses on a group as a functioning unit, the sociologist emphasizes the family as a unit of mutually interacting *people.* Whereas the systems theorist is more likely to focus on the behavior and direction of the family social unit, the sociologist is more interested in the influence of individual personalities on the group. Both the systems and sociological approaches are very concerned with the "sick" member's *role* in the group and the relationship between "sickness" and designated roles in the family unit.

Orford (1975) elegantly exemplified the sociological approach in his paper which argues against treating the alcoholic marriage as unique and separate from other marriages under stress. He points out that:

> Alcoholism in one partner is, however, only one amongst a number of circumstance which have been construed as crises to which marriage must adjust . . . . Whatever the specific factors involved, it is therefore possible to begin to see alcoholism in marriage not as a unique set of circumstances but as a set of circumstances which can be placed within a spectrum of events associated with marriage. Marriages complicated by alcoholism are exposed to a potentially crisis-producing series of events. But many of the reactions which then take place are shared by members of families exposed to other, similarly quite different, sets of stressful events. (pp. 4, 6)

Orford goes on to cite examples of investigations into the family's coping with burdens of economic depression and unemployment (Angell, 1936); mental illness (Clausen & Yarrow, 1955; Merrill, 1969); war, separation, and reunion (Hill, 1949): and bereavement (Eliot, 1948). Each crisis has its own unique properties of onset, degrees of impairment, and tendencies to engender externalization or internalization of blame (Hansen & Hill, 1969). Sociologists, however, argue strongly against any concept that implies that there is something very substantively different about alcoholics and people who marry them as compared to other marital pairs adjusting to severe stress.

EARLY STRESS THEORY LITERATURE

Until the 1950s, reports on spouses focused on the psychopathology or personality of the spouse as she existed prior to or separate from her husband's alcoholism. One notable exception is that of Mowrer, who in 1940 compared 25 wives of alcoholics to "normal" wives (Mowrer, 1940). A careful reading of Mowrer's paper reveals her impression that the attitude and behavior of the wives in the experimental group changed in response to the husband's behavior. Mowrer was one of the first to partially explain the clinical picture of the wife in terms of the situational stress of living with an alcoholic, but Mowrer was not explicit and she did not publish further on these innovative concepts.

The ensuing literature revealed little interest in expanding on Mowrer's idea until Joan Jackson (1954, 1956, 1959, 1962) wrote the landmark papers on the sociological *stress theory*. The stress theory explains the psychological profile of the wife as primarily a manifestation of adjusting to the prolonged and cumulative crisis of living with an alcoholic (a "crisis" can be defined as a condition of acute anxiety occurring when someone's habitual ways of coping are no longer sufficient and new solutions are required) (Finlay, 1972). Jackson objected to the preponderance of DPH and DH literature which had "advanced to the point that the alcoholic emerges as the innocent victim of his family" (Jackson, 1962, p. 472). The sociological approach was a major conceptual leap from the past alcoholic marriage literature and was in direct opposition to the *decompensation theory* (and DPH).

Jackson's revolutionary and refreshing formulations resulted from over 3 years of scrutinizing Al-Anon members. She attended hundreds of meetings and made verbatum recordings of each gathering or interview in an attempt to identify or describe the specific patterns of family reaction and adjustment to an alcoholic husband and father. Jackson concluded that the alcoholic's family of procreation goes through an adjustment experience that involves crisis, followed by disorganization, and then recovery and reorganization. Jackson claimed that there were seven basic successive stages in the modal course of family adjustment to alcoholism and she reported that all wives of confirmed *abstinent* alcoholics that she studied passed through or encountered these stages, although there was no fixed length of time for each stage. The following is a summary of Jackson's (1954) classic paper. The stages must be presented in series but the reader should bear in mind that these stages overlap and are very rarely as clear-cut as a written description.

Jackson's Seven Critical Stages of Family Adjustment to the Crisis of Alcoholism

Stage 1: Attempts to Deny the Problem

The prospective alcoholic drinks "inappropriately" either socially or alone which leads to rationalizations on the part of self or friends. The couple might discuss the apparent excessive drinking and both partners feel guilty, the alcoholic for his drinking and the spouse for her apparent exaggeration of the problem. As the inappropriate drinking continues, the spouse might seek advice of friends, but usually allows herself to be convinced that the problem is not serious. During this stage, the marital interaction is not disrupted and, in fact, may be better than usual as both partners try to compensate for the problem that they are denying. In our culture, many people have episodes of inappropriate drinking without going on to alcoholism. Accordingly, many couples experience a stage of denial or concern without ever going on to Jackson's next adaptive stage.

Stage 2: Attempts to Eliminate the Problem

Stage 2 begins when the husband's drinking results in the couple's relative social isolation, for example, less invitations to events at which liquor is served, limited serving of drinks when husband is present, awkwardness of friends when the general subject of alcoholism is discussed in the husband's presence, or the couple's self-imposed decreased socialization to avoid embarrassment.

As social isolation increases, so does marital conflict. The drinking becomes the focus of the family's thoughts and actions and drinking tends to be blamed for all family problems. The wife continues to cover up for husband's absenteeism, violence, etc., and she still refuses to seek outside help. During this stage, the couple experience progressive anxiety, anger, and distance from each other. Both search for reasons; the husband feels that his wife does not understand him and the wife feels that she has failed in her family obligation and role. The increased social isolation further reduces the already diminished low self-esteem for both alcoholic and his wife. There are still periods of sobriety, which only serve to help the family deny that the husband has lost control of his drinking. The family tries all kinds of behaviors and techniques to control the husband's drinking without enlisting outside help, for example, threats of divorce, hiding or emptying liquor bottles, hiding money, nursing his hangovers, and even trying to drink with him in an attempt to keep him under observation and control.

An important part of this stage is that the family still maintains their usual roles and the husband is still allocated the responsibilities of the head of the household. Since the wife is protecting the drinker, it is not at all uncommon for the children to experience mostly positive interactions with the husband, and this increased affection between children and father thereby furthers the wife's fear and isolation. During this stage the wife begins to feel self-pity, a feeling which will to some degree forever remain. Jackson compared this person to Whalen's (1953) "Suffering Susan" (see page 37).

Stage 3: Disorganization

In Stage 3, the wife begins to lose all hope and manifests a "what's the use" attitude. Stage 3 is characterized by chaos, anger, and fear. The wife fluctuates from nagging to frustrated emotional and behavioral disorder, as these become agents in the marital conflict. The wife no longer supports the husband as the head of the family, but she is confused about where to turn and worries about her lack of constructive behavior and her conflicted loyalties to her husband and children. By this time, some crisis has occurred in which help from outside the family is inescapable, and as a result, the family finds it progressively less difficult to seek help from the appropriate professionals or agencies.

Fear prevails in Stage 3. The wife fears for the emotional and physical well-being of her husband and her children and she is especially fearful of her own mental health, frequently comparing herself and her behavior to the person she was before alcoholism intruded:

> *The husband and wife both feel trapped in an intolerable, unstructured situation which offers no way out. The wife's self-assurance is almost completely gone. She is afraid to take action and afraid to let things remain as they are. (Jackson, 1954, p. 575)*

Jackson points out that during this stage the wife presents a clinical picture similar to Whalen's "Wavering Winifred" (see page 37).

Stage 4: Attempts to Reorganize in Spite of the Problem

Stage 4 begins either with a crisis that warrants action (e.g., a medical crisis or an episode of violence) or when chronic Stage 3 has become unbearable. Many wives leave at this point and go directly to Stage 5 ("efforts to escape the problem").

If the wife goes into Stage 4, she takes on the role of the father and head of the household and abandons her role as a wife. She is more aware of her pivotal responsibility for her childrens' welfare; she makes the major decisions and, in essence, controls the home.

In Stage 4, she no longer covers up; for example, now she locks him out of the house or refuses to pay his bail. She is no longer in conflict regarding her loyalties, and her decisions are invariably in favor of her children over the husband. The husband, on the other hand, becomes more socially and emotionally isolated from the family as the wife and children learn to function without his support.

> *There are fewer and fewer roles left for him to play. He becomes aware that the family members enjoy each other's company without him. When he is at home, he tries to enter the circle of warmth or to smash it. Either way he isolates himself further. (Jackson, 1954, p. 576)*

The children learn that they are not the cause of their father's drinking and they show progressively less respect for him as a father, frequently talking back to him, as they would to other children.

The alcoholism gets worse but the family is more secure, since the wife has assumed control and has brought more stability into the family unit. The wife has learned to seek emotional and financial help from helping agencies and groups, and in fact, she becomes quite knowledgable about where in the community she can get specific kinds of assistance. She meets other women in similar situations and is reinforced in her new behavior of putting herself and the children ahead of her husband. She no longer doubts her own sanity as she focuses on getting her own life and those of the children in order. Jackson says she is now behaving similarly to Whalen's (1953) "Controlling Catherine" (see page 37). With increased control comes increased self-confidence. No longer does she try to hide her husband's alcoholism. The wife and her children band together to protect themselves from the disgrace and social stigma which usually are markedly less than they feared. She becomes aware of how very much the husband needs her as his progressive drinking leads to increased social and family isolation. His desperate state makes it difficult for her to think of leaving him, although the continuing stress eventually leads to Stage 5.

Stage 5: Efforts to Escape the Problem

Stage 5 may be the end of the marriage. In this stage, the wife separates from the husband and may or may not attempt a reconciliation. The wife must struggle with all kinds of social, cultural, religious, familial, and environmental conflicts before arriving at the decision to leave. The events that lead to the end of a marriage in our culture are very complex and a description of this painful and private struggle between two people is beyond the scope of Jackson or of this book. The significant change that has occurred in the wife, however, is that she has by now achieved enough self-sufficiency and selfconfidence to see that life for her and her children can go on without the husband.

Stage 6: Reorganization of Part of the Family

The wife reorganizes the family as a unit without the husband. This reorganization is similar to other divorced families with some unique exceptions, such as the recurring sense of guilt that she has deserted a sick person. The increased public information system about alcoholism as a disease serves to compound this guilt.

Stage 7: Recovery and Reorganization of the Home and Family

Stage 7 occurs only if the husband achieves sobriety. Regardless of whether or not separation has preceded sobriety, the reorganization of the family as a whole is usually constructive but is also frequently a painful process within a climate of uncertainty for all family members. [Proponents of the de-compensation hypothesis (see Chapter 3) conclude that the difficulties of this stage are manifestations of the spouse's need for the husband to be actively drinking.] The husband and wife must learn that marriage without alcoholism is not without problems. The wife has to deal with the danger of becoming emotionally available and again vulnerable in the face of repeated broken promises and past disappointments; she must relinquish some of the head of household roles. The children must readapt to this uneasy truce, and recognize the father in the reinstated role from which he was excluded in Stage No. 4. The wife must again share the children and also realize that her husband, perhaps through the help of an agency, counselor, or fellowship, achieved sobriety, something the wife and children were never able to do for him. Also, the husband frequently is actively involved in helping other alcoholics and is usually more introspective than before, so that although the problem drinker is abstinent, the family in some ways will never be free of alcoholism.

Other Stress Theory Proponents

A frequent criticism of Jackson is that she did not quantify her observations but relied on subjective impressions. Sound research subsequent to Jackson's pioneer work, however, supports the general concept that the psychopathology seen in wives of alcoholics is as much or more the result of the stress of living with alcoholism in the family than the result of intrapsychic and personality factors that preceded the husband's uncontrolled drinking (Kogan & Jackson, 1965a).

Haberman's (1964) study, in which wives showed less psychophysiological symptoms during the husbands' period of abstinence compared to periods of drinking, has already been mentioned (see page 66).

Bailey, Haberman, and Alksne (1962) used the 22-item Index of Psychophysiological Disturbance (see page 66) which identified psychophysiological and psychoneurotic symptoms. Four groups were studied:

1. Twenty-three wives who were living with their alcoholic and actively drinking husbands who had never been separated.
2. Twenty-three wives who were living with their alcoholic husbands but the husbands had been abstinent for 6 months or more.
3. Twenty-three wives of alcholics who had been separated or divorced for more than 6 months.
4. Five hundred and thirty-seven women in a representative community sample who were married to nonalcoholics.

Groups 1, 2, and 3 were matched in age and length of marriage. Some striking findings of this study are that 65% of Group 1 had a high level of psychophysiological and psychoneurotic symptoms compared to 55% of Group 3, 43% in Group 2, and 35% in Group 4. Also, the incidence and frequency of these symptoms decreased markedly as husbands' drinking decreased; for example, 82% of Group 2 reported that in retrospect they experienced marked psychophysiological and psychoneurotic symptoms when their husbands were drinking compared to 43% at the time of the study when their husbands were sober. It is important to emphasize that all the respondents were answering in retrospect. It is also interesting to note that 82% of Group 2 reported symptoms in retrospect whereas 65% of the group (Group 1) questioned while the husband was drinking reported symptoms, suggesting again the caution that must be exercised in evaluating retrospective observations.

Kogan and Jackson (1965b) support the conclusion of Bailey et al. (1962). Kogan and Jackson administered the MMPI to three groups of women: Group 1 consisted of 26 wives of alcoholic husbands who had been abstinent for more than 12 consecutive months. Group 2 consisted of 50 wives of actively drinking alcoholics. Group 3 consisted of 50 wives married to nonalcoholics. The major finding was that the incidence of personality disturbance was greatest in Group 2, least in Group 3, and somewhere in between in Group 1. Kogan and Jackson (1965b) conclude that "the findings were most consistent with the psychosocial hypothesis which takes into account both personality and situational variables" (p. 494).

Bailey (1967), using the same 22-item questionnaire of psychophysiological and psychoneurotic symptoms mentioned on page 66, analyzed the symptom scores of 262 wives of alcoholics. The scores were compared to periods of husbands' drinking and sobriety. The wives of sober alcoholics were statistically significantly less symptomatic than the wives of actively drinking alcoholics and no different from a representative sample of control wives of nonalcoholics.

Paolino, McCrady, and Kogan (in press) have recently completed a pilot study which empirically assesses alcoholic marriages and concludes by strongly supporting the stress theory. Fourteen spouses of nonpsychotic hospitalized alcoholics were tested for psychopathology at three times: (1) when the alcoholic spouse was admitted to hospital, (2) 6 weeks after discharge, and (3) 6 months after discharge. The instruments used to measure the nonalcoholic spouse's psychopathology were the Psychological Screening Inventory (PSI) (Lanyon, 1970, 1973; Lanyon, Johnson, & Overall, 1974; Overall, 1974) and the "In General Form" of the Multiple Affect Adjective Checklist (MAACL) (Zuckerman & Lubin, 1965), both instruments having been shown in previous studies (Lanyon, 1970, 1973; Lanyon et al., 1974; Overall, 1974; Zuckerman & Lubin, 1965) to be reliable and valid measures of psychopathology. The Quantity Frequency Index (QF) (Jessor, Graves, Hanson, & Jessor, 1968) was used to measure the alcoholic's frequency of drinking. The QF score is a composite number reflecting the amount of alcohol consumed during the preceding 30 days. The Alcohol Impairment Index (AI) (Shelton, Hollister, & Gocka, 1969) was administered to determine an index that represented the degree to which the alcoholic was impaired during the preceding 30 days as a result of drinking. Examples of impairment are blackouts, days of work missed, quarrels, to name a few. Both the QF and AI were reported to have extensive reliability, validity, and normative data and have been used in the evaluation of federally funded alcoholism treatment centers (Jessor et al., 1968; Towle, 1974). The QF and AI were given to the alcoholics at the same time that the PSI and MAACL were administered to the spouses of the alcoholic. The results, to a statistically significant degree, were that the alcoholics' QF and AI scores dropped, the spouses' PSI started out as normal and did not change, and the spouses' Anxiety and Depression scales of the MAACL dropped at follow-up testing. Thus, this longitudinal empirical assessment of the couples involved in an alcoholic marriage shows that the spouse group either remained normal or improved on all psychopathology scales while the alcoholics' drinking dramatically improved as measured by the QF and AI. The authors are very cautious in making generalizations on a small study such as this, but at the very least one can conclude that the results support the stress theory and do not support the decompensation theory.

It can be concluded that the research of Haberman (1964), Bailey et al. (1962), Kogan and Jackson (1965b), Bailey (1967), and Paolino et al. (in press) strongly invalidates the decompensation hypothesis and supports the general concepts of the stress theory.

A More Specific Critique of Jackson's Work

Although well-designed stress theory research has supported Jackson's (1954, 1956, 1959, 1962) general concepts, there has not been support for Jackson's proposal that seven specific adaptive stages are experienced by most, if not all, families of abstinent alcoholics.

One major and frequent criticism of Jackson is that she observed, almost exclusively, Al-Anon members.[1] Several studies have shown important differences between Al-Anon and non-Al-Anon wives. For example, Pattison, Courlas, Patti, Mann, and Mullen (1965) reported their subjective impressions

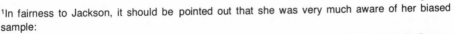

---

[1] In fairness to Jackson, it should be pointed out that she was very much aware of her biased sample:

> Yet there is no reason to believe that wives who, say, seek help through Al-Anon Family Groups are similar to wives who go to marriage counseling clinics, or those who join their spouses in psychiatric treatment at an alcoholism clinic. Nor can it be assumed that they have much in common with those who seek psychiatric aid for themselves or who end up in mental institutions. Wives of alcoholics who do not seek help, or who divorce their alcoholic spouses have not been studied. Hence we do not know if the apparent contradictions in certain research findings are attributable to differences in research techniques, sample sources, or the wives themselves. (Jackson, 1962, p. 480)

that "clinic" wives were less cooperative, of lower socioeconomic class, less intelligent and verbal, less likely to see alcoholism as a disease, and less self-reliant than Al-Anon wives.

Bailey (1965) compared 116 Al-Anon wives to 126 wives of alcoholics who had never attended Al-Anon meetings. Bailey reported that the Al-Anon wives were of a higher socioeconomic status, drank less, were better educated, and were less moralistic than the non-Al-Anon group. Also, the Al-Anon wives were more likely to see alcoholism as a combined mental and physical disturbance, whereas non-Al-Anon wives usually regarded alcoholism as solely a mental disease. Two years later, Bailey (1967) published a study in which psychophysiological and psychoneurotic symptoms were more frequent in 84 non-Al-Anon wives of alcoholics compared to 99 Al-Anon wives regardless of husband's drinking status.

Lemert (1960) (see page 49) and James and Goldman (1971) (see page 183) confirmed Jackson's general concept that the coping mechanisms of the wife as related to the husband's drinking change as the degree or style of drinking changes and that wives change their duties, responsibilities, and mental status as the various degrees of involvement with alcohol change in the husband. Lemert (1960) and James and Goldman (1971), however, also found no data to support the seven specific stages postulated by Jackson.

Lemert (1960) reported that his inability to duplicate Jackson's findings was because Jackson's seven stages were very specific to the kinds of wives who become active in Al-Anon. Lemert itemized 11 events that were associated with the family's adjustment to the stress of alcoholism and then asked each family about the sequencing of these items. Following analysis of his data, Lemert suggested that coping events tended to group together into early and late adjustment phases. Examples of early adjustment phases were awareness of the problem, attempts to control the problem, and social isolation. Examples of later adjustment phases were feelings of hopelessness, role changes, and divorce. Lemert (1960) observed a significant variety of sequencing of these adjustment events, however, and concluded by saying:

Seeking to factor the process of family adjustment to alcoholism into stages poses a problem similar to that which became the stumbling block in older evolutionary theories of cultural change. In order to demonstrate evolutionary stages and cultural development, behavior was often taken out of the context of a larger sociocultural situation. The exclusive emphasis upon cultural forms led the advocates of the theories to ignore such things as function, meaning and value of the behavior. This is not to say that the idea of some kind of temporal order in family adjustments to alcoholic crises must be abandoned. Nevertheless it is imperative to replace the concept of stages *with some other formulation, or to redefine "stage" in ways to make it more congenial to the data. (pp. 695 and 696)*

James and Goldman (1971) studied 85 wives of alcoholics. Using the approach of Orford and Guthrie (1968) as a point of departure, James and Goldman categorized the wives' coping patterns into four stages of husbands' drinking: social drinking, excessive drinking, alcoholismic drinking, and abstinence. The data analysis led to a categorization of the behavior of the wives into five patterns or styles of coping:

1. Withdrawal within marriage: This style included quarrels about drinking, avoidance of husband, sexual withdrawal, and avoidance of her own feelings.
2. Protection: Involved pouring out his liquor, insisting that he eat, and talking to his employer on husband's behalf.
3. Attack: This style included the wife initiating discussion about divorce and locking him out of the house.
4. Safeguarding family interest: Included paying his debts, giving him money, and keeping children out of his way.
5. Acting-out: Included getting drunk herself in an attempt to control his drinking, making him jealous, and threatening suicide.

"Withdrawal from marriage" was the most frequent style of coping, and in contrast to Jackson's (1954) observations, withdrawal was found in 50% of the cases, even when the husband was abstinent. Orford, Guthrie, Nicholls, Oppenheimer, Egert, and Hensman (1975) have recently offered some very interesting perspectives on the wives' withdrawal coping style. In a well-designed longitudinal empirical assessment of the relationship between wives' coping styles and their alcoholic husbands' treatment outcome, Orford et al. have shown that Withdrawal manifested by avoidance, sexual withdrawal, refusing to talk, feeling frightened, seeking outside help, making special financial arrangements, and contemplating terminating the marriage is most consistently associated with a relatively poor prognosis (this study is also discussed on page 97 of chapter 6).

James and Goldman (1971) also reported that all wives used more than one style; for example, almost all wives tried pouring out liquor (Protection style) and had argued with their husbands about drinking (Withdrawal style). All of the styles reached a peak during the alcoholic's periods of heaviest drinking. This finding that wives manifest more coping behavior when they have more with which they must cope has also been reported by Orford et al. (1975), whose research has shown that when 100 wives were assessed with respect to 56 specific coping style items, not one of those items shows a statistically significantly higher frequency in the group of alcoholics who had a *good* therapeutic outcome.

Before concluding this chapter, we would like to point out that except for Lemert (1960) (see page 49), none of the contributions of the alcohologists to the alcoholic marriage literature suggested studying the courtship period. Although we have no direct experimental evidence to prove our point, there are good theoretical reasons to support a strong recommendation that since alcoholism frequently precedes a marriage, research into adjustment to crises should begin with the period of courtship rather than with the marriage. It is the courtship that is the bridge between the life of the child in the family of origin, and the life of the adult in the family of procreation. The courtship period can be as revealing of what is wrong with the marriage as an analysis of the marriage period itself. The potential research of the courtship has not even begun to be realized.

SUMMARY AND DISCUSSION OF STRESS THEORY

There seems to be little doubt that the strain of alcoholism on family members engenders psychological symptoms in those members. The stress theory proposes that the behavior of the spouses is more a result of the strain of living with an alcoholic than the result of preexisting intrapsychic disturbances.

The early stress theory studies claim that the families adjusted in characteristic ways; but subsequent·research has strongly supported the concept that no single adjustment pattern is entirely typical of the alcoholic family. Each family and each family member react in different ways and to varying degrees.

Although Joan Jackson's general concepts regarding the stress theory are probably valid, we remain critical of generalizing about the "alcoholic wife" from data obtained from working almost exclusively with Al-Anon wives. It is our opinion that Al-Anon, with its focus on exhortatory methods and family recovery and its emphasis on self-inventory, self-help, and self-change, represents a biased sample of women who in many ways may be significantly different from other groups of alcoholic wives.

We recommend to future investigators that since it has been shown that alcoholism frequently preceded the marriage, the research into the adjustments and crises of the alcoholic should include the courtship period.

REFERENCES

Angell, R. C. The family encounters the Depression. New York: Scribner, 1936.

Bailey, M. B. Al-Anon family groups as an aid to wives of alcoholics. Social Work, 1965, 10, 68–74.

Bailey, M. B. Psychophysiological impairment in wives of alcoholics as related to their husbands' drinking and sobriety. In R. Fox (Ed.), *Alcoholism: Behavioral research, therapeutic approaches.* New York: Springer, 1967, pp. 134–142.

Bailey, M. B., Haberman, P., & Alksne, H. Outcomes of alcoholic marriages: Endurance, termination or recovery. *Quarterly Journal of Studies on Alcohol,* 1962, *23,* 610–623.

Clausen, J. A., & Yarrow, M. R. The impact of mental illness on the family. *Journal of Social Issues,* 1955, *11,* 3–65.

Eliot, P. D. Bereavement: Inevitable but not unsurmountable. In H. Becker & R. Hill (Eds.), *Family, marriage and parenthood.* Indianapolis, Indiana: Heath, 1948.

Finlay, D. G. Anxiety and the alcoholic. *Social Work,* 1972, *17,* 29–33.

Haberman, P. W. Psychological test score changes for wives of alcoholics during periods of drinking and sobriety. *Journal of Clinical Psychology,* 1964, *20,* 230–232.

Hansen, D. A., & Hill, R. Families under stress. In H. T. Christensen (Ed.), *Handbook of marriage and the family.* Chicago, Ill.: Rand McNally, 1969, pp. 782–819.

Hill, K. *Families under stress: Adjustment to the crisis of war separation and reunion.* New York: Harper, 1949.

Jackson, J. K. The adjustment of the family to the crisis of alcoholism. *Quarterly Journal of Studies on Alcohol,* 1954, *15,* 562–586.

Jackson, J. K. The adjustment of the family to alcoholism. *Marriage and Family,* 1956, *18,* 361–369.

Jackson, J. K. Family structure and alcoholism. *Mental Hygiene,* 1959, *43,* 403–406.

Jackson, J. K. Alcoholism and the family. In D. J. Pittman & C. R. Snyder (Eds.), *Society, culture and drinking patterns.* Wiley: New York, 1962.

James, J. E., & Goldman, M. Behavior trends of wives of alcoholics. *Quarterly Journal of Studies on Alcohol,* 1971, *32,* 373–381.

Jessor, R., Graves, T., Hanson, R., & Jessor, S. *Society, personality and deviant behavior.* New York: Holt, 1968.

Kogan, K. L., & Jackson, J. K. Alcoholism: The fable of the noxious wife. *Mental Hygiene,* 1965, *49,* 428–437. (a)

Kogan, K. L., & Jackson, J. L. Stress, personality and emotional disturbance in wives of alcoholics. *Quarterly Journal of Studies on Alcohol,* 1965, *26,* 486–495. (b)

Lanyon, R. I. Development and validation of a psychological screening inventory. *Journal of Consulting and Clinical Psychology, Psychology Monograph 35,* 1970(1), 1–24, Pt. 2.

Lanyon, R. I. *Psychological screening inventory manual.* Research Psychologists Press, New York: Goshen, 1973.

Lanyon, R. I., Johnson, J. H., & Overall, J. E. Factor structure of the psychological screening inventory items in a normal population. *Journal of Consulting and Clinical Psychology,* 1974, *42* (2).

Lemert, E. M. The occurrence and sequence of events in the adjustment of families to alcoholism. *Quarterly Journal of Studies on Alcohol,* 1960, *21,* 679–697.

Merrill, G. How fathers manage when wives are hospitalized for schizophrenia: An exploratory study. *Social Psychiatry,* 1969, *4,* 26–32.

Mowren, H. R. A psychocultural analysis of the alcoholic. *American Sociological Review,* 1940, *5,* 546–557.

Orford, J. Alcoholism and marriage: The argument against specialism. *Journal of Studies on Alcohol,* 1975, *36,* 1537–1560.

Orford, J. F., & Guthrie, S. Coping behavior used by wives of alcoholics: A preliminary investigation. *Proceedings of the International Congress on Alcohol and Alcoholism, Abstract 28th,* 1968, p. 97.

Orford, J., Guthrie, S., Nicholls, P., Oppenheimer, E., Egert, S., & Hensman, C. Self-reported coping behavior of wives of alcoholics and its association with drinking outcome. *Journal of Studies on Alcohol,* 1975, *36,* 1254–1267.

Overall, J. E. Validity of the Psychological Screening Inventory for psychiatric screening. *Journal of Consulting and Clinical Psychology,* 1974, *42,* 717–719.

Paolino, T. J., McCrady, B. S., & Kogan, K. B. Alcoholic marriages: A longitudinal empirical assessment of alternative theories. *British Journal of Addiction* (in press).

Pattison, E. M., Courlas, P. G., Patti, R., Mann, B., & Mullen, D. Diagnostic-therapeutic intake groups for wives of alcoholics. *Quarterly Journal of Studies on Alcohol,* 1965, *26,* 605–616.

Shelton, J., Hollister, L. E., & Gocka, E. F. The drinking behavior interview. *Diseases of the Nervous System,* 1969, *30,* 464–467.

Towle, L. H. Alcoholism treatment outcome in different populations. *Proceedings from the Fourth Annual Alcohol Conference of the NIAAA,* April 1974.

Whalen, T. Wives of alcoholics: Four types observed in a family service agency. *Quarterly Journal of Studies on Alcohol,* 1953, *14,* 632–641.

Zuckerman, M., & Lubin, B. *Manual for the Multiple Affect Adjective Checklist.* San Diego, Calif.: Educational and Testing Service, 1965.

5

The Application of Learning
Principles to the Alcoholic
Marriage

In this chapter we will examine the alcoholic marriage from the behavioral perspective. Sulzer (1967) was the first behaviorist to suggest the crucial role of the spouse in alcoholism. Basing his approach on learning principles, Sulzer instructed friends of an alcoholic to leave the bar if the alcoholic ordered a drink or attempted to consume an alcoholic beverage. Sulzer concluded by suggesting that involving the spouse in such procedures would be especially effective. It was not until 1972, however, that Miller reported an empirical study based on a behavioral approach to the alcoholic marriage. Thus, although learning theorists have analyzed alcoholism for many years (Conger, 1951, 1956; Kepner, 1964; Kingham, 1958; Voegtlin and Lemere, 1942), and behavioral approaches to the conceptualization and treatment of alcoholism have received increasing prominence in recent times (Hamburg, 1975; Hunt and Azrin, 1973; Miller, 1976; Miller and Barlow, 1973; Nathan and Briddel, 1977; Sobell and Sobell, 1973b), the behavioral approach to the alcoholic marriage is still in its infancy.

In order to appreciate the approach fully, the reader must first understand some of the basic principles of learning. Behavior therapists have explicitly derived their research and treatments from a defined set of learning principles. Behavioral research and treatment has also been significantly influenced by the findings of experimental–social and cognitive psychology. A detailed discussion of these principles, however, is beyond the scope of this book. What follows in this chapter is a description of the relevant basic principles of learning, a discussion of how these principles have been applied to the alcoholic marriage, and conclusions on the status of research and concepts in this area.

PRINCIPLES OF LEARNING

What Causes Behavior

The behavioral approach to psychopathology states that behaviors such as alcoholism are *learned* behaviors, understandable through the basic principles of learning. These principles are applicable to the whole range of human and animal behavior and can be systematically applied to both usual and unusual behaviors. Behaviorists strongly contend that it is possible to describe a behavior, describe the factors which maintain it, and, based on this analysis, to then introduce lawful manipulations which should change the behavior in predicted directions.

Behaviorists state that understanding is synonymous with control, and that the goal of treatment is to modify (control) undesired behavior. Understanding can be demonstrated in two different ways. First, one can manipulate the contingencies of reinforcement (discussed in detail on page 91) associated with a specific behavior or manipulate the stimuli which precede the behavior, and if the behavior changes, the change demonstrates that the analysis was correct. A second way of demonstrating understanding of a behavior is to create the same behavior in another organism by applying the set of conditions believed to have created the behavior in the original organism. If the same behavior pattern is created in the new organism, this also indicates understanding of the behavior originally observed. Of course, this latter method is of limited applicability in demonstrating a correct understanding of alcoholism in humans. It should be noted that this approach to the understanding of behavior is quite antithetical to the psychoanalytic approach, which states that the goal of psychoanalytic therapy is to understand and *not* to control. In fact, "controlling" a patient's behavior is considered antitherapeutic in the psychoanalytic therapeutic approach.

Any behavioral analysis of a problem considers five major elements: (1) events antecedent to the behavior; (2) organismic variables, including the biological state of the individual, drugs which the person is taking, the person's biochemical makeup, and cognitive mediational factors; (3) a description of the behavior; (4) a description of the consequences of the behavior; and (5) a specification of the relationship between the behavior and its consequences. The following sections will briefly describe these five basic elements of a behavioral analysis.

Stimuli

The environment is considered to be composed of a set of units called *stimuli.* This is in contrast to the behavior of the individual being studied, which is considered to be broken into units called *responses.* There are four different classes of stimuli. First, there are *eliciting* stimuli, which regularly precede and automatically lead to a particular response. For example, drinking enough alcohol to reach blood alcohol levels of 100–199 mg % results in incoordination, slowed reaction times, and ataxia. Through certain processes of learning, frequently called *respondant conditioning,* other stimuli can come to be associated with the same responses. For example, an individual may come to associate the sight, smell, and taste of alcohol with poor coordination, slowed reactions, and stumbling, and may learn to exhibit this same behavioral pattern at much lower blood alcohol levels than those which physiologically elicit such responses.

Discriminative stimuli comprise the second category. These stimuli regularly precede and accompany responses, but do not elicit them in the same manner as the eliciting stimuli. That is, the responses which follow are not reflexive. Rather, the presence of the discriminative stimulus serves to increase the probability that a certain response will occur. Therefore, these stimuli *control* behavior, but do not *elicit* behavior as eliciting stimuli do. Most people learn that it is appropriate to drink in certain situations, such as at parties or at dinner, but not in other situations, such as at work or when driving down the highway with a policeman in the next car. Many alcoholics learn not to drink in front of their spouses, and become adept at hiding liquor and drinking under stimulus conditions which do not include the spouse. In each of these examples, the probability of the drinking response is high only in the presence of certain environmental events, such as the party in the first instance, or the absence of the spouse in the second example, and is low under the other conditions described. Discriminative stimuli acquire the property of increasing or decreasing the probability of a response through their consistent association with reinforcers or punishers (described in detail on page 176). The probability of drinking at parties but not at work may be determined primarily by the positive reinforcement accorded to the drinker at a party (he's a regular guy, the life of the party) and the punishment that frequently accompanies drinking on the job.

Neutral stimuli comprise the third set of stimuli. These include any environmental events which occur, but which have no relationship with the behavior. For example, although the presence of the alcoholic's spouse might have a significant effect on the probability of occurrence of his drinking, the presence of the family parakeet is unlikely to have a significant effect on the drinking.

The fourth class of stimuli is made up of *reinforcing stimuli,* or reinforcers. These are environmental events which follow responses of the organism. These stimuli are considered under the discussion of reinforcers.

The reader will recall from chapter 2 that psychoanalytic theory discusses another type of stimulus, the stimulus associated with instinct theory.

The Organism

There are two major classes of organismic variables. First, there is the group of physiological, genetic, neurological, and biochemical variables. These variables form the substrate of behavior, and must be accounted for. If a person has alcoholic hepatitis, or Wernicke–Korsakoff syndrome, the behaviorist recognizes that these physiological states must be considered and treated as well as behaviors related to environmental stimuli.

The second category of organismic variables is comprised of those related to self-statements (thoughts), standards that the individual has for self-evaluation, and feeling states. For example, an alcoholic may believe that he should be able to supply his wife with any luxuries she desires (a standard for evaluation of his competency as a husband). If he is unable to do so, he may think himself a failure as a husband (self-statement) and experience feelings of anxiety or depression. These private events are considered to be behaviors subject to the same principles of learning as are public behaviors. This view of thinking is in marked contrast to the psychoanalytic view of the mind, in which thought is believed to reflect unconscious needs and impulses and in which internal processes are regarded as the primary cause of all behavior.

Learning theorists have been leery of attributing explanations of behavior to such internal events. Even Bandura (1969), who has been a major force in emphasizing the importance of private events, warns that:

> The common practice of invoking spurious inner states or agents as determiners of behavior has also produced justifiable wariness of inferential variables. After a given response pattern has been attributed to the action of a psychic homunculus, the search for controlling conditions promptly ceases. Although the use of the more colorful animistic entities in explanatory schemes is declining, the tendency to offer new descriptive labels for behavioral phenomena in the guise of explanations remains a flourishing practice. (p. 38)

Skinner (1953) stated more emphatically:

> The objection to inner states is not that they do not exist, but that they are not relevant in a functional analysis. We cannot account for the behavior of any system while staying wholly inside it; eventually we must turn to forces operating upon the organism from without. (p. 35)

Recent research provides evidence for the role of such private events in controlling behavior. Bandura (1969) critically reviewed the literature in this area, and emphasized that such factors as verbal mediators, concept formation, imaginal mediators, and arousal mediators can be demonstrated to have a significant effect on behavior.

Responses

The behavior of an individual is conceptualized as being broken into segments called *responses*. A response is a behavior of the organism which occurs following a private event such as a thought or feeling or an environmental event. There are two major types of responses: *operants* and *respondants*. Respondants are also called reflexive responses. Respondants occur in reaction to eliciting stimuli, such as stumbling and poor coordination (respondant) following ingestion of significant amounts of alcohol (eliciting stimulus). The frequency of occurrence of a respondant depends primarily on the frequency of occurrence of its eliciting stimulus. The environmental events which follow a respondant generally do not affect the frequency of a respondant. The fact that the stumbling resulted in falling down the stairs and breaking a leg would not change the probability of occurrence of stumbling at high blood alcohol levels (although it might affect the amount the individual drinks in the future). As noted (see page 87) in the discussion of eliciting stimuli, respondants can be conditioned to new stimuli. This is called respondant conditioning.

The second type of response is the *operant*. This is behavior which simply occurs without an environmental eliciting stimulus. Drinking a glass of wine, hugging one's spouse, or calling work to say that one's alcoholic spouse is sick and not coming to work are all operant responses. The frequency with which an operant response occurs is affected by the consequences of that response and by the occurrence of antecedent discriminative stimuli. Events which follow an operant and which lead to an increase in the probability of the occurrence of that operant are considered to be *reinforcers*. For example, if the alcoholic drew his wife into his arms and kissed her after she made the phone call to his place of employment, she might be more likely to make such phone calls in the future. Events which follow an operant and which serve to decrease the probability of that response are considered to be *punishers*. To continue with the foregoing example, if the alcoholic's boss got angry at the wife for not letting the husband call for himself, the probability of her making such calls in the future might be lower.

In examining a response, we can look at various dimensions of the response, such as the length, frequency, magnitude, or pervasiveness of its occurrence. The relevance of these dimensions varies with the behavior. For example, in analyzing drinking responses, one might consider how long the alcoholic takes to drink one drink (length), how often he drinks (frequency), how large a sip he takes (magnitude), or in how many situations he drinks (pervasiveness).

Consequences

As noted, environmental stimuli which follow operants in a contingent relationship and which serve either to increase or decrease the probability of occurrence of these operants are called *consequences*. There are two basic types of consequences. Those that increase the probability of occurrence of the behavior are called reinforcers; those that decrease its probability are called punishers. The consequences of operant responses are considered to be an essential factor in determining whether or not the behavior is likely to occur again.

Reinforcers function in two different ways, as diagrammatically shown in Figure 5.1. First, if the *appearance* of a stimulus following a response results in an increase in the probability of occurrence of that response, it is called a *positive reinforcer*. The example of the alcoholic kissing his wife after she covered for him with the boss would most likely be a positive reinforcer. If, on the other hand, the *disappearance* of a stimulus consequent on the response leads to an increased probability of occurrence of the response, this is also considered a reinforcer and is considered a *negative reinforcer*. For example, if the same alcoholic husband complained and kept badgering his wife to make the phone call and stopped the complaining and badgering when she did finally call, the cessation of his behavior contingent on the completion of the phone call would serve to negatively reinforce the phoning behavior and increase the probability of the occurrence of future cover-up phone calls.

The concept of punishment (see Figure 5.2) is sometimes confused with that of negative reinforcement. The main differences between the two lie in the *temporal relationship* between the aversive event and the response, and in the effect of the aversive event on the response. (Inspection of Figures 5.1 and 5.2 will help to clarify this concept.) That is, if the response (telephone call) terminates the aversive event (complaining and badgering), the cessation of the event (stopping badgering) is a negative reinforcer and increases the probability

Positive reinforcement:

antecedent stimulus —— response —— positive consequence —→ increased likelihood of response

Negative reinforcement:

antecedent stimulus —— response —— termination of negative consequence —→ increased likelihood of response

—Temporal relationship
—→ Causal relationship

Figure 5.1   Reinforcement.

antecedent stimulus —— response —— negative consequence ——→ decreased likelihood
of response

—Temporal relationship
——→ Causal relationship

Figure 5.2   Punishment.

of the phoning behavior. If the aversive event (badgering) *follows* the occurrence of the response (phone call) and decreases the probability of occurrence of the response, however, then the event is considered to be a punisher.

Reinforcers and punishers can be either primary unconditioned reinforcers or secondary conditioned reinforcers. Stimuli such as food, water, and relief from pain are primary unconditioned reinforcers in that they are able to reinforce behavior without the individual's having had any particular experience with these stimuli in the past. Conditioned reinforcers, on the other hand, acquire their capacity to reinforce behavior during the life and experiences of the individual. For example, there is nothing innately reinforcing about money, but within our culture it serves as a secondary reinforcer because of the association of money with other desired reinforcers, both primary ones such as food and secondary reinforcers such as alcohol, entertainment, clothing, possessions, and homes.

As noted earlier (see page 87) in this discussion, most operant responses are not reinforced indiscriminately, but only under highly discriminated circumstances. Getting intoxicated, jovial, and loquacious at a New Years' Eve party would be more likely to result in laughter, attention, and slaps on the back than would the same behavior during a visit from one's mother-in-law. Therefore, most operants occur at high frequency under circumstances in which the probability of reinforcement is high for the behavior, and occur very infrequently under conditions in which the probability of reinforcement is low.

Contingencies

The word *contingency* refers to the relationship between a response and its consequence. The time of occurrence of the consequence in relation to the response, the frequency of occurrence of the consequence, and other factors all affect the future occurrence of the response. For example, if the contingent relationship is such that the behavior is immediately followed by a positive reinforcer but is then followed after a delayed period of time by a punisher, it is most likely that the behavior will be maintained at a high rate, because of the immediacy of the positive reinforcement. The immediate reinforcing effects of alcohol ingestion seem to be more powerful in maintaining drinking than are the delayed, long-term punishing effects of alcohol abuse, such as loss of health, job, or spouse. Also, it has been demonstrated that when reinforcement occurs on an intermittent or partial reinforcement schedule, such that the behavior is reinforced on only some occasions, the behavior will continue for a longer time upon withdrawal of that reinforcer than would a behavior which had been reinforced at every occurrence.

Summary

There are five basic components to consider in analyzing a problem behavior from the point of view of learning principles: (1) the stimuli which precede a behavior (either discriminative stimuli or eliciting stimuli); (2) organismic factors such as genetic, physiological, and cognitive factors; (3) the nature of the response; (4) the consequences of that response; and (5) the relationship between the consequence and the response. Behaviorists regard these as the essential factors to consider when analyzing any behavior.

RESEARCH APPLICATION OF LEARNING PRINCIPLES TO THE ALCOHOLIC MARRIAGE

There have been two major approaches to research on the application of learning principles to the alcoholic marriage. The first body of research has encompassed studies of the processes of the alcoholic marriage. These studies identify reinforcers and punishers within the marital relationship which might affect the drinking response. Currently, there is very little research in this area. The second body of research has included studies of the effects of *treatment* of couples in which the principles of treatment have been derived from the principles of learning. If a researcher or therapist has completed such an accurate analysis of the problem behavior and the factors maintaining it that he can apply these principles and actually control the drinking behavior and marital interaction, indirect support is provided for the principles.

Process Studies of the Alcoholic Marriage

The earliest discussions of the role of the family in maintaining drinking behavior which incorporated behavioral principles were provided by Ward and Faillace (1970). Although they presented their views as a systems theory approach to alcoholism, many of their statements point to possible reinforcers for the drinking behavior:

if a family member has had a long history of heavy drinking there were many interactions within the family which occurred in response to his drinking, some of which may come to provide positive reinforcement of drinking. Some of these family responses fall into patterns showing powerful reinforcing effect [sic] on drinking behavior. (p. 685)

Ward and Faillace (1970) suggested several mechanisms through which the wife's behavior might maintain certain cognitions of the alcoholic. For example,

The wife and mother of the man alcoholic are intimately involved in the patterns of his illness, and often contribute considerably to its perpetuation, as do the father and husband of the woman alcoholic. The wife may deny to herself and to others that her husband has a drinking problem, which permits and reinforces the alcoholic's wish to similarly deny his problem. (p. 686).

Thus, these authors suggested that the wife's behavior may serve to reinforce self-labelings of the alcoholic as a nonproblem drinker. In addition, Ward and Faillace suggested that the wife has two major responses to the "disrupted drunken behavior" (p. 686) of the alcoholic which maintain the behavior through positive reinforcement or the elimination of punishers for drinking. The wife may respond to the "husband's pleas of physical illness, his shame, guilt or remorse with either sympathy and forgiveness, or anger and punishment" (p. 86). Ward and Faillace suggest that either of these responses may serve to reinforce the drinking response. If the wife forgives the husband, the husband learns that his wife will be kind to him for being drunk, provided he is remorseful and sick. Thus, drunkenness followed by "remorse" is powerfully positively reinforced. Her kindness and understanding also serve to protect him from the negative consequences of the drinking. Conversely, if the wife punishes her husband for his drinking by criticizing him, berating him, or becoming angry, the guilt and shame which he feels for having been drunk are relieved, and he therefore feels considerably less anxious. In this paradigm, the wife's behavior serves to reduce the aversive consequences of the drinking by decreasing its punishing value.

Ward and Faillace provide fascinating speculation about the role of the spouse in the reinforcement or punishment or drinking behavior. Their article is a theoretical and speculative statement, however, and no data are provided to support their arguments. Even more unfortunately, almost no studies have been done since that time to explore any of the variety of reinforcers which they suggested. There have been only two empirical studies which systematically examine behavioral processes of interaction in alcoholic marriages (Becker & Miller, 1976; Hersen, Miller, & Eisler, 1973). Because of the paucity of studies in this area, these two studies are now discussed in some detail.

The subjects in the Hersen et al. study were four couples in which the husband was hospitalized in the VA hospital for alcoholism. The couple were videotaped while sitting side by side on a loveseat discussing the husband's alcoholism and other topics. Each topic was discussed for a 6-minute interval in which a drinking problem-related discussion was alternated with a nondrinking problem discussion. Two measures were coded from the videotape. The first was the rate of looking at the spouse, which was defined as one of the pair turning his/her head 45 degrees from the forward position toward the spouse and focusing his/her eyes between the top of the head and the chin of the spouse. The second measure was the total duration of speech for each member of the pair. They found that the behaviors of the alcoholic husbands were not affected by the content of the discussions. The wives looked at their husbands for a longer duration of time when discussing alcohol-related topics, however. There was a consistent pattern in which duration of looking increased each time alcohol was discussed and decreased when nonalcohol-related topics were discussed. Hersen et al. (1973) concluded:

It would be tempting to conclude the results of the present study lend credence to the contention that the wife of the alcoholic reinforces aspects of his drinking problem. If this were the case in the present study, the wife's looking would function in the role of a positive reinforcer. It is likely that an interactive pattern may exist in which the husband's speech content is a discriminative stimulus for the wife, resulting in increased looking. The looking may then serve as a positive reinforcer for the husband, resulting in continued alcohol-content speech. (p. 519)

They further caution the reader that these data are at a descriptive level, and that additional research is needed.

The Hersen et al. study is an empirical demonstration of the existence of behaviors which could be construed as reinforcing drinking behavior. The limitations of this study must be noted, however, and it must be regarded as preliminary rather than definitive for several reasons. First, there is no evidence that looking behavior is actually a positive reinforcer for drinking or alcohol-related speech. The reader will recall (from page 90) that a reinforcer is defined as a stimulus which, on presentation following a response, leads to an increased probability of occurrence of that response. There is no evidence to date that such looking behavior does serve to reinforce the drinking response in this manner. Second, Hersen and co-workers used no controls, and it is not known whether or not it is common to pay more attention to any problem which has been disruptive to a couple's life and which has led to a hospitalization than to neutral topics which are currently of minimal interest to the couple. Third, it is not known whether such behavior occurs outside of the laboratory. Therefore, it cannot be concluded that the looking behavior is an important reinforcer in maintaining actual drinking behavior outside of the hospital, even if it were demonstrated that it could potentially serve as a reinforcer in the laboratory setting. Finally, since Hersen et al. provide no statistical analysis of their results, no statement can be made about the statistical significance of the differences in looking which they observed.

Becker and Miller (1976) improved the original design of Hersen's group by increasing the number of subjects, utilizing controls, and analyzing the results statistically. Their 12 couples consisted of 6 couples in which the husband was hospitalized for alcoholism at a VA hospital, and 6 in which the husband was hospitalized at the same facility for anxiety neurosis or depressive neurosis and had no known problems with alcohol. Couples were matched in age, education, duration of present marriage, and previous hospitalizations. The procedures were identical to the earlier study, in having the couples sit next to each other and discuss alcoholism and other topics in alternate 6-minute blocks. These authors measured several additional dimensions of behavior, however, including duration of looking, duration of speech, number of positive and negative statements, number of interruptions, frequency of touching, and requests for new behaviors.

The results of this study were quite different from the results of the Hersen et al. study, although the methodology was quite similar. The reader will recall that husbands in the Hersen group's study showed no changes in their behavior when the topic of discussion changed. Becker and Miller found that husbands as a group (alcoholic and nonalcoholic) talked more during the alcohol-related discussions than during nonalcohol discussions. In addition, husbands talked as much as their wives during alcohol-focused talk, but talked less than their wives when the topic was not related to alcohol. The reader will further recall that the wives in the Hersen study increased their duration of looking during alcohol-related conversations, but did not change their duration of speech. Becker and Miller found, in contrast, that the wives as a group talked more during nonalcohol-focused discussions. These authors also found that the wives in both groups looked at their spouses more than the husbands did during a discussion of alcohol than during the discussion of other topics. These workers did not find, however, that the wives of alcoholics looked at their husbands or spoke longer (than wives of nonalcoholics) during alcohol-related conversations than during nonalcohol-related conversations.

On only one variable did the alcoholic couples differ from the nonalcoholic couples. Becker and Miller found that alcoholic husbands and their wives interrupted significantly more frequently than did the nonalcoholic group, no matter what they were talking about. There were no significant differences between the groups or between the husbands and wives on positive or negative statements, touching, or requests for new behavior.

The Becker and Miller study suggests that there may be significant differences between husbands and wives in verbal interactional behavior, but this is certainly not a new or surprising finding. That they found so few differences in interactions between alcoholic and nonalcoholic couples may suggest that couples in which there is some behavioral disorder manifest dysfunctional communication patterns, no matter what the dysfunctional behavior is. The hypothesis that the wives' looking behavior reinforces the alcohol-related discussion and therefore maintains the alcoholic's drinking in some way is, however, brought under question by these results. Were the looking behavior a consistent reinforcer for alcohol discussion and drinking, then we would have to predict that the nonalcoholic couples also had alcohol problems of which the experimenters were unaware. Becker and Miller apparently screened their subjects carefully, however, and this is not a particularly tenable hypothesis. One possible explanantion of the similarity of the two groups during alcohol discussions is that the nonalcohol topics may have been so uninteresting or impersonal that the couples had little reason to look at each other during these discussions. Since the other topics are not enumerated in the article, the tenability of this hypothesis cannot be evaluated.

Certain further refinements could still be introduced into this research program. First, nonpsychiatric controls could be included. In addition, the nonalcoholic couples could discuss the husband's main psychopathology in the same way that the alcoholic couples were discussing the alcoholism. In this way, the behaviors of couples in relation to a major, current area of conflict could be compared more directly.

Two other studies have examined behavioral responses of wives to the drinking behavior of the alcoholic. James and Goldman (1971) were interested in Orford and Guthrie's (1968) five coping styles of the wife of the alcoholic, described in chapter 4. The reader will recall that the styles included safeguarding family interests, withdrawal within marriage, attack, acting out, and protection. Telephone interviews with 85 wives who had sought help for their alcoholic husbands included questions related to the five coping styles, and questions about problems created by or contributed to by their husband's alcoholism. Four different stages of the husband's drinking were explored: social drinking, excessive drinking, alcoholismic drinking, and abstinence. All the wives reported using more than one of the coping styles described, with withdrawal and protection being the styles used most frequently. Withdrawal within marriage is similar to what Ward and Faillace described as an approach that would decrease guilt and shame and therefore decrease negative consequences of drinking which might otherwise decrease drinking. The protection style is one which could provide positive reinforcement for the drinking, and therefore increase the probability of drinking. This study suggests that the wives of alcoholics report engaging in behaviors which may reinforce drinking. Contingency relationships between these behaviors and the drinking behavior of the alcoholic are unknown, however. Furthermore, the wives did not report systematic, controlled attempts to apply these various strategies. If they engaged in these behaviors on an aperiodic basis, the behaviors could be intermittently reinforcing the drinking behavior. As noted previously, intermittent reinforcement is quite powerful in maintaining any behavior pattern.

More recently, Orford, Guthrie, Nicholls, Oppenheimer, Egert, and Hensman (1975) attempted to discriminate the coping styles of the wives of alcoholics from situational determinants of the coping behaviors. They studied 100 wives of alcoholics referred for outpatient treatment for alcoholism. Wives answered 56 questions related to the coping styles described by Orford and Guthrie. The spouses indicated whether or not they had engaged in these behaviors in the last 12 months, rating each behavior on a four-point scale from "yes often" to "yes sometimes" to "yes, once or twice," to "no." They also rated the husbands' drinking outcome after a 12-month period, rating 28 subjects as having a "good" outcome and 29 as having a "bad" outcome. "Good" outcome was defined as when both the husband and wife agreed that there were less than 10 weeks of the year when excessive drinking occurred, and they both described the drinking problem as slight or as much better. A "bad" outcome was one in which both agreed that more than half of the year had been taken up with excessive drinking, and they had both described the problem as considerable or as little changed. Eleven more subjects had insufficient data, and 32 were not classifiable into the categories of good or bad outcome.

Orford et al. (1975) found 10 unique factors which described coping behaviors. They then attempted to determine if it were possible to identify certain behaviors of the wives which were consistently associated with good or bad outcome in regard to drinking. They found 35 behaviors for which bad-outcome wives were above the median in stating that they had engaged in that behavior, although only six of these behaviors were statistically significant. Only 11 behaviors were associated with good outcome, and none of these was statistically significant. Factors significantly correlated with bad outcome included having arguments about problems related to drinking, telling the husband he must leave, the wife fearing that she could not face going home, refusing to share the bed with her husband when drunk, consulting a lawyer about separation and divorce, and hiding things so that the husband could not sell them. These data, at first glance, do not bode well for a learning conceptualization of the alcoholic marriage. Were learning conceptualizations to be accurate, one would expect that withdrawing attention (such as not sleeping with a drunken husband) contingent upon drinking should be associated with a more positive outcome by providing aversive consequences for continued drinking. The data of Orford et al., then, merit further discussion here to assess their implications for a behavioral conceptualization of the alcoholic marriage.

Two factors attenuate the significance of their findings. First, Orford and co-workers found that there was a significant and positive correlation between most of the coping behaviors associated with poor outcome and the extent of beratings, threats, arguments, etc., which the wife reported as resulting from the husband's drinking. In contrast, wives whose husbands had a good outcome described significantly less hardship prior to treatment. Orford et al. suggested that the data support the notion that wives tried more ways to cope when they had more with which they had to cope. That is, when the husband's drinking was quite severe and disruptive, they attempted more coping behaviors. Since these were husbands who had a poorer prognosis, the likelihood was low that these coping behaviors would be successful. The second concept which calls into question whether these behaviors actually have an effect on drinking is the concept of contingency (discussed on page 91). The temporal relationships between the wife's behaviors and drunkenness or sobriety are unknown. If arguments occurred only when the husband was sober, this would provide punishment for the sober behavior. Threatening divorce or telling the husband he must leave, and not following through on this threat in action, could teach husbands only to ignore their wives' verbal behavior, and would not have very much effect on the drinking behavior. Refusing to share the bed with him when he was drunk, however, should be a behavior which would punish drunkenness. Unfortunately, the efficacy of this withdrawal of attention cannot be fully evaluated, since the wives did not report whether this was a consistent behavior pattern or a response in which they engaged only intermittently. If they refused to share the bed at times, but at other times did sleep with their drunken husbands, the husbands would then be on an intermittent reinforcement schedule, which would provide extremely powerful reinforcement for the drinking behavior to continue. Therefore, although the work of Orford et al. is one of the most comprehensive attempts to date to study the behaviors of the wife in response to a drinking husband, the frequency of the wives' responses and contingency relationships were not explored. As Orford and co-workers readily acknowledged, a self-report questionnaire is a very crude instrument for making this kind of assessment, and the details of the wives' responses to their drinking are yet to be elucidated in studies with careful observations and controls.

Only one investigator has attempted to quantify antecedents to drinking within the marital relationship. Hore (1971a, b) examined the relationship between different types of environmental stresses and relapses from sobriety. Through interviews, he identified 52 stressful life events among 14 alcoholics over a 6-month period. About one-third of these stressful events were disturbances in interpersonal relationships, such as quarrels with spouses or lovers. Hore reported that the correlation between the *number* of stressful events and the frequency of relapse was not significant. Further examination of the frequency of relapse following each type of stress, however, revealed 16 *interpersonal* stress events among the 14 subjects over the 6 months. *One hundred percent of these interpersonal stresses were followed by a drinking relapse within 2 weeks,* whereas the percentage of relapses following the other types of stresses was considerably lower. This study clearly identifies interpersonal stresses as a predictable antecedent to drinking.

The final study to be examined in this section was completed by McNamara (1960). McNamara emphasized cognitive or labeling factors in the maintenance of drinking behavior:

The interpretation that is placed on alcoholism by the alcoholic and his spouse will be viewed, in part, as one of the "effective" causes of alcoholism. A distinction has been made between "original" and "effective" causes of deviant behavior, in which it is pointed out that certain consequences of deviant behavior, especially the societal response to the deviation (the "effective" causes) are equally, if not more importantly, determinative of the course of the deviance. (p. 461)

McNamara discussed the disease concept of alcoholism, carefully differentiating evidence for the disease concept from the therapeutic value of this concept. He weighed both the advantages and disadvantages of the disease concept for the alcoholic and for the wife of the alcoholic and concluded that one of the most important drawbacks to the disease concept is that the alcoholic becomes labeled as a "sick person" and especially a "mentally sick" person. McNamara (1960) emphasized that this label is unacceptable to many people because American society values individual responsibility heavily. He suggested:

Perhaps, in a society such as ours, a more suitable approach would be to suggest an interpretation of alcoholism as a problem in adjustment, as a problem in learning. . . . This approach is more consistent with the value placed on individualism and might prove in the long run to be much more effective for both the alcoholic and his wife. (p. 465)

He suggested that viewing alcoholism as a learned response would decrease the likelihood of insulating the alcoholic from experiencing the consequences of drinking, make it less likely that the spouse would treat her husband as a helpless, sick person because of his terrible disease, and also would emphasize the personal responsibility of the alcoholic in obtaining and continuing in treatment. McNamara made a very cogent attempt to focus on labeling factors for the alcoholic couple, but did not detail the actual cognitive sequences and how these cognitions would specifically affect drinking behavior or marital interactions. Therefore, although McNamara's article is pioneering in suggesting a focus on cognitive factors, more work in this area is sorely needed.

Application of Learning Principles to the Treatment of the Alcoholic Marriage

There have been several reports of the application of behavioral principles to the treatment of the alcoholic marriage. These studies have all been multifaceted, using many behavioral techniques without specifying the active elements in therapy. Such an approach is quite reasonable, but eventually research will have to pinpoint the specific effective aspects of the treatment packages. In the first treatment study, Cheek, Franks, Laucius, and Burtle (1971) attempted to teach wives to modify the consequences of the alcoholic's drinking behavior. They also attempted to teach wives to become less disturbed by tension-arousing situations related to the drinking of the alcoholic husband. Although not stated, it could be inferred that decreasing wives' arousal to the drinking would also decrease the likelihood of their engaging in behaviors which could either reinforce the drinking through attention or precipitate further drinking because of the aversive nature of their behaviors. Of 158 wives or parents of previously hospitalized alcoholics whom they invited to participate in the program, 27 agreed to take part, although seven of these never attended a session. The authors do not explain the low participation rate. Only three subjects attended more than five meetings. The program involved lectures and written instructions about the principles of behavior modification, presentation of a method of identifying and recording behaviors, group discussions focused on analyzing the problems of interaction within the home of the alcoholic, especially emphasizing faulty systems of reinforcement, and deep muscle relaxation and desensitization. Wives saw modest changes in their own and spouse's behavior, especially identifying "better communication." They did not report any difference in drinking behavior, nor were any significant changes reported on any of the assessment instruments.

There were several difficulties with this study which probably contributed to the low effectiveness of the program. First, the attendance rate was extremely low, perhaps because the meetings were on Sunday afternoons. The immediate aversiveness of going to a hospital for treatment on a Sunday may have been more powerful than any delayed reinforcing qualities of the program. It is unlikely that any participants would have benefited maximally from the program with such low attendance. Second, although the program apparently emphasized a behavioral analysis of problems in the homes, it is not clear how much of the focus was on drinking behavior, marital interactions, or other difficulties. With 10 2-hour meetings, it perhaps would have been more effective to focus on one to two problem behavior systems. Third, the authors stress that the behavior modifier (the wife) and person whose behavior was to be modified (the alcoholic husband) were of similar stature, which is not the case when teachers or mental health workers are used as behavior modifiers. The authors suggested that the wives felt that they might lower their husband's esteem if they attempted to manipulate his behavior in a nonreciprocal relationship and therefore did not consistently apply the principles which they had learned.

Miller (1972) attempted to circumvent a variety of these difficulties in a case study of a single couple where the husband was a 44-year-old alcoholic who had been consuming 4 to 6 pints of alcohol weekly for 2 years. Miller involved both the husband and the wife in treatment, and established both of them as behavior modifiers for the other's behavior. The first step in treatment involved defining an acceptable limit to the alcoholic's drinking (defining the nature of the response). This couple decided that two drinks was an acceptable limit of drinking for any one day. They also defined only one stimulus complex in which drinking was acceptable—when the spouse was present. Thus, the presence of the spouse served as a discriminative stimulus for appropriate drinking for which the alcoholic would receive positive reinforcement.

The therapist and couple then established a contract in which there were negative consequences to the alcoholic for exceeding the two-drink limit or drinking in other than the defined stimulus situation. The alcoholic was punished for drinking inappropriately by having to pay his wife a large monetary fine, and by having her withdraw her attentions contingent on his drinking inappropriately. In addition, the husband also was to provide negative consequences to his wife for certain inappropriate behaviors. In this case, when the wife had previously made verbal or nonverbal negative comments about her husband's drinking or nagged him, these behaviors had led to increased drinking on the husband's part. Therefore, the negative consequence (punishment) for these behaviors was the husband's withdrawal of attention from his wife. In addition, the contract included positive reinforcers which the couple provided to each other for engaging in desired behaviors such as drinking appropriately, or speaking in friendly tones. Therefore, they were each receiving contingent positive reinforcements for desired behaviors, and contingent punishment for undesired behaviors.

The contract therefore was designed to lead to an increase in the probability of occurrence of the desired behaviors, and a decrease in the occurrence of the undesired behaviors. This contract was written and signed, and drinking came down to the desired, defined level within a few days. A 6-month follow-up revealed that the drinking continued at that desired level.

Hedberg and Campbell (1974) compared a behavioral family counseling approach with other behavioral treatments for alcoholics. Their subjects were 73 alcoholics, 10 of whom dropped out of the study and 14 of whom were referred to another treatment facility before the fourth treatment session. Therefore, their final sample included 49 subjects, 45 male alcoholics and 4 female alcoholics. Subjects were randomly assigned to one of four experimental groups, which included systematic desensitization (Wolpe, 1969) to individualized hierarchies;

covert sensitization (Cautela, 1967); electric shock therapy (Davidson, 1974); or behavioral family counseling. Systematic desensitization is a procedure whereby the subject is taught to become deeply relaxed, and then to imagine fear-eliciting scenes in a gradual progression from mildly to extremely fear provoking. Through respondant conditioning, the individual is supposed to pair the new response of relaxation with the previously anxiety-arousing scene. The anxiety-arousing situations treated were ones which were judged to be antecedents to drinking. Covert sensitization and electric shock therapies are both aversive conditioning procedures whereby the aversive stimulus is paired with alcohol consumption, and thus should serve to decrease the probability of the drinking response. In covert sensitization this pairing is done in imagination whereas in electric shock therapy the pairing is between actual alcohol consumption and painful but harmless electric shocks. The behavioral family counseling focused on increasing positive verbal exchanges, assertive training to enable the couple to express their wishes and dissatisfactions to each other more directly, behavioral rehearsal of the new skills which they were being taught, behavioral contracts similar to the type that Miller used (as just described), and teaching the couples the principles of learning, especially the roles of positive reinforcement and punishment. This treatment was based on the premise that these couples had negative verbal interactions which led to drinking behavior. If the couples could learn responses (other than the negative verbal interactions) such as talking more positively to each other and expressing their wishes more clearly in some of these difficult situations, the negative interactions and therefore the drinking would decrease. Hedberg and Campbell were trying to modify antecedents in order to decrease drinking. Teaching the couple the roles of reinforcement and punishment would help them learn to provide positive reinforcement for desired behaviors such as sobriety, and punishment for undesired behaviors such as excessive drinking. The contracts were a way to formalize this contingent application of reinforcers and punishers. Each couple chose a treatment goal of either abstinence or controlled drinking, and the authors found at 6-month follow-up that 80% of those treated with behavioral family counseling with a goal of abstinence had attained their goal, and 60% of those with the goal of controlled drinking had achieved their goal. Overall, 74% had attained their treatment goal, and another 13% were rated as much improved. Systematic desensitization also led to quite positive results, with an overall goal attainment of 67% and another 20% being much improved. Covert sensitization and electric shock therapy were much less effective.

Finally, in the most comprehensive approach reported to date, Miller and Hersen (1975) studied a single couple whom they treated with a broad spectrum behavioral approach. The authors suggested that excessive drinking in an alcoholic marriage serves as an antecedent stimulus to increased marital tension, which in turn is an antecedent to increased problem drinking, continuing in a never-ending circle. They described alcoholic marriages as being characterized by avoidance of the partner and a high frequency of quarrels about drinking, and suggested that behaviors related to excessive drinking were reinforced via increased attention, with appropriate behaviors being ignored. The treatment strategy was similar to that of Hedberg and Campbell (1974) in teaching couples "adaptive social interactional skills" (Miller and Hersen, 1975, p. 1), giving them controlled practice in using these skills, and scheduling these new interactions to occur in the natural environment through behavioral contracting.

The alcoholic husband in this couple was a 49-year-old hospitalized male with a 10-year history of alcoholism, arrests, and car accidents due to drinking. The husband had been drinking approximately a pint to a fifth of hard liquor a day. The wife had stated that she would divorce her husband if he did not obtain treatment at this time. The first phase of treatment involved a careful assessment of the behaviors associated with the drinking, which involved interviews, a 20-minute videotape of the couple discussing problem and nonproblem areas, and a tape recording of a mealtime conversation in the home. This analysis revealed that there was a minimum of positive interactional statements, an excess of non-goal-directed alcohol-related conversation, especially talking about the past and threats about drinking, and an absence of positive suggestions to deal with the drinking. Miller and Hersen also found that the wife talked much more than the husband, and that she interrupted frequently. The investigators have no comparative data on normal couples, but their study of this couple provides some support for their assessment that the alcoholic marriage is characterized by a lack of positive verbal interactions, a high frequency of negative interactions around the drinking, and ignoring of appropriate behaviors.

There were three components to treatment. First, social skills training was instituted in which the couple learned how to negotiate agreements by observing a male/female cotherapist team model negotiations. The social skills training included being taught how to compromise, how to offer concrete solutions to problems rather than engaging in non-goal-directed drinking conversation, and how to use positive comments to reinforce each other. The training also included instruction in simple nonverbal behaviors such as making eye contact, smiling and listening attentively to the other, and touching each other. They were also encouraged to make simple positive statements and to learn how to apply these positive verbal and nonverbal behaviors contingent on appropriate verbal interactions from the other partner, such as compromising and offering solutions. It was expected that teaching these skills would decrease the frequency of many of the marital antecedents to drinking, and would lead to positive reinforcement for more appropriate behavior.

The second element of treatment included assertive training in which the couple were taught to express their personal rights and feelings directly, making eye contact, expressing appropriate affect, compromising, and asking the other to change behavioral patterns rather than her or his personality. The assertive training was also seen as a way to enable the couple to obtain more desirable reinforcers from each other.

Finally, the couple negotiated behavioral contracts in which they agreed to engage in new behaviors which the other had requested, and which were reinforced by the partner who had requested the new behavior. These contracts were designed to systematically increase the probability of occurrence of the desired interactional behaviors. A 9-month follow-up revealed that the husband was abstinent at that time, that he was taking Antabuse daily, and that both reported that they were going out at least twice a week, that they sat and talked in the evenings at least three times a week, that the wife had stopped mentioning the past and was generally more pleasant, and that the couple had handled several problems quite well.

The Miller and Hersen study is important even though it is only a single case report. The significance of the study lies in the fact that a complete behavioral analysis of the marital interaction was completed which focused both on drinking behavior, the response of the spouse to the drinking behavior, and the lack of alternative responses to the negative verbal interactions which led to drinking. Based on this very careful analysis, a treatment program was designed to provide positive consequences for behaviors alternative to drinking and negative consequences for the drinking behavior. Therefore, contingency management and providing alternative skills to deal with problem situations (antecedents) in combination led to a very successful treatment outcome. There is no way to be certain that their interventions led to the behavioral changes, however, since there were no controls for the effects of the passage of time, the wife's ultimatum that her husband seek treatment, the role of Antabuse, or other unknown changes in the couple's situation. Using a multiple baseline design (Hersen & Barlow, 1976) in which only one problem behavior at a time was treated while the other behaviors were monitered, or using a control group design in which several similar couples were studied with some receiving treatment while others awaited treatment would lead to more unambiguous, readily interpretable results.

SUMMARY AND CONCLUSIONS

At the beginning of this chapter, five major components of a behavioral analysis were discussed: antecedent stimuli, organismic variables, the nature of the response, consequences of the response, and the contingency relationship between a response and its consequences. In this section, the results in each of these areas will be summarized. From an examination of the behavioral data on the alcoholic marriage, it is evident that there is a paucity of well-controlled studies to test the validity of such an analysis.

Antecedents

The data strongly suggest that many antecedents to drinking lie within the marital relationship of the alcoholic. The work of Hore (1971a,b) demonstrates a high frequency of drinking relapse following interpersonal conflicts with spouse or lover. The case studies of Miller (1972) and Miller and Hersen (1975) further suggest that the marital stresses which serve as antecedents take the form of spouse nagging, excessive talk about alcohol and past alcoholic transgressions, and attempts at communication which do not result in satisfactory conflict resolution or goal attainment for either partner. The only empirical support for these contentions, however, comes from three treatment studies (Hedberg & Campbell, 1974; Miller, 1972; Miller & Hersen, 1975) in which modification of these antecedents was one of the elements which led to a decrease in drinking behavior. There are limitations to the support which these studies provide, however. First, in all three studies a multifaceted approach to treatment was utilized, so it is not possible to determine whether the modification of antecedents alone was an active effective element in changing the drinking behavior and marital relationship. In addition, since none of these studies utilized either no treatment controls or single-case designs (Hersen & Barlow, 1976), the influence of the passage of time or other occurrences is unknown, and may have been primary contributing factors to the successful treatment outcome in these cases.

Behaviorists emphasize the importance of an individual and unique analysis of each case. Therefore, one would not expect a behaviorist to define the identical antecedents of drinking as occurring in every alcohol-troubled marital relationship. The research reviewed, however, has pointed to classes or categories of behavior which are potential antecedents. Detailed studies which attempt to delineate antecedents or systematically modify potential discriminative stimuli for drinking and studying the effects of such modification on the drinking response, would help to demonstrate the validity of this analysis.

Organismic Variables

Organismic variables have been largely neglected in the behavioral alcoholic marriage literature. Only McNamara (1960) has suggested that labeling the excessive drinking as a learned behavior would facilitate treatment because the alcoholic would be less shielded from the consequences of his excessive drinking. There have been no studies which have attempted to identify the labeling of the alcoholic couple in regard to drinking behavior. For example, what is the spouse's cognitive response to an alcoholic's drinking episode? Or, what are the alcoholic's cognitions about his drinking and marriage—does he consider the effects of the impending drinking bout on his marital relationship, does he say to himself that he has angry feelings toward his spouse and therefore will drink to express his anger at her? The area of organismic variables is extremely difficult to study, but it has become increasingly evident in recent years that the neglect of cognitive variables in a behavioral analysis may lead to mechanistic or ineffective treatments.

Nature of the Response

The nature and form of the drinking response in relation to the alcoholic marriage has also been a neglected area of research and speculation. Miller (1972) and Hedberg and Campbell (1974) both gave couples the option of selecting a drinking goal of moderate or controlled drinking rather than abstinence. The question of whether or not an alcoholic can learn to drink in a controlled manner is not of specific relevance to this chapter, although it is an area of research and much debate at this time. The role of the spouse both in helping to define what is an appropriate response, and being involved in the task of teaching the alcoholic how to exhibit that appropriate response has, however, been relatively ignored. For example, in much of the controlled drinking research (Ewing, 1974; Sobell & Sobell, 1973a) the alcoholic is actually taught how to drink in a controlled manner, learning to sip drinks rather than gulp them, space drinks over a period of time, and drink only in defined social situations such as parties or bars. The role of the spouse in teaching controlled drinking has largely been ignored.

Another aspect of the definition of the response which has been ignored is whether the nature of the drinking response changes in relation to marital events or the presence of the marital partner. That is, does the frequency of drinking change, does the form of the response change, or does the magnitude of the response change? If indeed this were the case, it would point to further questions about the role of the spouse in moderating or maintaining drinking behavior.

Consequences

The consequences of drinking within a marital relationship have been an area of much speculation and most of the behavioral alcoholic marriage research. Ward and Faillace (1970) and Orford et al. (1975) have provided the most comprehensive and exhaustive detailing of possible spouse behaviors which could maintain drinking, including attention to the drinking behavior in a variety of forms, ignoring appropriate and desirable behaviors, protecting the alcoholic spouse, to name a few. The work of Hersen et al. (1973) is suggestive in illustrating one possible reinforcer which the spouse provides for the drinking behavior, i.e., looking at the alcoholic when discussing his alcoholism, but this study is not definitive. Becker and Miller's (1976) findings contradict the earlier findings of Hersen and co-workers, and do not support the concept that the spouses of alcoholics consistently engage in specific attentional behaviors which reinforce the drinking. The three treatment studies reviewed have all attempted to modify the consequences of drinking through behavioral contracts so that there would be negative consequences of drinking or reinforcement for other more appropriate behaviors. The same criticisms of the studies discussed in regard to antecedents are of relevance here in that it is not known if it was the modification of consequences, the teaching of new skills in order to modify the antecedents, or unknown maturational or extraneous variables which led to the successful treatment outcome in these cases.

Contingencies

A final major question involves the contingent relationships between spouse behaviors which are potential reinforcers or punishers and the actual drinking behavior. Orford et al. (1975) described a variety of spouse behaviors which potentially could reinforce or punish drinking, but whether or not they were consistent in their behavior, or inconsistent and noncontingent is a crucial unknown factor at this time. Without a response to this question, one cannot fruitfully address the question of whether behaviors of the spouse are actually reinforcing and maintaining the drinking behavior.

In conclusion, it can be stated that a behavioral analysis of the alcoholic marriage is a promising approach in that it provides an articulated set of constructs on which research and treatment can be based, that the research to date is quite supportive of a behavioral analysis, that the few treatment studies of alcoholic marriages based on these principles have been extremely successful, and that there are no significant data to date which provide contradictory evidence to such an analysis. A great deal of research needs to be done, however, to fully validate this conceptualization of the alcoholic marriage.

REFERENCES

Bandura, A. *Principles of behavior modification.* New York: Holt, 1969.

Becker, J. V., & Miller, P. M. Verbal and nonverbal marital interaction patterns of alcoholics and nonalcoholics. *Journal of Studies on Alcohol,* 1976, *37,* 1616–1624.

Cautela, J. R. Covert sensitization. *Psychological Reports,* 1967, *20,* 459–468.

Cautela, J. R., & Kastenbaum, R. A reinforcement survey schedule for use in therapy, training and research. *Psychological Reports*, 1967, *20*, 1115–1130.

Cheek, R. E., Franks, C. M., Laucius, J., & Burtle, V. Behavior-modification training for wives of alcoholics. *Quarterly Journal of Studies on Alcohol*, 1971, *32*, 456–461.

Conger, J. J. The effects of alcohol on conflict behavior in the albino rat. *Quarterly Journal of Studies on Alcohol*, 1951, *12*, 1–29.

Conger, J. J. Alcoholism: Theory, problem and challenge. II. Reinforcement theory and the dynamics of alcoholism. *Quarterly Journal of Studies on Alcohol*, 1956, *17*, 296–305.

Davidson, W. S. Studies of aversive conditioning for alcoholics: A critical review of theory and research methodology. *Psychological Bulletin*, 1974, *81*, 571–581.

Ewing, J. A. Behavioral approaches for problems with alcohol. *The International Journal of the Addictions*, 1974, *9*, 389–399.

Hamburg, S. Behavior therapy in alcoholism. *Journal of Studies on Alcohol*, 1975, *36*, 69–87.

Hedberg, A. G., & Campbell, L. A comparison of four behavioral treatments of alcoholism. *Journal of Behavior Therapy and Experimental Psychiatry*, 1974, *5*, 251–256.

Hersen, M., & Barlow, D. H. *Single case experimental designs: Strategies for studying behavior change.* Oxford: Pergamon, 1976.

Hersen, M., Miller, P. M., & Eisler, R. M. Interactions between alcoholics and their wives: A descriptive analysis of verbal and nonverbal behavior. *Quarterly Journal of Studies on Alcohol*, 1973, *34*, 516–520.

Hore, B. D. Factors in alcoholic relapse. *British Journal of Addiction*, 1971, 66, 89–96. (a)

Hore, B. D. Life events and alcoholic relapse. *British Journal of Addiction*, 1971, *66*, 83–88. (b)

Hunt, G. M., & Azrin, N. H. A community-reinforcement approach to alcoholism. *Behavior Research and Therapy*, 1973, *11*, 91–104.

James, J. E., & Goldman, M. Behavior trends of wives of alcoholics. *Quarterly Journal of Studies on Alcohol*, 1971, *32*, 373–381.

Kepner, E. Application of learning theory to the etiology and treatment of alcoholism. *Quarterly Journal of Studies on Alcohol*, 1964, *25*, 279–291.

Kingham, R. J. Alcoholism and the reinforcement theory of learning. *Quarterly Journal of Studies on Alcohol*, 1958, *19*, 320–330.

McNamara, J. H. The disease conception of alcoholism: Its therapeutic value for the alcoholic and his wife. *Social Casework*, 1960, *41*, 460–465.

Miller, P. M. The use of behavioral contracting in the treatment of alcoholism: A case report. *Behavior Therapy*, 1972, *3*, 593–596.

Miller, P. M. *Behavioral treatment of alcoholism.* Oxford: Pergamon, 1976.

Miller, P. M., & Barlow, D. H. Behavioral approaches to the treatment of alcoholism. *Journal of Nervous and Mental Diseases*, 1973, *157*, 10–20.

Miller, P. M., & Hersen, M. Modification of marital interaction patterns between an alcoholic and his wife (unpublished manuscript).

Nathan, P. E., & Briddell, D. W. Behavioral assessment and treatment of alcoholism. In B. Kissin & H. Begleiter (Eds.), *The biology of alcoholism* (Vol. 5). New York: Plenum Press, 1977.

Orford J., & Guthrie, S. Coping behavior used by wives of alcoholics; a preliminary investigation. *Proceedings of the International Congress on Alcohol and Alcoholism, 28th,* 1968, p. 97.

Orford, J., Guthrie, S., Nicholls, P., Oppenheimer, E., Egert, S., & Hensman, C. Self-reported coping behavior of wives of alcoholics and its association with drinking outcome. *Journal of Studies on Alcohol,* 1975, *36,* 1254–1267.

Skinner, B. F. *Science and human behavior.* New York: Macmillan, 1953.

Sobell, M. B., & Sobell, L. C. Alcoholics treated by individualized behavior therapy: One year treatment outcome. *Behavior Research and Therapy,* 1973, *11,* 599–618. (a)

Sobell, M. B., & Sobell, L. C. Individualized behavior therapy for alcoholics. *Behavior Therapy,* 1973, *4,* 49–72. (b)

Sulzer, E. S. Behavior modification in adult psychiatric patients. In L. P. Ullman & L. Krasner (Eds.), *Case studies in behavior modification.* New York: Holt, 1967, pp. 196–200.

Voegtlin, W. L., & and Lemere, F. The treatment of alcohol addiction. *Quarterly Journal of Studies on Alcohol,* 1942, *2,* 717–803.

Ward, R. F., & Faillace, L. A. The alcoholic and his helpers. A systems view. *Quarterly Journal of Studies on Alcohol,* 1970, *31,* 684–691.

Wolpe, J. *The practice of behavior therapy.* Oxford: Pergamon, 1969.

6

Systems Theory Approaches to the Alcoholic Marriage

This chapter will examine the alcoholic marriage from the perspective of general systems theory. General systems theory approaches to psychopathology have received increasing attention in only the past 25 to 30 years. These approaches have developed in response to the explosion of scientific information and knowledge in this century and the need for an approach that attempts to integrate knowledge from such diverse fields as biology, psychology, anthropology, sociology, ethology, linguistics, and cybernetics. The perspective of general systems theory was first associated with the alcoholic marriage in 1959 (Bullock & Mudd, 1959; Mitchell, 1959) and was only systematically applied to alcoholic marriages in the 1970s (Gorad, 1971; Gorad, McCourt, & Cobb, 1971; Steinglass, Weiner, & Mendelson, 1971a, b). Thus, these applications are relatively new, and data and theoretical applications are currently evolving. In order for the reader to comprehend the alcoholic marriage systems theory literature, it is necessary first to have an understanding of the conceptual approach and theoretical constructs of systems theory. What follows is a brief description of these concepts, a discussion of their application to the alcoholic marriage, and conclusions about the status of systems theory in the alcoholic marriage field.

AN OVERVIEW OF THE GENERAL SYSTEMS THEORY

Definitions

Systems theory assumes that all important people in the family unit play a part in the way family members function in relation to each other and in the way the symptom finally erupts. The part that each person plays comes about by each "being himself." (Bowen, 1974, p. 115)

Thus, a central concept of systems theory is that, in order to understand individual behavior, it is essential to understand the significant group in which a person lives, the relationships within that group, and the importance of any particular individual's behavior to maintaining the group, or system. Therefore, the target for change is the whole system, not any individual member of a system. Whereas traditional individually oriented therapists would label the person initially seeking help as the *patient,* the systems theorist would call him the *identified patient* to indicate that the whole system, and not the individual, is the *real patient.*

A system is considered to be more than the behaviors and personalities of the individuals within the system; the system is considered to have properties beyond those of the individual members which arise from the interactions of the individual members.

The systems theorist's approach requires a focus on the observable *facts* of the relationship. That is, the family systems theorist is interested in describing *what* happened in any family interaction, *how* it came about, *when* the behaviors of the individual members occurred in relation to one another, and *where* the behaviors or incidents occurred. The systems theorist avoids intrapsychic motivational explanations of *why* an interaction or family event occurred and instead attempts to focus on the interrelationships among behaviors in contrast to the psychoanalytic approach which focuses on the interrelationships between component parts of the minds of the individual members of the system.

A formal definition of a system is given as "a set of objects together with relationships between the objects and their attributes" (Hall & Fagan, 1956). Objects are defined as the parts of a system, and attributes are considered to be the properties of the objects. For example, in an alcoholic family, the objects would be family members, and their attributes would include such things as intelligence, skills, affective responsiveness, and so on.

Roles

A family is considered to be made up of certain roles. All families have some roles which must be fulfilled, such as those of provider, parent, or homemaker. These roles generally are the focus of sociological studies of families. Families, however, also have a variety of emotional roles, to which the members are "assigned." For example, in many marital relationships, the husband often fulfills an instrumental task-oriented role, whereas the wife fulfills an expressive, emotional, relationship-oriented role. Families may also have roles such as "troublemaker," "denier," or "calm decision maker." Many families also include the role of the sick patient, which is often the role of the alcoholic in an alcoholic marriage. That is, the family structure would require that one member of the family not function capably, according to his supposed abilities, and rather would engage in unpredictable, socially unacceptable behaviors. This role might allow others in the family to assume the role of caretaker, knowing parent, or angry accuser. Systems theory emphasizes that any system requires a variety of roles in order to function.

In a family, the various members are assigned these roles. The "assignments," however, can shift from individual to individual, although the roles within the family as a unit generally do not change. Thus, a systems theorist might suggest that the concept of decompensation of the spouse following an alcoholic's sobriety would not be an expression of the spouse's *individual* intrapsychic need for the alcoholic to remain an alcoholic, but rather would be an expression of the *system's* need to include the role of sick member. That is, since the alcoholic was no longer "sick," someone else had to take this role. This need would *not* reflect the intrapsychic unconscious conflicts of any particular family member, as the psychoanalyst might claim, but rather would reflect the "unconscious" need of the whole system for a sick member.

Rules

Families are considered to be rule-governed systems just as psychoanalytic theory considers the mind to be governed by certain principles. A discrete body of rules can be derived which describes the typical behavior patterns of the family.

The observation of family interaction makes obvious certain redundancies, typical and repetitive patterns of interaction which characterize the family as a supraindividual entity. (Jackson, 1965, p. 590, italics in the original)

For example, in an alcoholic marriage, the rule of the system might be that the couple could only express strong affectionate feelings toward each other after the alcoholic had completed a drinking spree. At other times, affective expressions would be disallowed. Or a rule of the system might be that the wife is allowed to work outside of the home when the alcoholic husband is drinking, hospitalized, or otherwise severely disabled from the drinking. At times when the alcoholic is functioning in a relatively less disrupted manner, the wife would be required to give up her job and return to her home. Clearly, these rules are not often discussed and deliberately decided upon. Rather, they evolve from the needs of the system. Some rules may be overt and understood by all members of the system, however, whereas other rules are covert and unrecognized by members of the system.

Although the concept of rules may seem to be rather obscure, careful consideration makes it clear that couples must develop some relatively easy means of making decisions in areas in which decisions must be made repeatedly. For example, if there were no rule, decisions about the frequency of sex or the initiator of sexual interaction would have to be worked out each time the couple had sexual contact. Who earned money and who worked would have to be negotiated over and over again, were there not some rules to decide these roles. Jackson (1965) cogently described the necessity of rules to govern a relationship when he proposed a hypothetical pair of individuals who were carbon copies of each other. He stated,

if such a pair were to live together, it is obvious that they would have to evolve differences which did not before exist. The first time they approached a door that must be entered in single file the dye would be cast. Who is to go first? On what basis is this decision to be made? (p. 591)

The Contribution of the Individual to the Establishment of the System

Bowen (1974) described what he believed to be the contribution of the individual to the initial establishment of any system. He emphasized the concept of differentiation of the self, which is defined as the "degree to which the person has a 'solid self' or solidly held principles by which he lives his life" (Bowen, 1974, p. 117).[1] The degree to which any individual is differentiated is related to the level of differentiation of his or her parents, his or her relationship with them, and how the individual has handled unresolved attachments to the parents in his own adult life. An individual can seldom reach a level of differentiation much higher than that of his parents. Marriage involves the establishment of a relationship between two individuals who have usually selected a mate at a level of differentiation similar to their own. The level of differentiation of the parents predicts the overall degree of differentiation in the new family. Therefore, in a family with a low level of differentiation, the family members lacking the "solid self" to which Bowen refers would frequently ascribe their own characteristics or feelings to other members of the family.

In the initial stages of the establishment of a relationship, the individuals involved begin to bargain for different roles in the family, and also begin to establish rules for their interaction. The level of differentiation, needs, and conflicts of each individual in the developing system will affect the types of roles and rules negotiated for that system. Over time, these roles and rules become fixed as relatively enduring roles and rules of the system. The identity of the

---

[1]A more detailed discussion of Bowen's concept of differentiation is included in Appendix C.

individual occupying any role may change at different times in the life of the system, but the roles themselves change much less frequently.

Homeostasis

Any system is exposed to stresses and various external pressures to introduce change into the system. Systems theory suggests that all family systems operate to maintain a certain level of equilibrium, which is intended to "minimize the threats of disruption and pain" (Meeks & Kelly, 1970, p. 400). This equilibrium is established in order to maintain the family unit. Therefore, any attempts to introduce change into the system will lead to resistance or compensatory changes within the system. For example, if one member of a family were to become alcoholic and was functioning at a reduced level, there would be automatic compensations in the family so that other members of the family would assume additional functions and responsibilities for a period of time. The homeostasis of a system is similar in concept to the psychoanalytic mentalistic view of homeostasis among the component parts of the mind.

The most striking examples of homeostasis have been noted by family therapists:

> *It has been frequently observed that, in response to the treatment of a single family member other members tried to sabotage, or become a part of his treatment, as though they had a stake in his illness. (Meeks & Kelly, 1970, p. 399)*

Thus, if a therapist working individually with an alcoholic attempts to help him toward sobriety and fuller functioning, this would threaten the equilibrium of the system, because the role of sick member would no longer be fulfilled, and any established rules which had required the alcoholic to be sick would be in jeopardy. The homeostasis of the *system* would be jeopardized. Therefore, systems theory predicts that the family might behave in ways either to return the alcoholic to his drinking, or to provide another sick member to fulfill that role in an attempt to maintain the system. The pro-DPH theorist (described in chapter 2) might also predict that a spouse would fight the recovery or become ill herself, but would make this prediction because the spouse's *intrapsychic* homeostasis would be threatened, rather than the family *system* homeostasis.

Communication

Patterns of communication are the most observable aspects of family interaction. Communication occurs on both verbal and nonverbal levels. These multiple channels of communication provide the opportunity for the individual to transmit conflicting messages. For example, an alcoholic, when drunk, might fondly put his arm around his wife and tell her that he loves her, which would be his verbal communication. If she has repeatedly expressed her disapproval of his drinking, however, his other nonverbal message, his drunkenness, would convey a different, hostile message to her.

Patterns of communication clearly reflect the interactive processes in the family system. Who speaks to whom, sequences of communication, the congruence or incongruence between the verbal and nonverbal modes all provide significant data on family roles and rules. Patterns of communication, once begun, develop into chains of interaction with varying behavioral outcomes. An initial communication leads to some response in the receiver which in turn leads to a response in the initial message sender. The result is a continuing feedback process in which a system may negotiate roles, or establish rules of interaction. For example, to continue the description of a drunken alcoholic embracing his wife, his initial information transmission might be translated as, "I don't really love you, and besides I think you're a fool, because I think that you believe what I say to you." The wife's response may be to stiffen her body, but also to smile and respond verbally, "I love you too." This message might be translated as, "I think you're as big a fool because I think *you'll* believe what *I* say." This message may lead in response to feelings of anger in the alcoholic, which might in turn lead to hostile words, resulting in anger in the wife, which in turn could lead to argument, further drunkenness, physical abuse, threats of divorce, and so on.

Communication, then, is clearly a complicated process; merely describing what people say to one another does not adequately describe communication within a system.

The Role of Symptoms

In the systems framework, symptoms are regarded as having a significant function. In fact, the symptom is considered to be adaptive and protective for the maintenance and functioning of the family system, even though it may cause emotional pain for the individual experiencing it, for other members of the system, or both. This concept is similar, on the intrafamilial level, to the psychoanalytic concept of symptoms which serve the important function of defending a person from the expression of unacceptable id drives, and consequent greater impairment of functioning.

The symptom may serve one of four possible roles within a system:

1. The symptom may assure acceptance into the family. A father who is not able to fulfill traditional roles to maintain his place in the family, such as those of provider or calm decision maker, might only be excused from these roles and therefore accepted within the family system if he is sick. He may become an alcoholic in order to assure his acceptance in the family system.

2. The symptom may also serve to cement role differentiations within a family. For example, a couple may have conflicts over who will have control of the relationship, in terms of decision making, status, and freedom within the relationship. This conflict may continue, or be resolved by one of the two members developing a symptom, such as alcoholism, which makes that person unable to compete effectively for the role of controller within the relationship. Therefore, this symptom would make it clear that one member of the couple would have control within the relationship and that the other has abdicated this control, through symptoms.

3. A third possible role for a symptom may be as a signal that there is stress or strain within the system. A system may have been functioning fairly well by its old rules and roles, but then may be subjected to stress, such as moving to a new location, physical illness in a member of the family, financial setbacks, and the introduction of a new child into the family, to name a few. The system might not have already established rules and roles to accommodate the changes fully, and one member of the system might develop symptoms such as alcoholism which would indicate that the system was not adapting well to the stress.

4. A final possible adaptive role of symptoms is as responsibility-avoiding maneuvers. Haley (1963) has stated that a symptom has two primary characteristics. First, the symptom has an extreme influence on other persons. Second, the individual indicates that in some way he cannot help the behavior in which he is engaging. This combination, having extreme influence on another person and also saying that the individual has no control over it, actually leads to powerful control over the relationship. For example, if an alcoholic is drunk and engages in offensive verbal and nonverbal interactions, and at the same time makes it clear that he is drunk, this cripples others with whom he is interacting. It is difficult for them to stop his behavior, and it is difficult for them to ignore it. At the same time, they may feel hesitant or guilty about reprimanding him or becoming angry at him, because he would be regarded as not knowing what he was doing because he was drunk. Because few alternatives are available to persons in this situation, they are rendered relatively impotent and out of control of the situation and relationship.

Determining what role the symptom is playing is a difficult task for the therapist, as is discussed in chapter 7. It should be noted here, however, that a symptom may initially develop in response to stress, but may become a relatively enduring aspect of the system.

Variations within Systems Theory

Different researchers and theorists have emphasized different aspects of systems theory as just described. In the following section systems theory and research in the alcoholic marriage will be studied from five systems perspectives:

1. *General interactional approach.* Many authors have focused on the importance of interaction in the family and have treated the couple or whole family without explicitly deriving the rationale for this approach from systems theory. The studies reviewed in this area are treatment studies which provide general support to the notion of whole family involvement but are not necessarily specific to systems theory.

2. *Descriptive studies of the alcoholic system.*   Several researchers have explicitly used the concept of a system to direct their attention to observational and descriptive studies of alcoholic families during periods of intoxication. Conclusions from these studies have contributed data supportive of many systems concepts.
3. *Family roles.*   Some researchers have attempted to specify what roles are available in an alcoholic family, and to study the results of interactions among these roles. Results from these studies have been supportive of use of the concept of family roles, but generally have been derived from somewhat weak research methodologies.
4. *The individual's contribution to the system.*   Since theorists in this area have not yet researched their conceptualizations, the literature reviewed is of a speculative nature and therefore provides no unambiguous information relevant to systems notions.
5. *Communications patterns.*   Studies of communication patterns in alcoholic marriages have focused primarily on alcoholism as a responsibility-avoiding communication. Data in this area have provided some of the clearest support for certain systems concepts.

RESEARCH ON SYSTEMS THEORY APPLICATIONS TO THE ALCOHOLIC MARRIAGE

General Interactional Studies

As noted, several researchers have recognized the significance of the family system in the understanding and treatment of alcoholism without explicitly deriving their approach from general systems theory. These workers can best be described as subscribing to an interactional rather than individual approach, and therefore their work can reasonably be regarded as providing support for the most fundamental of systems notions, the importance of inclusion of the relevant system in treatment.

Burton and Kaplan (1968a,b) reported on the effects of couples' treatment on alcoholism. The couples approach was grounded in the belief that alcoholism and marital conflict were interrelated, although explicit systems concepts were not described. In the first of two studies, Burton and Kaplan (1968a) compared the effects of group couples therapy and individual psychotherapy for one or both members of the marital couple. Their follow-up criterion was the response to the question "Do you feel that you (your husband/wife) got something out of counseling?" (p. 77). They found, in couples in which only one had received individual counseling, that 43% answered affirmatively to this question, whereas when both partners had received individual counseling, 50% responded affirmatively. Those who had received group counseling responded positively 76% of the time. Although no statistical analysis was done of these results, it is of interest to notice that couples' counseling led to a higher percentage of positive subjective feelings about the outcome of therapy than the individual counseling did, even when both members of the couples received individual treatment. Treatment of individuals versus treatment of couples, however, was completely confounded by the factor of individual versus group therapy, and therefore no definite conclusions can be drawn as to which was the active ingredient in treatment. These results, however, do support the concept that it may be important to treat the total alcoholic marriage system in order to effect positive changes within the behavior and feelings of an individual.

A second study (Burton & Kaplan, 1968b) was based on the assumption that excessive drinking and family pathology were mutually reinforcing, and that the question of which came first was not of relevance to treatment. Based on the notion that circular and nonproductive interactions, rather than intrapsychic pathology, were the core of the couples' problems, Burton and Kaplan (1968b) focused their group counseling sessions on the interaction between husband and wife, considering drinking only in terms of the overt and covert role that it played in the relationship. They followed 73.3% of 47 couples at 9 to 77 months after they had terminated group therapy (the mean follow-up time was 39 months). They found that 75% reported fewer problems in their marriage, 47.4% reported that they had experienced none of the negative consequences of drinking, and 55.6% reported that the drinking had decreased or that abstinence had been maintained to the followup period. Burton and Kaplan also found, at follow-up, that the fewer the number of areas of considerable disagreement between a couple, the greater the probability would be that drinking had decreased. Their data suggested that one to two areas of considerable disagreement (at the conclusion of treatment) was the maximum possible in order for couples to have experienced a decease in drinking. Unfortunately, Burton and Kaplan have no control group to allow an unambiguous conclusion that treating the couple as a unit actually led to decreases in drinking and marital conflict.

Burton and Kaplan's studies represent one of the first systematic attempts to evaluate the value of couples therapy in the treatment of alcoholism. There are limitations to their work, however, and their results must be regarded as suggestive rather than conclusive. First, they did not utilize a no-treatment control group to study the effects of time and self-initiated recovery. Second, in their first study, which employed an individual treatment control, the mode of delivery of treatment (individual versus group) was confounded by the couples versus individuals treatment comparison. A third limitation of their work involves the method of obtaining follow-up data, in that the counselors, rather than unbiased uninvolved interviewers, obtained follow-up data (Burton & Kaplan, 1968a). The effects of the couples' desire to please their counselor is an uncontrolled complicating variable. They also relied solely on subjective self-report to evaluate the efficacy of treatment. Biases in reporting, based on desire to please or appear in a positive light, faulty memory, and so on, might have slanted responses in an unknown way. Finally, the specific content of the treatment was not reported in these studies. Therefore, it would be impossible to replicate their work, which makes its scientific value somewhat limited.

In two uncontrolled clinical studies, Smith (1969) and Gallant, Rich, Bey, and Terranova (1970) reported on the degree of success of two group therapy programs which included spouses of alcoholics in treatment. Smith's work included having wives attend group therapy while their alcoholic husbands were in the hospital. The aims of the groups were to help spouses understand the process of alcoholism and its treatment, to help them understand their relationship with their husband and how this might influence the drinking, and to overcome feelings of rivalry with the treatment facility when their husbands were in treatment. Fifteen of 23 wives to whom the program was available attended. Of those 15, 11 of their husbands were abstinent 15 months after hospital discharge. However, only one of the eight husbands of the nonattenders was abstinent at that follow-up. Smith concluded that it did not bode well for the outcome of treatment for the wife to be uninvolved in treatment. It is not possible, however, to make a causal statement about these results, because it is not known if the successful outcomes were due to the groups which the wives attended, or due to their willingness to attend groups. That certain wives were willing to attend groups may in itself have been a favorable prognostic sign even before treatment was initiated. More controlled studies in which spouses were randomly assigned to attend or not attend group therapy would clarify this question.

Gallant et al. (1970) utilized group couples therapy for couples in which one partner had a drinking problem. They treated 118 couples, with goals of treatment being to penetrate denial of drinking and to help the couple improve the quality of their relationship. Their results were somewhat less encouraging than those of Burton and Kaplan (1968a) in that they found that 44.92% of this sample were abstinent and relating well at follow-up, 34.74% were considered to be treatment failures, and the outcomes of 23.4% of the couples were unknown. Burton and Kaplan's (1968b) follow-up data, however, were based on only 39 of the 47 subjects in the original sample. If those for whom follow-up data were not available are included in the calculations of drinking outcome, Burton and Kaplan's adjusted results suggest that 46% had decreased their drinking or had maintained abstinence at follow-up, 23% showed no change, 14% were worse, and 17% were unavailable for information. These results are almost identical to those of Gallant et al. (1970). Parenthetically, it should be noted that a large proportion of couples who were not interviewed were probably treatment failures who may not have been located for follow-up because of loss of job, loss of home, geographical escape, or avoidance of the interviewer because of the shame and embarrassment associated with continued drinking or marital tension.

Cohen and Krause (1971) assigned 298 cases to two treatment groups. In one group, treatment was based on the disease concept of alcoholism; the other group of caseworkers used a "traditional" approach in which the alcoholism was viewed as a symptom of family problems. Follow-up data, obtained at least 6 months after the end of treatment, and based on interviews with the nonalcoholic wives, suggested a greater decrease in drinking in the disease-oriented group than in the traditional group. In the intact marriages (30% of both groups were separated at follow-up), however, the wives treated by the traditional workers reported more sexual satisfaction, more satisfaction with their husbands as husbands and fathers, and fewer employment problems. It would appear that wives reported improvement in the areas focused on in treatment (alcoholism in the disease approach; marital conflicts in the traditional approach) and that changes in the two areas (drinking and general satisfaction) were relatively independent.

Paolino and McCrady (1976) reported on an alcoholic woman and her husband who were treated conjointly while living together in a psychiatric hospital. Although the authors reported an uncontrolled case study, they suggested that their intensive, 24-hour involvement of the "normal" spouse in treatment led to a variety of beneficial results: (1) use of ward staff for immediate feedback about interactional patterns; (2) freedom to explore hostile and other frightening feelings with a sense of security that the hospital staff would not allow destructive results to ensue; (3) instillation of hope; (4) lack of disruption of the marital system at a time of stress; (5) increased continuity from inpatient to outpatient treatment.

In a controlled evaluation of the joint hospital admission concept and of the general efficacy of couples versus individual treatment, McCrady, Paolino, Longabaugh, and Rossi (submitted for publication) reported on treatment outcome for 33 couples randomly assigned to individual treatment for the alcoholic, couples treatment, or couples treatment plus a joint admission.

All alcoholics in the study began treatment as inpatients in a private adult psychiatric hospital. After hospital admission, all couples were pretested on a battery of assessment devices, including the Psychological Screening Inventory (PSI) (Lanyon, 1973), the Multiple Affect Adjective Checklist (MAACL) (Zuckerman & Lubin, 1965) and the Marital Adjustment Inventory (MAI) (Manson & Lerner, 1973). Each member of the couple was also interviewed privately and individually to complete the Quantity–Frequency (QF) and Alcohol Impairment (AI) indices (Armor, Polich, & Stambul, 1976). After this pretreatment assessment, each couple was interviewed, the nature of the study was explained, and informed consent was obtained. As already noted, couples were then randomly assigned to joint admission, couples, or individuals treatment groups. All began immediately in group therapy (couples, individual patients, and individual spouses for the first two groups, individual patients only for the third group), and joint admission spouses moved into the hospital. All continued in the appropriate therapy groups after hospital discharge. Follow-up data identical to the pretreatment data were obtained 6 weeks and 6 months after hospital discharge.

McCrady et al. found trends suggesting that involvement of the couple led to more successful treatment outcome in terms of drinking, but small sample size and large variability made their findings tentative rather than conclusive. They found no evidence of differential effectiveness of the treatments in the number of self-reported marital problems, experience of depression, anxiety, or hostility, or degree of psychopathology at 6-month follow-up.

In sum, the work of Burton and Kaplan (1968a,b), Smith (1969), Gallant et al. (1970), Paolino and McCrady (1976), and McCrady et al. (submitted for publication) suggests that couples group therapy where alcoholism is a problem may lead to successful treatment outcome in greater than or equal to 45% of the cases treated. Since none of these groups utilized no-treatment controls, and only McCrady et al. utilized appropriate individual treatment controls, it is impossible to conclude whether such treatment increases, decreases, or has no effect on the overall success of treatment. Additionally, Cohen and Krause's (1971) results suggest that subjective data may be highly dependent on the expectations of the treatment personnel. A further limitation of these studies is that all were based on self and spouse retrospective self-report. The effects of denial, intentional distortion, and faulty memory may have distorted the results to an unknown degree.

All of these studies were loosely based on the concept that involving the couple in treatment was important in changing drinking, but were not explicit in deriving their treatments and hypotheses from general systems theory. The first study which explicitly derived treatment from systems theory concepts was reported by Meeks and Kelly (1970). They treated five families in which either the husband (four families) or the wife (one family) had a drinking problem. They treated the family as a unit, with treatment focusing on helping the families to communicate openly and to understand interactional patterns. They found, of the five families whom they treated, that in two the drinking member remained abstinent, and in three there was a substantial improvement in the drinking. As with the other studies mentioned, there was no control group with which to compare these results, and the data gathered were subjective and impression-istic.

Finlay (1974) summarized the literature on the systems approach to treating the alcoholic marriage, reviewing four studies which he considered relevant to the question of treatment of alcoholism as an illness versus as an interactional problem:

> *Thus the studies compare the marriage of a "one up–one down" view of interpersonal malfunctioning [alcoholism as an illness] and an "everybody in the same boat but with different oars" perspective [alcoholism as an interactional problem] and consider their relative usefulness as designs for action. (p. 399)*

He reviewed the four treatment studies described earlier (Burton & Kaplan, 1968a,b; Cohen & Krause, 1971; Gallant et al., 1970; Smith 1969) and also reported on a study by Gerard and Saenger (1966) which found that having the spouse or other relatives involved in the initial evaluation for treatment enhanced continued clinic attendance. Finlay concluded that there was strong support for the interactional approach to treating alcoholism. Unfortunately, he reviewed no studies which included controls.

In a more recent review, Steinglass (1976) traced the history of family treatment approaches to alcoholism from 1950 to 1975. He reviewed some of the early alcoholic marriage literature described in chapter 2, and then intensively reviewed both controlled and uncontrolled clinical reports of couples or family approaches to the treatment of alcoholism. Steinglass (1976) concluded:

> *Although every study we have mentioned concludes with an enthusiastic statement encouraging greater use of family therapy it is also apparent that very little hard evidence exists at this point demonstrating either the efficacy of family therapy by itself or the comparative value of family therapy versus traditional forms of therapy in the treatment of alcoholism. (p. 116)*

Descriptive Studies of Interpersonal Systems Involving Alcoholics

Beginning in 1971, a group of researchers at the National Institute of Mental Health (NIMH) and Georgetown University began reporting on a series of studies based on actual observations of interactions within alcoholic families during periods of intoxication. The systems theory focus on family interactive behavior rather than individual behavior provided the framework for these studies.

The earliest studies of this group (Steinglass et al., 1971a,b; Weiner, Tamerin, Steinglass, & Mendelson, 1971) focused on father–son and brother–brother interactions. Although these were not direct studies of alcoholic marriages, this early work laid the groundwork for later study of alcoholic marriages, and thus is of direct relevance to this chapter.

Weiner et al. (1971) described a research protocol for observation of drinking behavior which they used throughout their early work. The first phase of this study was the baseline in which no alcohol was available and predrinking data were collected. Baseline was followed by 14 days of ad libitum alcohol ingestion, in which the alcoholics could drink up to 1 quart of 100-proof alcohol. The third phase involved alcohol withdrawal. Data collection was primarily through observations during individual and conjoint meetings with two staff psychiatrists.

In their first work, Weiner et al. (1971) studied a father and son who were both alcoholics. During baseline, the father and son reacted to each other with "separateness, aloofness and distrust" (p. 1648). During the conjoint sessions the son was described as verbally abusive toward his father, with the father responding passively. During drinking, however, the interactions changed, with the son initially expressing more ambivalent feelings toward his father, which his father responded to with open expressions of affection. They described several vignettes of intense emotional interaction, and concluded "thus behind the sober veneer of coolness, distance, irritability and truculent independence lay an intense desire to hate, love and be loved once the drinking began" (p. 1649). The father and son also talked openly about issues, such as the mother's prostitution, which were not discussed during sober periods. Finally, they observed switching of roles, in which one of the pair would be drunk and childlike, and the other would be relatively sober and caretaking. Postdrinking, however, they reported that the pair quickly returned to their predrinking interactional pattern.

In interpreting these data, Weiner and his associates focused on differences between the alcoholic's sober and drunken personality. They also hypothesized that more direct data about the wife of the alcoholic could be obtained by observing her behavior when the husband was drinking, rather than relying on retrospective reports. Finally, they suggested that drinking might serve as a signal of stress in the system. These authors, however, also considered individual interpretations of their results, however, by suggesting that "alcohol may be used as a stabilizing factor, helping to satisfy *unconscious intrapsychic needs* [italics ours], solidifying and clarifying role performance, controlling aggression, etc." (p. 1650). In other words, they considered the alcoholism in terms of its meaning for the intrapsychic as well as the interpersonal system.

In their later work, the group gradually moved toward a more totally interactional conceptualization. In their next papers (Steinglass et al., 1971a,b) they more intensively examined the systems approach for its potential in interpreting data about alcoholic interactions. As they began to think of alcoholism as a mechanism to maintain system homeostasis, provide structure to the system, and as a communicational mode, they derived the question, "Is the alcoholic's behavior truly self-defeating or unsuccessful as a means of social adaptation, or do we view it this way because we employ a wrong frame of reference?" (Steinglass et al., 1971a, p. 402). This study (Steinglass et al., 1971a) reports on observations on two pairs of brothers while drinking. In one relationship, while one brother initially appeared dominant with the other submissive, these roles reversed during the drinking period. In the second pair of brothers, however, one of the brothers remained sober throughout the drinking period, and actually encouraged his brother to drink very heavily. Derived from these observations, the authors concluded that the alcoholic marriage or family was an operational working system. They suggested that a system was initially established in which each partner selected and manipulated the other and adjusted her/his own behavior so that there was a complementary relationship in terms of needs, strengths, etc. In such systems, drinking is used to maintain the system, serving either as a signal of stress or strain, or as an integral part of the workings of the system. If the drinking is an integral part of the system, it may be used to satisfy unconscious needs (such as the expression of affection in the father–son pair), to cement power distributions or role differentiations (as in the second pair of brothers), to provide scapegoats for aggression, or to express cultural attitudes toward alcoholism. Steinglass et al. (1971b) also noted, however, that in all three familial pairs whom they studied, the dyads discontinued regular interaction right after the study ended. Since all pairs, when sober, were shown videotapes of their drunken interactions, the possible deleterious effects of the feedback had to be considered. They suggested that the drinking systems were actually very rigid and brittle systems which had very few mechanisms by which to maintain homeostasis in response to external pressures, other than to flee from the external pressures.

The systems concepts just described were reiterated by Davis, Berenson, Steinglass, and Davis (1974) in a theoretical nonempirical article. In addition, these authors expanded their conceptions to include learning concepts, asserting that alcohol abuse had adaptive consequences which were sufficiently reinforcing to maintain the drinking behavior. The nature of the adaptive consequences varies from individual to individual, being potentially intrapsychic, intracouple, intrafamily, or larger systems maintenance. Davis et al. (1974) reported on four clinical ways in which alcohol abuse could be adaptive, citing (1) a wife's assertiveness when drunk, (2) the family's laughing and having a great deal of fun when the father got drunk, (3) a man in a therapy group whose speech became more audible, and who was attended to more fully when drunk than when sober, and (4) two brothers in which drinking allowed one of them to become aggressive, and the other one to come to his rescue and maintain their family relationship.

Thus, as observational data accumulated, this NIMH group began to conceptualize alcohol abuse from both a systems and behavioral viewpoint. The consequences of excessive alcohol ingestion were considered reinforcing, and this reinforcement maintains the drinking behavior. What makes the consequences reinforcing, however, involves both intrapsychic and social systems needs.

Steinglass, Davis and Berenson (1975), and Wolin, Steinglass, Sendroff, Davis, and Berenson (1975) reported observational data on married couples. In these studies, they admitted couples in which one was alcoholic to a self-contained living unit within a hospital. All couples had been married and living together at least 5 years without separation, and alcohol problems were self-diagnosed by at least one member of the couple.

In the first study (Steinglass et al., 1975) 10 couples were admitted to the hospital, following 2 weeks of three times a week outpatient groups. They stayed in the hospital for 10 days, then had a subsequent 3 weeks of twice weekly outpatient groups. The groups then reconvened every 6 weeks over a 6-month period. The inpatient stay was designed to simulate "a homelike atmosphere" in which the couple shopped, fixed their own meals, planned their schedules, decided sleeping arrangements, and so on. Alcohol was freely available the first 7 of the 10 days of the hospitalization. Direct observations of the couples revealed that drinking was heavy in the first 3 to 4 days, and then decreased to almost none throughout the rest of the inpatient stay. All the alcoholics apparently reproduced the drinking patterns which were characteristic of their drinking outside the hospital, solitary drinkers being solitary drinkers on the ward, tavern or party drinkers being social drinkers on the ward. By the third or fourth day, the observers were able to identify "repetitive and predictable patterns of alcohol consumption and intoxicated behavior from couple to couple" (Steinglass et al., 1975, p. 5). These investigators noted that the specific patterns varied and that they were distinguishable and different from their sober interactions. Their clinical observations were coded through an "interaction summary," but they unfortunately do not report data from this instrument. They did, however, describe a case which illustrated many of their concepts, in which the husband of a female alcoholic expressed physical affection and tenderness to her only when she was drinking.

In a second study, Wolin, Steinglass, Sendroff, Davis, and Berenson (1975), utilizing a similar research design, reported on the results of a "family tree," in which they traced the genealogy of the family for four generations. They also asked the husbands and wives to recall family reactions around drinking. They concluded that the significance of the family incidence of alcoholism was quite apparent in the seven couples whom they studied, and that the couples appeared to be repeating the interactional style and patterns expressed in the parental or grandparental families. They gave clinical examples of this conclusion. These conclusions are reminiscent of Bowen's (1974) contention that the level of differentiation of the parents determines that of the family, and therefore of the children.

The contribution of the observational studies is significant. They are the first to report on observations of interactions of alcoholic couples or other natural family systems when the alcoholic was actually drinking. The researchers involved in these studies have derived at least six very interesting hypotheses from these observations:

1. Family interactional behavior during drinking episodes is "highly patterned" (Steinglass, 1976, p. 105) and very different from sober family behavior.
2. Alcoholism should be viewed with an eye to determining how it affects the interactional life of the family, rather than the intrapsychic or social functioning of the alcoholic or spouse.
3. Alcoholism serves as an "organizing principle for interactional life within these families" (Steinglass, 1976, p. 106).
4. Alcoholism produces predictable if not enjoyable patterns for the family, and therefore serves a stabilizing function.
5. The family should be the patient.
6. If the therapist does his assessment carefully, he will be able to identify adaptive consequences of the drinking which maintain it regardless of the original etiology of the problem.

Each of these propositions must be regarded as a working hypothesis at this time. Observational studies have led to the generation of these hypotheses, and contradictory data are not evident. Support, however, is also scanty. It should be recalled that Steinglass et al. (1975) reported the use of an interactional summary, but have not yet reported the results of this summary. We must await with eager anticipation the results of these more systematic research efforts.

Family Roles

Transactional Analysis (TA)[2] (Berne, 1961, 1973) is a theoretical approach to the understanding of human behavior, originally grounded in Freudian theory. It has extended psychoanalytic concepts to the interpersonal realm, has created a popular language to express these extended concepts, and has emphasized the relationships among individual needs, family roles, and family rules for interaction. Through the work of Steiner (1969), TA represents the major application of the concept of family roles to the alcoholic marriage.

It is Steiner's thesis that alcoholics engage in recognizable and repetitive interpersonal sequences involving alcohol which have the express purpose of

---

[2]A more thorough exposition of the concepts of Transactional Analysis can be found in Appendix D.

producing a certain interpersonal payoff. Alcoholism is the end result of the alcoholic "game," a systematic set of rules and interactional sequences, rather than being an entity in itself. The unique contribution of the TA approach is to integrate the payoff, or reinforcement, with roles and with individual needs.

Each individual's life is considered to be governed by a "script," which is a life plan, assumed in childhood, that serves as a blueprint for the person's future. Each script involves certain provisions or beliefs about one's own and others' worth. The alcoholic's position is best described as "I am no good and I know it, but you are no good either and, since you don't seem to be aware of it, I am going to expose you" (Steiner, 1969, p. 923). This position, not determined by an alcoholic's current relationships, but rather by his early childhood experiences, determines the roles he assumes in relationships. The alcoholic engages in transactions with other people which allow him to confirm his position about the world, other persons, and himself.

There are three types of repetitive interactional sequences ("games") characteristic of the alcoholic. In all three games, the alcoholic manages to put himself in a position of being disapproved of, which allows the others who disapprove of him to feel virtuous and blameless, even though they actually are not. There are several roles, or "players," in each of the games. All games include an "Alcoholic" player and someone to fill the roles of "Persecutor," "Patsy," "Rescuer," or "Connection." (All role titles are capitalized in TA terminology to emphasize that they have identifiable characteristics.)

Since it is not essential to describe each variation of the alcoholic game, an example will suffice. In the aggressive variation of the alcoholic game, "Drunk and Proud of It," the Alcoholic player demonstrates that others are no good by getting them so angry that they show their impotence and foolishness. For example, a "Drunk and Proud" alcoholic might stay out late at night or lose large sums of money playing poker, which results in his wife reproaching him (taking the Persecutor role) the morning after. The alcoholic might then apologize, placing the wife in the position of either continuing to be the Persecutor or accepting his apology, which would put her in the role of Patsy.

In the "Lush" variation of the alcoholic game, the partner more frequently vacillates between the role of Persecutor and Rescuer, usually bolstered up by a Rescuer or Patsy helping professional. The nonalcoholic spouse, in this paradigm, is considered to be unable to give affection, and feels guilty about this. Therefore, this partner will quickly switch from the role of Persecutor to that of Rescuer, in response to his/her own feelings of guilt. Thus, the spouse of an alcoholic is seen as either persecuting the alcoholic for his alcoholism, attempting to rescue him through taking care of him, or playing the role of the fool either by forgiving him for inappropriate behavior or by ignoring it. The interactions between alcoholic and spouse are initiated primarily by the alcoholic's individual needs to confirm his own inadequacy and to expose the inadequacies of others. Parenthetically, it should be noted that Steiner (1969) and Ward and Faillace (1970) also comment that the helping professional may get caught up in the alcoholic's script and usually assumes the role of Persecutor, Patsy, or Rescuer. Both Steiner (1969) and Ward and Faillace (1970) emphasize that therapists often vacillate between the roles of Rescuer and Patsy, and become Persecutors and punishers of the alcoholics when they are angry, having discovered that they unknowingly have been playing one of these other two game roles.

There have been two experimental studies of the TA roles of alcoholics and their spouses. Albretsen and Vaglum (1971, 1973) studied 12 hospitalized wives of alcoholics, in order to determine the roles which the women played before they experienced the symptoms which led to their psychiatric hospitalization, and to study possible changes in their roles prior to becoming patients. Most of the women were hospitalized for depression and suicidal ideation or acts, although some also experienced other types of psychiatric symptoms. Before symptoms occurred, Albretsen and Vaglum observed that 2 of the 12 wives were Patsys, 6 were Rescuers, and 4 were Alcoholics. In almost all these individuals, the authors found that the spouse had, prior to their developing "symptoms," shifted from the original role to the role of Persecutor. There were two possible outcomes of assuming the role of Persecutor: sobriety and an improved marital relationship, or destruction or loss of the alcoholic spouse. These two outcomes are contradictory, but Albretsen and Vaglum believed that these outcomes expressed conflicted desires of the wives. This conflict between possible outcomes was intolerable for the wives and so they escaped the conflict inherent in the Persecutor role by developing symptoms and assuming the patient role themselves. Follow-ups of 11 of the 12 women 2½ to 3 years later (Albretsen & Vaglum, 1973), revealed that five were experiencing psychiatric symptoms at the time of follow-up. They found that an additional five were in the Rescuer role, and one was in the Persecutor role. All the Rescuers were symptom free.

Albretsen and Vaglum categorized the roles of the wives of alcoholics by examining their behavior prior to hospitalization and labeling it according to the TA roles, but unfortunately do not report the specific criteria they used to assign these roles. Their results, which suggested that wives do not tolerate the Persecutor role easily, are not readily predictable from Transactional Analysis concepts about the alcoholic interaction, but must be explained by additional concepts about individual needs and conflicts.

A completely different study of the applicability of Transactional Analysis to alcoholism was provided by Griffith, Martin, Crowder, and Edwards (1968). They suggested that a crucial test of the accuracy of the TA viewpoint of the alcoholic marriage would be to use these concepts to develop a substitute game which did not have the destructive results which the current alcoholic game had. Were this feasible, and were the alcoholic to then function without alcohol, this would suggest that the game analysis was correct. The substitute game they selected involved the use of Antabuse. The specific instructions for the use of Antabuse included the following:

1. The wife gave her husband Antabuse each day.
2. If he took his Antabuse, she was allowed to say nothing positive or negative about his drinking behavior.
3. If the alcoholic did not take his Antabuse, he had to leave home until he was willing to take it.
4. If he refused his Antabuse and did not leave, the wife was to argue about the Antabuse in the same manner that she used to argue about his drinking.
5. If the wife forgot to administer the Antabuse, the husband was to say nothing, not take it on his own, and drink if the wife forgot to give it for too long a period of time.
6. The drug dosage was determined only by the physician involved in the case.
7. Antabuse was to be discontinued after 1 year.
8. For 2 years, 1 year on Antabuse and 1 year off Antabuse, the couple were to visit the clinic once a month for a 15-minute appointment.
9. The husband could drink either by leaving home or could drink when taking Antabuse if he desired.

The rules of the new game were designed to eliminate the roles of Persecutor or Rescuer for the wife, and were designed to eliminate the transactional payoff for drinking to the alcoholic. Specifically, by not allowing the wife to talk about drinking, much of the Persecutor role was eliminated. Similarly, by specifying circumstances under which drinking was actually acceptable, much of the impetus for the Rescuer role was reduced.

At 12 months, 76% of the alcoholics were abstainers. Griffith et al. (1968) also suggested that intense destructive game behavior was noted only in couples where the alcoholic was still drinking. They described various means by which the alcoholics or their spouses undermined the substitute game, but noted that these were rare. Griffith and co-workers (1968) concluded "most wives . . . were not provocative, were generally supportive, and rarely forgot to give Antabuse. Most would make a rare statement about drinking" (p. 13).

In conclusion, it can be said that there are certain prescribed roles in an alcoholic marriage which may be characteristic of this relationship. Whether these roles are unique for the alcoholic transaction or are characteristic of a variety of transactions is not an answerable question at this time. Furthermore, although the data are congruent with TA descriptions of the roles in an alcoholic marriage, the data must be regarded as circumstantial, and as gathered in a relatively unsystematic and uncontrolled manner.

Contribution of the Individual to the Establishment of the Alcoholic System

Bowen (1974) focused on the individual's original degree of differentiation as contributory to the level of functioning of the system. Persons who become alcoholic are regarded as handling emotional attachments to their parents by "denial of the attachment and by a superindependent posture which says 'I do not need you. I can do it myself' " (p. 119). There are several possible results of this approach to life, all of which are ultimately dysfunctional. Such an individual might become extremely involved in work, behave extremely responsibly toward his family, deny his need for attachments to others, and become very emotionally isolated. Turning to alcohol would be one way to gain relief from this isolation. Because of the basic denial of attachments to the parents, the person who becomes alcoholic will carry out this same posture of emotional distance with his spouse. A second alternative outcome of this posture of denial of attachment would be for the individual to become overly attached to his parents in an immature, clinging fashion and never achieve a productive life. Bowen suggested that treatment in either case should focus on decreasing emotional distance from the parental family which could allow for closer emotional ties in the current family, and decreasing the degree of anxiety in the family which contributes to the drinking.

Although Bowen's intriguing concepts are presented as a systems approach, the parallels between his approach and a psychoanalytic one are of interest. For example, the process of denial of unconscious wishes is fundamental to psychoanalytic theory. Bowen emphasized the significance of denial of attachment to parents as fundamental to the alcoholic's posture. Further, the defense of reaction formation is also a part of the psychoanalytic theory. Bowen's discussion of the emotional distance and independence of the alcoholic appears to be similar to reaction formation against the unconscious wish for attachment. The most important difference between Bowen's and psychoanalytic views of the individual lies in the former's emphasis on the interdependence between individual processes and the development and maintenance of the family system. Further, the elaborate psychic apparatus of the psychoanalyst is not Bowen's interest, whereas the structure of the family is much more so.

Thus, Bowen's primary contribution to the alcoholic marriage systems literature lies in his recognition of the importance of individual needs in the alcoholic system. He unfortunately has not well developed the notions for the alcoholic system.

Communication Approaches

As discussed in the first section of this chapter, communication is the observable data by which the functioning of any system can be understood. Communication also provides the mode by which roles and rules within a family system are established, negotiated, and maintained.

Gorad et al. (1971) used communications concepts to look at the interpersonal effects of drinking and drunkenness. Their basic premise was that drunken behavior transmits messages to the persons around the drunken individual, and that these messages both contain information and have an effect on other persons. Drunkenness as a communication functions in the following manner in any interaction, marital or otherwise. First, the person broadcasts the message that he is drunk through slurred speech, unsteady gait, smell of alcohol on his breath, and so on. However, the drunken message also states that the individual is not really himself, because of his drunkenness, and therefore may do things and say things for which he claims no responsibility. Therefore, he may send messages which he would not send otherwise, such as "take care of me," or behave in a seductive manner. The combination of engaging in such behaviors, and at the same time giving the clear message that he is not responsible for what he is doing, actually gives the alcoholic great control over the relationship in which he is interacting at the time of his drunkenness. The usual response of the sober spouse is to let the inebriated spouse set the rules, say or do what he wants, and to follow his lead.

Gorad et al. suggest, at an individual level, that the primary feature of alcoholic communication is this avoidance of responsibility for communications. In fact, they suggest that even when the alcoholic is not intoxicated, he engages in a variety of responsibility-avoiding devices in his communication, such as ambiguous messages or taking back what he has said. In relationships it would be deduced that the alcoholic is involved in a struggle for control or dominance, because he must resort to indirect responsibility-avoiding mechanisms as a means to gain control of the relationship. When the control/dominance struggle is occurring, and the alcoholic is losing with direct tactics, this may precipitate drinking bouts as an attempt to gain control of the relationship. When the drinking occurs, the spouse is confronted with her lack of control over the relationship and the alcoholic's behavior. Bullying does not work, and it is very difficult for a spouse to ignore drinking behavior because of its extreme effect and its potential for generating anxiety and discomfort in the spouse. Therefore, the alcoholic is almost guaranteed a temporary victory in the struggle for control by becoming drunk. The spouse, in contrast, does not utilize indirect responsibility-avoiding methods. Therefore, casual observation of alcoholic marriages would suggest that the spouse is in control, whereas detailed observation would reveal that true control resides in the alcoholic. That is, it might seem that the spouse is in control in the instance in which she is taking care of her drunken husband, but in fact he has manipulated the situation so as to cause her to take this role.

Gorad (1971) tested these hypotheses through an experimental analog of decision making, cooperation, and competition in 20 alcoholic couples and 20 normal control couples. Briefly, he hypothesized that (1) the alcoholic uses responsibility-avoiding behaviors when interacting with his wife; (2) the wife of an alcoholic uses a more direct, responsibility-accepting style of communication than her husband; and (3) the interaction between the alcoholic and wife is marked by the inability to function as a unit for mutual benefit with either rigidity of complementarity or escalation of symmetry as the primary interactional mode. If rigidity of complementarity is the mode, then partners would assume reciprocal roles (such as winner/loser), and never vary from the roles. In escalation of symmetry, partners would assume similar roles (such as winner/winner) and would not modify their approach even if it were clear that it was not a successful approach to a given situation.

The experimental analog which Gorad designed is somewhat complicated to describe, but, as the experiment tests crucial communications concepts, a detailed explanation of the procedure is provided here. In the procedure, each husband and wife sent messages to each other. Each selected one of three message cards, "Win," "Secret Win," or "Share." They showed their choices to the experimenter, who then communicated this choice to the partner. Each combination of messages resulted in a different payoff. Win–Share or Secret Win–Share resulted in a large monetary payoff to the individual selecting the Win or Secret Win card, and no money to the partner. Share–Share resulted in a more modest monetary payoff to both partners and Win–Win, Win–Secret Win, and Secret Win–Secret Win resulted in no monetary payoff.

Couples were instructed that the experimenter might occasionally change one of their selections to Secret Win (he never did in actuality). Thus, if one of the couple chose Secret Win, the partner could never be certain what the other player's choice had been. Thus, Secret Win can be regarded as a responsibility-avoiding, competitive message. Win can be seen as a responsibility-accepting competitive message, and Share as a responsibility-accepting, cooperative message.

Gorad found that the alcoholic men played Secret Win (the responsibility-avoiding communication) significantly more often than did the normal husbands, and that the alcoholics' wives used Secret Win significantly less than their husbands. There were no differences between normal wives and normal husbands or between normal wives and alcoholic wives in their use of the Secret Win alternative. He also found that the alcoholic couples won significantly less money than the normal couples, and that they used the Share–Share combination significantly less than did the normal couples. These alcoholic couples also interacted through escalation of symmetry in that they more often used combinations such as Win–Win, Win–Secret Win, or Secret Win–Secret Win. These results support the hypothesis that the alcoholics use a responsibility-avoiding competitive communication much more frequently than nonalcoholics. In contrast to the wives, the alcoholics used responsibility-avoiding communications while the wives used responsibility-accepting, competitive communications more frequently.

The relationship between behavior in this analog study and behavior in actual ongoing interactions is completely unknown. Gorad provided no validity data to suggest that the behaviors in this game have any correspondence with actual ongoing behaviors. In addition, many comments of Gorad et al. about the alcoholic's individual responsibility-avoiding style across situations are untested and unexamined, either in the theoretical paper or in Gorad's experimental analog study. Finally, there was no attempt to compare these alcoholic couples to other conflicted relationships. Communications theory suggests that in *any* relationship, when one member is experiencing symptoms the symptoms serve a responsibility-avoiding function (Watzlawicz, Beavin, & Jackson, 1967). Therefore, there should be conflict over control and dominance in the relationship. If this were so, the alcoholic marriage would not be at all unique in regard to communicational patterns. This conclusion is indirectly supported by the findings of Becker and Miller (1976) discussed in chapter 5, in which few differences in communication were found between alcohol-conflicted and other psychiatric problem-conflicted marriages. Communications theory provides no reason why alcoholism would be the symptom in some marriages, whereas depression, schizophrenia, or psychosomatic symptoms would prevail in other marriages. The theory simply describes what is currently happening, without offering hypotheses as to etiology of symptoms.

In a less structured simulated game situation, Kennedy (1976) studied 28 married couples, in which 11 husbands had been hospitalized for alcoholism in the last year, 6 wives had been hospitalized for psychiatric problems within the last year, and 11 couples had not been hospitalized for either alcoholism or any other psychiatric problems. Kennedy found that the psychiatric couples used a rigid cooperative style in playing, whereas normals tended to be competitive. Alcoholic couples did not show a consistent pattern, but rather showed a much greater variability and range of scores than either the psychiatric or normal couples. When the author divided the alcoholic couples into those originally selected from an outpatient setting and those from an inpatient setting, however, he found apparent uniformities within the two subgroups. Outpatient couples generally showed a competitive pattern of play, which tended to escalate. These findings are very similar to Gorad's (1971) findings of escalation of symmetry within his alcoholic couples. Inpatient couples tended to be more cooperative, although not as much as the psychiatric couples were. Kennedy suggested that these differences in interactional style might reflect differences in the stage of the husband's alcoholism.

From a completely different communications perspective, Hanson, Sands, and Sheldon (1968) looked at the amount of information which was transmitted and received congruently within alcoholic couples. In contrast to the communications approach described in which all behavior is regarded as communicative, Hanson et al. suggested that alcoholic marriages in fact had unequal communication, in which the spouse communicated more about him or herself than did the alcoholic partner. They suggested that the result of this disparity in communication was that much of the alcoholic's life went on separate from that of the spouse, excluding the spouse from important emotional experiences.

Nineteen couples in which the male partners were alcoholics filled out a questionnaire in which they described their own feelings, their relationships with others, and information about their activities. They filled out these questionnaires both for themselves and for how they thought their spouses would respond.

Hanson et al. found that the alcoholics were able to predict their spouse's responses better than the spouses could predict those of the alcoholic. In the area of symptoms and emotions, the wives of the alcoholics were unable to predict accurately any of their husband's responses. The women also saw their husbands as having more negative self-concepts than those which they reported about themselves, and they also underestimated the amount of activities in which their husbands engaged. Overall, the wives rated their husbands much more negatively than the alcoholics rated themselves. Hanson et al. concluded that communications between an alcoholic and his spouse were primarily unidirectional, going from the spouse to the alcoholic.

The difficulties with this study are myriad. First, previous studies (Jourard, 1959; Jourard & Landsman, 1960) revealed that men do not disclose themselves as much as women. Hanson et al. made no comparisons between the discrepancies in their couples and the discrepancies found in most other couples. In addition, these spouses were experiencing anger and frustration at their husbands at the time of the experiment. Therefore, that the wives would describe their husbands in more negative terms than the husbands would describe themselves might not in fact reflect inaccurate perceptions, but might more parsimoniously be seen as expressions of their anger and frustration at their husbands' drinking. Finally, other research has suggested that person perception research is not based so much on accurate perceptions of the individual but on stereotypes of male and female, husband and wife behavior. This factor is also not parcelled out in these results.

In conclusion, communications research would suggest that alcoholic couples' interactions are characterized by a certain competitive style of interaction, but that this style may only be characteristic of certain stages of alcoholism, and that the degree of accurate assimilation of communications is disparate in the couple. Since the studies have not yielded uniform results, however, these conclusions must be regarded as highly tentative.

SUMMARY AND CONCLUSIONS

In this section is presented a summary of the diverse data viewed in the preceding section that uses the organizational structure of the introduction to systems theory sections of this chapter. A critique of the status of systems theory approaches to the alcoholic marriage concludes the chapter.

Roles

There are several alternate ways of considering the interaction between alcohol ingestion and family roles. Alcohol ingestion can serve to clarify roles, but not determine a particular role for the alcoholic (Steinglass et al., 1971a, b; Weiner et al., 1971). Or it could be argued more emphatically that being an alcoholic is a defined family role, with certain characteristics, such as a goal of proving the alcoholic's and others' lack of worth (Albretsen & Vaglum, 1971, 1973; Steiner, 1969). There may also be defined spouse roles that interact with the characteristic alcoholic role. There are not sufficient data, however, to conclude that alcoholism defines any particular role, or in fact clarifies roles at all.

The need of the system for an alcoholic member has not been firmly established. If this were a necessary family role, another member would assume the same role if the alcoholic achieved abstinence. Neither the work reviewed in this chapter, the research on decompensation of the wife following her husband's abstinence (see chapter 3), nor attempts to eliminate the role of alcoholic (Griffith et al., 1968) prove that the role of alcoholic is essential to the maintenance of the family.

Thus, the concept of family roles is of theoretical interest, and directs attention to enduring behavioral patterns which are determined by other than intrapsychic needs. Supporting data, however, are scant and contradictory at present.

Rules

As discussed in the introduction to this chapter, family rules describe typical repetitive behavioral patterns of interaction within a family. No study has directly addressed or attempted to define the rules which characterize an alcoholic marriage. Griffith et al. (1968) created new rules for interaction in alcoholic couples, and found that these new rules were ones which could support abstinence. The rules that were being replaced were not clearly defined, however.

Contribution of the Individual to the Establishment of the System

The role of the alcoholic's individual needs in determining the system may be quite varied. The individual alcoholic may have a need for affective expressiveness, both of an affectionate and an assertive or aggressive type (Bowen, 1974; Steinglass et al., 1971a, b, 1975; Weiner et al., 1971). The need to prove others' worthlessness (Steiner, 1969) may be a variation of the need to express aggressiveness.

Alternately, the alcoholic's primary need could be to avoid responsibility for his actions, and to attempt to control or dominate interactions (Gorad, 1971; Gorad et al., 1971).

In summary, most authors have suggested the need for affection or the expression of aggression as the primary individual need which the individual alcoholic brings to the system in which he or she is involved. Direct experimental data proving that these are needs, however, are lacking, although Gorad's data on responsibility avoidance, and the observations by Steinglass, Weiner, and Wolin and their groups of affectionate and aggressive displays in alcoholic dyads provide some support to these concepts.

Homeostasis

Alcoholism can be conceptualized as necessary for the maintenance of family homeostasis (Davis et al., 1974; Steinglass et al., 1971a, b). The alcoholic system may be a basically brittle system which deals with attempts to introduce change through avoidance or escape from these change-inducing agents (Steinglass et al., 1971a, b). Only subjective clinical observations support these contentions. There are also no direct data supporting the belief (Meeks & Kelly, 1970) that other family members try to sabotage treatment in order to maintain the family system. As noted in discussing family roles, there are no data suggesting that another sick member is provided to fulfill the alcoholic role if the alcoholic maintains abstinence.

Communication

There have been no studies of actual patterns of communication, in terms of sequences of speech, and/or congruence or incongruence between verbal and nonverbal communicational modalities which were based on systems concepts. The clearest data about communicational patterns suggest that the alcoholic's communication is characterized by avoidance of responsibility, especially in comparison to the wife of an alcoholic (Gorad, 1971). Additionally, the communication patterns in alcoholic marriages seem to reflect conflict for control and dominance in the relationship, suggesting that role relationships and rules around dominance have not been firmly established in such marriages

(Gorad, 1971; Kennedy, 1976). Very preliminary data suggest that the wife of the alcoholic may actually receive less information about her spouse than vice versa (Hanson et al., 1968). This may reflect the alcoholic's style of avoidance of responsibility for his communications, so that the clearness and directness of any communications from an alcoholic to his spouse are blurred and hard to interpret. Data in the communications area have been carefully gathered, but the range of applicability is still somewhat constricted due to the small number of studies completed.

The Role of Symptoms

In systems theory, symptoms have been regarded as essential to the maintenance of a family system. This is in contrast to the psychoanalytic model that conceptualizes symptoms as essential to the maintenance of the mind (psychic apparatus) of the individual person. As reviewed under the concepts of homeostasis and family roles, there are no data which suggest that elimination of the alcoholic role leads to dissolution of the family system. Alcoholic symptoms have various functions, including maintenance of the system, signaling stress and strain in the system, cementing or clarifying roles in the family, or allowing the expression of otherwise unacceptable behaviors and feelings (Steinglass et al., 1975; Weiner et al., 1971). Although such changes have been observed during experimental intoxication studies with alcoholic families, the *necessity* of the alcoholism for these behaviors has not been firmly established. The relationship between teaching families to allow these other behaviors to be exhibited without alcohol and changes in drinking behavior has not been firmly established.

A variety of the treatment studies reviewed, however, do suggest that there is some relationship between drinking behavior and marital conflict. There may be an inverse relationship between the number of marital problems and degree of drinking (Burton & Kaplan, 1968a, b).

A Final Overview

As can be seen from this summary, data supporting general systems theory approaches to the alcoholic marriage are sparse. What data exist do support this approach. It might be more fruitful, however, to regard systems theory as an orientation which provides a different framework for thinking about the alcoholic marriage, rather than a set of theoretical constructs which can be proven or disproven through empirical research. That is, systems theory provides a different framework for examining the alcoholic marriage, emphasizing aspects of relationships such as roles, rules, and homeostasis which are not attended to in other approaches.

In general, systems theorists are reluctant to argue that there is *one* explanation for any problem behavior. Rather, they state that looking at the system, and considering such concepts as communication, roles, and the adaptive function of symptoms, will lead to a correct conceptualization of each individual case, on which treatment interventions can be based. Systems theorists, however, do not argue, for the most part, that there is any one role, rule, or communication pattern which should characterize all alcoholic systems. Although some regularities have been noted, the diversity of potential roles, rules, etc., is more striking than the similarity.

It should be emphasized that hard data gathered to date have not been impressive, and that frequently the very broadness and multifaceted nature of systems theory has led to some confusion in interpreting data. This diversity and broadness is the greatest strength of systems theory, because it expands our thinking about the meaning of human behavior and its context. Such broad-based thinking makes the derivation of testable hypotheses an unusually difficult task, however.

Finally, several studies suggested that a positive outcome for treatment was associated with couples approaches to treatment for the alcoholic marriage. Although initially these data seem impressive, two factors suggest that they may not be exceptional outcome results. First, almost all the studies involved middle-class couples who were employed, and whose marriages were still intact. These factors are both known to be statistically associated with positive treatment outcome no matter what the treatment approach. Second, in a comprehensive review of the literature on the efficacy of treatment for alcoholics, Emrick (1975) concluded that, with any kind of treatment, the likelihood of successful outcome in terms of decreased drinking or abstinence is about 60%. Although Emrick's review did include studies of alcoholic couples treatment, his review suggests that these data may not be unique.

Therefore, without a clear explication of systems theory principles or research supporting it, either in terms of the efficacy of treatment or the concepts, we would have to conclude that this is an approach with promise, but not much firm support.

REFERENCES

Albretsen, C. S., & Vaglum, P. The alcoholic's wife and her conflicting roles—A cause for hospitalization. *Acta Sociomedica Scandinavica*, 1971, *1*, 41–50.

Albretsen, C. S., & Vaglum, P. The alcoholic's wife and her conflicting roles II. A follow-up study. *Scandinavian Journal of the Society of Medicine*, 1973, *1*, 7–12.

Armor, D. J., Polich, J. M., & Stambul, H. B. *Alcoholism and treatment.* Santa Monica, Calif.: Rand Corp., 1976.

Becker, J. V., & Miller, P. M. Verbal and nonverbal marital interaction patterns of alcoholics and nonalcoholics. *Journal of Studies on Alcohol*, 1976, *37*, 1616–1624.

Berne, E. *Transactional analysis in psychotherapy.* New York: Grove Press, 1961.

Berne, E. *What do you say after you say hello?* New York: Bantam Press, 1973.

Bowen, M. Alcoholism as viewed through family systems theory and family psychotherapy. *Annals of the New York Academy of Sciences,* 1974, *233,* 115–225.

Bullock, S. C., & Mudd, E. H. The interrelatedness of alcoholism and marital conflict. 2. The interaction of alcoholic husbands and their nonalcoholic wives during counseling. *American Journal of Orthopsychiatry,* 1959, *29,* 519–527.

Burton, G., & Kaplan, H. M. Group counseling in conflicted marriages where alcoholism is present. Client's evaluation of effectiveness. *Journal of Marriage and the Family,* 1968, *30,* 74–79. (a)

Burton, G., & Kaplan, H. M. Marriage counseling with alcoholics and their spouses. II. The correlation of excessive drinking behavior with family pathology and social deterioration. *British Journal of Addictions,* 1968, *63,* 161–170. (b)

Cohen, D. C., & Krause, M. S. *Casework with the wives of alcoholics.* New York: Family Service Assoc. of America, 1971.

Davis, D. I., Berenson, D., Steinglass, P., & Davis, S. The adaptive consequences of drinking. *Psychiatry,* 1974, *37,* 209–215.

Emrick, C. D. A review of psychologically oriented treatment of alcoholism. II. The relative effectiveness of different treatment approaches and the effect of treatment versus no treatment. *Journal of Studies of Alcohol,* 1975, *36,* 88–108.

Finlay, D. G. Alcoholism: Illness or problem in interaction? *Social Work,* 1974, *19,* 398–405.

Gallant, P. M., Rich, A., Bey, E., & Terranova, L. Group psychotherapy with married couples: A successful technique in New Orleans alcoholism clinic patients. *Journal of Louisiana Medical Society,* 1970, *122,* 41–44.

Gerard, D. L., & Saenger, G. *Outpatient treatment of alcoholism: A study of outcome and its determinants.* Toronto, Canada: Univ. of Toronto Press, 1966.

Gorad, S. L. Communicational styles and interaction of alcoholics and their wives. *Family Process,* 1971, *10,* 475–489.

Gorad, S. L., McCourt, W. F., & Cobb, J. C. A communications approach to alcoholism. *Quarterly Journal of Studies on Alcohol,* 1971, *32,* 651–668.

Griffith, J. D., Martin, R., Crowder, W. A., & Edwards, M. *The effect of game substitution on the interactions between alcoholics and their spouses.* Paper presented at the APA Annual Meeting, Boston, May 1968.

Haley, J. Marriage therapy. *Archives of General Psychiatry,* 1963, *8,* 213–234.

Hall, A., & Fagan, R. Definition of a system. *General Systems Yearbook,* 1956, *1,* 18–28.

Hanson, P. G., Sands, P. M., & Sheldon, R. B. Patterns of communication in alcoholic marital couples. *Psychiatric Quarterly,* 1968, *42,* 538–547.

Jackson, D. D. Family rules. *Archives of General Psychiatry,* 1965, *12,* 589–594.

Jourard, S. M. Self-disclosure and other cathexis. *Journal of Abnormal and Social Psychology,* 1959, *59,* 428–431.

Jourard, S. M., & Landsman, M. J. Cognition, cathexis and the "dyadic effect" in men's disclosing behavior. *Merrill–Palmer Quarterly of Behavior Development,* 1960, *6,* 178–186.

Kennedy, D. L. Behavior of alcoholics and spouses in a simulation game situation. *Journal of Nervous and Mental Disease,* 1976, *162,* 23–34.

Lanyon, R. I. *Psychological Screening Inventory manual.* Research Psychologists Press, New York: Goshen, 1973.

Manson, M. P., & Lerner, A. *The Marriage Adjustment Inventory manual.* Los Angeles, Calif.: Western Psychological Services, 1973.

McCrady, B. S., Paolino, T. J., Longabaugh, R. L., & Rossi, J. *Effects on treatment outcome of joint admission and spouse involvement in treatment of hospitalized alcoholics.* Submitted for publication.

Meeks, D. E., & Kelly, C. Family therapy with the families of recovering alcoholics. *Quarterly Journal of Studies on Alcohol,* 1970, *31,* 399–413.

Mitchell, H. E. The interrelatedness of alcoholism and marital conflict. 4. Interpersonal perception theory applied to conflicted marriages in which alcoholism is and is not a problem. *American Journal of Orthopsychiatry,* 1959, *29,* 547–559.

Paolino, T. J., & McCrady, B. S. Joint admission as a treatment modality for problem drinkers: A case report. *American Journal of Psychiatry,* 1976, *133,* 222–224.

Smith, C. G. Alcoholics: Their treatment and their wives. *British Journal of Psychiatry,* 1969, *115,* 1039–1042.

Steiner, C. M. The alcoholic game. *Quarterly Journal of Studies on Alcohol,* 1969, *30,* 920–938.

Steinglass, P. Experimenting with family treatment approaches to alcoholism, 1950–1975: A review. *Family Process,* 1976, *15,* 97–123.

Steinglass, P., Weiner, S., & Mendelson, J. H. A systems approach to alcoholics. A model and its clinical application. *Archives of General Psychiatry,* 1971, *24,* 401–408. (a)

Steinglass, P., Weiner, S., & Mendelson, J. H. Interactional issues as determinants of alcoholism. *American Journal of Psychiatry,* 1971, *128,* 275–279. (b)

Steinglass, P., Davis, D. I., & Berenson, D. *In-hospital treatment of alcoholic couples.* Paper presented at the American Psychiatric Association 128th Annual Meeting, Anaheim, California, May 5, 1975.

Ward, R. F., & Faillace, L. A. The alcoholic and his helpers. A systems view. *Quarterly Journal of Studies on Alcohol,* 1970, *31,* 684–691.

Watzlawicz, P., Beavin, J. H., & Jackson, D. D. *Pragmatics of Human Communication.* New York: Norton, 1967.

Weiner, S., Tamerin, J. S., Steinglass, P., & Mendelson, J. H. Familial patterns in chronic alcoholism: A study of a father and son during experimental intoxication. *American Journal of Psychiatry,* 1971, *127,* 1646–1651.

Wolin, S. J., Steinglass, P., Sendroff, P., Davis, D., & Berenson, D. Marital interaction during experimental intoxication and the relationship to family history. In M. M. Gross (Ed.), *Alcohol intoxication and withdrawal.* New York: Plenum, 1975.

Zuckerman, M., & Lubin, B. *Manual for the Multiple Affect Adjective Checklist.* San Diego, Calif.: Educational and Testing Service, 1965.

7

Treatment Implications

The preceding chapters have focused on several theoretical approaches to the alcoholic marriage, and much of the empirical evidence available which supports or challenges the various perspectives. In this, the final chapter, some *practical* implications for the treatment of alcoholism will be derived from this body of literature. It is our impression, based on the research evidence reviewed, that the behavioral perspective offers some of the most promising concepts and techniques developed to date. This assessment, coupled with the lack of supportive evidence for the DPH and DH, has led to a focus in this chapter on behaviorally oriented assessments and treatments. Systems, psychoanalytic, and sociological perspectives, however, offer ideas for enrichment of treatment which would not be suggested by a strictly behavioral viewpoint. What is presented in this chapter is not a treatment "package," to be applied to every alcoholic marriage, but rather some ideas and techniques which may be highly applicable to some alcoholic marriages, and of limited usefulness for others.

This book was written because of our strong opinion that regardless of the theoretical perspective from which the alcoholic is conceptualized, we believe that the alcoholic's drinking and marriage are inseparably related. The role of the spouse in the development, maintenance, and treatment of alcoholism has been emphasized repeatedly, and the discussion of treatment will highlight this relationship, rather than a total treatment for alcoholism. This means that the discussion does not focus on medical aspects of treatment, in terms of detoxification or treatment of the medical diseases associated with chronic alcoholism, and has very little to say about treatment for unmarried alcoholics, subjects worthy of a volume in themselves.

This chapter will focus on four major areas: (1) entering treatment and "motivation" for treatment, (2) assessment of the alcoholic marriage, (3) the delivery of treatment, and (4) the therapeutic relationship.

ENTERING TREATMENT AND "MOTIVATION" FOR TREATMENT

The issue of motivating the alcoholic for treatment has been often discussed and debated. Alcoholics as a group generally have the reputation of being "poorly motivated" and "difficult to treat." Such generalizations have left a stigma on alcoholics that is frequently passed on from one generation of mental health professionals to the next. The alcoholic's infamous reputation for being poorly motivated seems to be related to three factors: (1) denial or lack of labeling of alcohol as a significant problem, (2) supposedly poor treatment outcome, and (3) lack of involvement in psychoanalytically oriented, introspective treatments. The following subsections discuss each of these motivational issues and, where appropriate, treatment strategies designed to address these concerns.

"Denial"

"Denial" has been one of the most used and abused words in the field of alcoholism. At times, the term denial has referred to the alcoholic's lack of labeling his drinking as problematic. In the disease concept of alcoholism (Jellinek, 1951) the suggestion is made that each person must "bottom out," that he must suffer the severe pain of uncontrolled alcoholism, with all the accompanying miseries of lost jobs, lost family, lost friends, severe physical illness, and so on. Proponents of this approach argue that only at this point will the denial be broken and will the alcoholic be truly motivated for treatment. From a behavioral point of view, this concept suggests that the alcoholic must experience in an immediate and severe way the negative consequences of his drinking. From a psychonanalytic point of view, this same belief would be explained by saying that the defense mechanisms of the alcoholic have undergone a major reduction in their effectiveness consequent to these severe results of the alcoholism.

Often, the family and particularly the spouse of an alcoholic appear to contribute to maintaining this denial. Virtually every theoretical approach reviewed in the preceding chapters has described this phenomenon. The psychoanalytically oriented views (DPH and DH) suggest that the spouse of the alcoholic is an emotionally disturbed person who employs psychic defense mechanisms that support the alcoholic's continued alcoholism in order to survive emotionally herself. Therefore, she would be expected to engage in behaviors that would maintain his alcoholism. In order to be able to deal with the alcoholic's denial, the spouse would also need to obtain treatment in order to work through her needs for an alcoholic mate. The spouse would have to engage in intensive psychotherapy and, with the help of a therapist, come to understand, accept, and reduce the painful intensity of her intrapsychic needs to be married to an alcoholic, whether those needs were to dominate, to defend herself from her inadequacy, fulfill masochistic needs, or whatever. If she were able to attain these changes in psychic processes, then she would be free to change her behavior and therefore to allow the alcoholic to experience the consequences of his drinking in a way that would penetrate his denial of the problem.

The behavorial approach, as already noted would suggest that denial is actually a shorthand label for describing a person who has not fully experienced the negative consequences of his drinking, in a way that would lead to the belief that it was a significant problem. For a spouse to help her alcoholic mate to experience the consequences of his drinking, she could begin to rearrange his consequences to make immediate consequences of drinking unpleasant, and the consequence of sobriety more pleasant:

Mr. and Mrs. A. were a young married couple with a 3-year-old daughter. Mr. A. often would stop at a bar after work, and drink to the point of intoxication. He would somehow manage to return home, late at night, either by walking, driving, or being driven by a friend. However, he would virtually always pass out on the front lawn of his house. Mrs. A., a petite, frail woman (in contrast to her rather burly husband), would always wait up until he returned home, and then drag her unconscious husband into the house, down the hallway, and into their bedroom. She would then undress him, clean him up if he had messed himself by urination or vomiting, and put him to bed. In the morning, she would call his boss, stating that he would not be in that day because of a cold or some other medical problem, and would bring him juice and talk quietly.

On rare occasions, Mr. A. would return home immediately after work. In those days, Mrs. A. would frequently be in her housecoat, watching afternoon soap operas. As soon as he would appear, she would begin to berate him for his bouts of drunkenness, and then withdraw and refuse to talk to him further.

Clearly, Mrs. A. was unknowingly providing strong reinforcement for her husband's drinking behavior, and strong punishment for him to come home sober after work. Not surprisingly, Mr. A. stated that he did not have an alcohol problem, that he only "had a few beers with the guys." Through counseling, Mrs. A. needed to learn to allow her husband to lie on the front lawn if that was where he ended up, to not clean him up, and not cover for him at work. In this way, he would strongly experience the many very obvious negative consequences of his drinking, and, as a result, would be likely to show a decrease in his "denial."

Many spouses have somehow learned this principle on their own, and have implemented it in creative and humorous ways. For example:

Mr. and Mrs. B., a couple in their mid-forties, had been married for 2 years. Mr. B. was drinking daily to the point of intoxication, experiencing blackouts, and had numerous car accidents, which he usually did not remember. One night, Mr. B. ran over a small maple sapling planted next to their driveway. Mrs. B. quietly brought the broken top of the tree into the house, and placed it in a vase in the middle of the dining room table. She stated nothing. Through a series of such episodes, Mr. B. suddenly began to show a decrease in his "denial," and became highly "motivated" for alcohol treatment.

Maxwell (1976) cites numerous examples of such an approach.

Interestingly, Al-Anon (Al-Anon Family Headquarters, 1971) makes very similar suggestions to the spouses of alcoholics, although their theoretical rationale is quite different. They emphasize the importance to the spouse of disengaging from the alcoholism, not attempting to control it, and not responding to it. From the behavioral perspective, the Al-Anon philosophy results in spouses withdrawing reinforcement from the drinking behavior, although Al-Anon also discourages active punishment for drinking behavior.

A similar approach (Johnson, 1973) suggests that the alcoholic be forcefully confronted with the negative consequences of his drinking which have already occurred. For example, a calm presentation to the alcoholic, at a sober time, of the various missed appointments, arguments, hurts (both physical and emotional), accidents, personal injuries, and so forth, might also increase temporarily the negative consequences of the drinking enough that the alcoholic would willingly seek treatment.

Although discussion to this point has focused on the alcoholic's denial and the spouse's role in helping him decrease that denial, the reader should recall that the systems perspective would argue that the denial is not in the individual but in fact is in the whole system if the alcohol abuse is playing a significant role in the maintenance of family roles and system homeostasis. Thus, some form of stress would have to be introduced from outside the system in order to threaten this homeostasis enough to require treatment. A threat of loss of job, a driving while intoxicated (DWI) arrest, followed by court-ordered treatment, or diagnosis of a dangerous medical condition, might provide sufficient external stress to upset the balance of the system sufficiently to lead to treatment.

Prognosis for Successful Treatment Outcome

The second aspect of motivation described earlier was that of the reputed poor treatment outcome for alcoholism. Often, in a rather circular argument, therapists and researchers alike have argued that those alcoholics who have a poor treatment outcome were not "motivated" for treatment at the time of presentation to the treatment agency. This means that motivation can only be determined after the treatment is terminated and is used post hoc as an explanation (or perhaps therapist rationalization) for poor treatment outcome.

The issue of poor treatment outcome must be more thoroughly examined. Emrick (1975), in a recent review of over 300 published papers on treatment outcome for alcoholics, concluded that any type of treatment intervention strategy is more effective than no treatment at all. Specifically, he found that combined abstinence and decreased drinking rates for treated alcoholics was about 60%. Industrial alcoholism programs are reporting success rates of 70 to 80%, behavioral treatment programs have been routinely reporting 70% or greater improvement rates (Hedberg & Campbell, 1974; Hunt & Azrin, 1973; Sobell & Sobell, 1976). Therefore, the myth of untreatability appears to be just that, a myth. The treatment outcome in chronic, skid-row populations has most typically been much poorer, with many studies reporting success rates of only 10 to 15% (Chafetz, 1974). Even this poor outcome rate, however, has been challenged by recent research findings (Miller, 1976). "Poor motivation" has frequently been an easy excuse used to "explain" poor treatment outcome in difficult populations. Sadly, the belief that treatment outcome for alcoholics is poor because of their poor motivation has impeded the overall progress and interest in alcoholism treatment among many professionals.

Motivation for Introspective Treatment

The third aspect of poor motivation concerns the treatment for which an alcoholic is poorly motivated; i.e., for what type of treatment is he poorly motivated? One of the reasons alcoholics have been described as poorly motivated may be because of the conclusion by many psychoanalytically oriented therapists that alcoholics are not good candidates for psychoanalysis or mentalistic, insight-oriented treatment (Blum, 1966). The label of "poorly motivated" applies to a specific kind of motivation for insight-oriented therapy and the intensive intrapsychic introspection inherent in this approach. Thus, with alcoholics, treatment leaning toward more action-oriented approaches may lead to profoundly different treatment outcomes.

"Motivating" the Spouse

Up until this point, discussion has been on issues of motivating the alcoholic for treatment, techniques for motivation, and the manner in which the spouse can be helpful and indeed instrumental in this motivating process. No mention has been made of motivating the spouse herself for treatment, and in fact major behavior changes for the spouse have been suggested as if they would be easy for her to implement. The stress theory perspective has very cogently and clearly illustrated, however, that the spouses are themselves under enormous pressure and experiencing much psychological discomfort. To expect them to make major changes in their own behavior patterns, which would elicit hostility from their alcoholic husbands, condemnation from family and friends, and embarrassment in front of family, friends, and neighbors, is a great deal to ask of these women. Additionally, they are having to fulfill virtually all of the sociologically defined roles in the family, those of provider, homemaker, decision maker, and parents, and many of them are experiencing significant anxiety, depression, or other psychophysiological symptoms at this time. Therefore, if these women or their alcoholic spouses do come to the attention of treatment personnel, initially supportively engaging these women in treatment is an essential step. Providing or guiding them to agencies that can provide them with some relief for practical problems would be an initial step in helping to decrease their problems enough for them to begin to engage in productive work and treatment. For example, referral to one of the many child-care/child-support agencies now proliferating, such as homemakers' services, child care centers, or women's centers, might help. Additionally, helping them with financial problems through referral to welfare, vocational rehabilitation, or loan services would further reduce the burden of anxiety associated with these practical issues. Although many therapists might argue that it is not the task of the therapist to provide such guidance and that, in fact, providing such guidance might be countertherapeutic if it interfered with helping the wife to learn to develop her own resources further (a principle most consistently followed in psychoanalysis), this would be the most direct implication of the stress theory view of the spouse (a view that has significant empirical support). At the point at which the spouse has some decreased anxiety over role burden and practical issues, she most likely will be more receptive to treatment interventions which combine support with rather structured treatment to enable her to develop and implement the strategies described herein to help motivate her alcoholic spouse toward treatment.

In such treatment of the spouses of alcoholics, the power of group therapy in this process cannot be minimized (although specific research support for this assertion does not currently exist). The opportunity for modeling of appropriate behavior or role playing anticipated negative interactions with the alcoholic spouse, all important from the behavioral viewpoint; developing the strengths of the "healthiest" member of the system through identification with other group members, a viewpoint promoted by Bowen (1971); and opportunity for mutual identification, catharsis, and confrontation of spouse denial, elements essential in psychoanalytically oriented therapy, would all be available in a spouse therapy group. Of course, the actual content and structuring of the therapy would vary tremendously depending on the orientation used.

ASSESSMENT

Assessing the marital relationship, alcoholism, and the interface and interdependence between the two is an essential first step toward treatment interventions. Assessment is an ongoing process during treatment, and the therapist's assessment of various factors often changes as new information appears and the couples engage in a wider range of behavior, or as they report a wider range of behavior to the therapist. The therapist, however, needs to make an initial and rather thorough assessment on which to base initial treatment strategy. This section discusses assessment from three points of view: (1) the marital history and its implications; (2) specific issue or topic areas to consider in assessment; and (3) various techniques of assessment, such as interviews, observations, structured tasks or games, and structured tests.

Marital History

From virtually every theoretical perspective, the sequencing of events prior to and during the marriage is of crucial significance. This secion will highlight some of the information that is most essential to obtain in the marital history, and its implications for the various theoretical perspectives.

The related questions of when drinking problems began relative to the date of marriage and whether or not the spouse was aware of these problems if they predated marriage are of special significance. With some couples, it is abundantly clear that the problematic drinking preceded the marriage, or that it began well into the marriage. When drinking problems predated the marriage, it would be difficult to argue that the spouse played a significant role in the establishment of the alcoholism and drinking pattern, although, as mentioned in chapter 4, the role of the courtship period in the development of the relationship and the alcoholism is usually forgotten by both clinicians and researchers. When the alcoholism predated the marriage, the therapist must consider three major factors. First, what was the system in which the alcoholic was involved at the time of the establishment of the drinking pattern? Is this system still operative, and in fact is the drinking behavior still fulfilling functions for that system, whether it was the system of the family of origin, a previous marriage, or a nonfamilial system, such as a work group or stable social group? Concomitantly, the therapist would want to consider whether there were certain stresses which led to the drinking or reinforcers which maintained it. The second factor to consider is whether the reinforcements which originally maintained the drinking behavior, or the systems which originally required the drinking, are still major operative systems. If so, the therapist would want to consider involving these systems in the treatment, rather than what at first glance would appear to be the most significant system (the current marriage). If these factors are no longer operative, then it is incumbent upon the therapist to determine what factors are currently operating to maintain the drinking. The third issue to consider is that when the alcoholism did predate the marriage, the entire marital relationship has included drinking as a significant factor. Such a couple has never learned how to talk, work, make love, relax, or care for their children without the ever present specter, if not the actual presence, of drunkenness.

The constant tension associated with the unpredictability of the alcoholic, the difficulty of long-term and day-to-day planning of family activities, results in a distorted and unpleasant marital history.

In attempting to restructure such a relationship without alcohol, the therapist and couple are faced with the arduous task of building a new relationship, rather than attempting to reestablish previous and perhaps more productive modes, with modifications in them. Regardless of whether therapy would be intrapsychically or environmentally oriented, therapy with such a couple involves the difficult learning of new ways to relate and live together.

In cases in which the spouse was aware of the alcoholism prior to the marriage, the therapist needs to be alert to a special subset of expectations such a spouse might have had about marriage. Frequently, we could speculate that the spouse expected to be able to change her alcoholic partner, sadly believing that he only needed to be married and happy in order to stop drinking, but thoroughly lacking any means to effect that change in her partner. Such spouses often tried very hard to change the drinking, and consequently, when appearing for therapy, feel discouraged, angry, and hopeless. Assuming that the spouse genuinely wants the alcoholic to discontinue his problematic drinking behavior (of course, the DPH and DH would suggest that on some level she does not want him to discontinue his pattern), a significant task for the therapist would be to help such a spouse decrease her fantasy of omnipotence, and at the same time to increase her hope that she can effect change.

Most ominously, some spouses may have known about their partner's alcoholism prior to marriage, and not regarded it as of much concern. Their own models of marriage (parents, grandparents, aunts, uncles) may have been of alcoholic marriages, or they may not have regarded alcoholism as a disruptive element in marriage. In such a marriage, alcoholism might be an integral part of the system, and attempts to change would involve not only the drinking but also the degree of the couple's comfort and acceptance of alcoholismic drinking. It is unlikely, without an externally generated crisis such as described earlier in this chapter, that such a couple would even appear for treatment.

When alcoholism predated the marriage with the nondrinking partner being unaware of the alcoholism, communicational patterns must be even more closely attended to. Either the alcoholic was able to keep a very significant aspect of his existence extremely private, most likely by excluding the spouse-to-be from many activities or interactions, and/or the spouse was unusually insensitive to the frequent communications from the alcoholic which would provide cues about his problems. Communications research (reviewed in chapter 6) does suggest ineffective transmission of information from an alcoholic to his wife, once the relationship is established. In either case, it is less likely that such a couple has developed and maintained effective ways to communicate with each other verbally or nonverbally, and it is likely that the other's ability to read such communications accurately is impaired.

Finally, consider the couple in which alcoholismic drinking developed after the onset of the marriage. This may be a very hopeful condition for treatment. First, such a couple has had a time in their marriage characterized by nonalcoholismic drinking. Although it cannot be assumed that that marriage was harmonious previously, at least the couple have had some opportunity to work, love, and play without disruptive drinking. If the couple had had any degree of success in those endeavors, the therapist might be able to help them reinstate some of those original interactions rather than having to rebuild completely.

When the alcoholism postdated the onset of marriage, a particularly detailed marital history should be obtained. First, the therapist needs to obtain a detailed chronological review of symptom development, with specific dates and times of the occurrence of various problems being pinpointed very carefully. Many couples, when first asked about the onset of drinking will give such answers as "about 6 years ago," "it seems like forever," or other such nonspecific answers. The more specific the therapist can help the couple to be, the more helpful the assessment. For example, if the onset of the drinking problems was rather insidious, and seemed to begin quite early in the relationship, this would suggest that the drinking might be an integral part of the functioning of the family system. Conversely, if the problematic drinking began later in the relationship, and the onset was more sudden, it might more readily be seen as an expression of a stress upon the family system.

Concomitantly with obtaining information about the onset of drinking, it would be important to obtain information about other major events in the extended family throughout the life of the marriage. Births, deaths, serious illnesses, or other additions or losses in the extended family are all of significance. One area that some systems theorists have especially emphasized is that the stresses or changes may not be in the nuclear family, but rather may be in some aspect of the extended family. Often, when the therapist obtains a detailed history, the relationship between family conflict and drinking becomes quite clear to the therapist very quickly, although this relationship is often obscure to the family members themselves. Considering what events seem to be most strongly related to the onset of alcoholismic drinking provides the therapist with clues to the particular role the alcohol may be playing in the family system, or what individual conflicts may have been aroused at the time, and therefore what individual needs are being met both for the alcoholic and spouse through the drinking behavior.

Another highly significant aspect of the marital history concerns what has transpired when or if the alcoholic has attempted to stop drinking on his own, or with previous treatment. The therapist would be most interested in knowing what was the subjective experience of the spouses during an abstinent period, that is, were they experiencing less discomfort and less psychic pain, or did either of them experience an increase in psychological disturbance. If there was such an increase, this provides ample warning to the therapist to be aware that it will probably occur again, and that specific individual or system homeostasis will be threatened by attempts to achieve abstinence. Therefore, treatment would have to focus both on the achievement of abstinence and on the concomitant resolution of the issues related to the drinking which appear to be exacerbated when the person is not drinking. Specific focus on the spouse's behavior during the abstinent period would also be of great interest. Was she able to provide positive support and acceptance to her partner when he attempted to stop drinking, or did she repeatedly remind him of past alcoholic transgressions and her own anger and hurt feelings over his drinking behavior? Although certainly no spouse would be expected to be mute on such topics, the degree of emphasis on these would be especially important to know:

Mr. K. obtained treatment for his alcoholism, after a 6-year history of drunkenness, unemployment, and violent outbursts toward his wife while drinking. After a 3-week hospital stay, in which his wife was involved on an almost daily basis, he returned home with great hope for maintaining abstinence. At their first outpatient session, the wife stated "It's about time he stopped drinking, he can't imagine what a hell life has been for me. He just has not thought about me or the children at all in the last 6 years." At the second outpatient session, after Mr. K. had experienced an episode of impotence, she stated "I don't know what kind of a man you are. I could understand your having trouble when you were drinking, but now it just doesn't make any sense. Do you have a girlfriend?" Such negative, nonsupportive comments on Mrs. K.'s part, while reflecting her own frustration, anger, and depression, did not bode well for Mr. K.'s attempts to attain and maintain abstinence.

Different theoreticians would explain Mrs. K.'s negative behavior in different ways. The DPH and DH adherent would suggest that her nagging, questioning, and lack of positive efforts represent a matrix of psychic defense mechanisms that reflects unconscious needs to keep her alcoholic spouse sick. The systems theorist would blame the system's need for a sick member, and would predict that Mrs. K. would soon become symptomatic if Mr. K. were to somehow maintain abstinence. Behaviorists and stress theorists would argue that she did not know a more effective way to react to his changed behavior. *No matter what the explanation, this pattern would suggest that such a couple cannot maintain sobriety without specific attention to such destructive interpersonal patterns of response.*

A further question for the marital history is what factors precipitated the return to drinking. Were there identifiable, extrafamilial factors which triggered the renewed drinking, or were the precipitants specific to the marital family context?

In the K. family, the specific trigger which led Mr. K. to resume abusive drinking was the behavior of his 15-year-old son from a previous marriage. Mr. K. had reported feeling extremely guilty about having divorced his first wife, and therefore not being as available to his children as he would like. He and his son were working on a motorcycle one day, and Mr. K.'s son said "Dad, would you like me to get you a beer?" Mr. K. took the drink, and quickly returned to his alcoholism and drinking pattern.

In this example, we can surmise that the specific individual difficulty which Mr. K. had with his son, perhaps combined with the buildup of repeated negative comments from his spouse, and his lack of dealing with any of these stresses in a fashion which would lead to their resolution or diminution, most likely led to his return to drinking.

Current Marital Issues to Consider in Assessment

One of the most consistent issues studied in the alcoholic marriage research, and one which has repeatedly found empirical support, is the issue of control, dominance, or dependence. Theorists of persuasions as diverse as systems theory and psychoanalytic theory have suggested, and supported through empirical research (reviewed in chapters 2 and 6), the notion that there is an ongoing struggle for control in such marriages. The struggle may occur on various levels, and these various levels need to be assessed very carefully. The first level is that of actual sociological role distributions within the alcoholic marriage. For example, who is dominant in regard to finances, household management, child rearing practices and decisions, decisions about employment, where the couple lives, how many children in the family, and ways to pursue leisure time are all areas in which certain aspects of dominance can be evaluated.

The second level for assessment in the area of dominance involves communication patterns. For example, observations of which of the marital partners answers first when a question is asked, which opinion is accepted by the couple, who interrupts whom, who states opinions, who disagrees and the effect on the partner of disagreement, and who speaks the most are all aspects of communication which may reflect dominance within the relationship.

A third level of dominance and dependence involves the subjective psychological sense of dominance and dependence which each member of the couple holds. Although their psychological sense may not correspond with realities or the therapist's assessment of the distributions of roles and communication patterns, the couple's subjective view of who is dominant in the relationship and their own reactions to that assessment are of significance.

The second major issue to consider in assessment is the area of communication patterns. Whether or not couples are able to state effectively to their partner their opinions, feelings, or wishes in a manner which is comprehensible, and which is heard by the marital partner is of crucial significance. In addition to examining the efficiency and effectiveness of communicational exchanges, the therapist needs to look at the content of these exchanges also. For example, the behavioral perspective raises the question of whether or not there are significant affectional exchanges in which the members of the couple express positive feelings toward each other and about each other's behavior. Additionally, the behavioral perspective would examine nonverbal communicational interchanges, such as smiling, looking at the partner, indicating agreement, and various other means of reinforcing the partner's verbal expressions. Further, the effectiveness of the couple in solving problems is one heavily emphasized by the behavioral perspective. A variety of inefficient problem-solving behaviors have been identified, such as negative, critical, sarcastic talk (Miller, 1976), talk about past alcoholic transgressions (Miller, 1976), interrupting, humiliating the other person, or putting them down (Jacobson, b, in press), talking about the problem or its cause rather than trying to generate solutions or talking about who is responsible for the problem (Jacobson, b, in press), sidetracking (Jacobson, b, in press), vague, ambiguous communications (Jacobson & Martin, 1976), or obtrusive vocal characteristics, such as loud talk, fast talk, a monotone, sing-song speech, slow talk, overtalking (Thomas, 1977). Many of these dysfunctional communication patterns can be identified through interview; specific techniques for structured assessment are discussed in the following section.

A third area to examine in the current marital relationship is the degree of pleasurable experience in the relationship, especially in proportion to the degree of displeasurable experience. The behavioral view of marriage suggests that satisfying marriages involve a relative maximization of rewards and a minimization of negative interchanges. Stuart (1969) described marital discord as a function of a low rate of exchange of positive reinforcers, which results in each spouse becoming less attractive to the other, and thus the overall relationship becoming less attractive. A further extension of this concept is the concept of reciprocity and coercion. In reciprocity, rates of reward will be reciprocated on an equal basis. In coercion, there is inequitable exchange in which one member's behavior is under positive control and the other member uses aversive control. Robinson and Price (1976) found that much of the variation in daily reports of marital satisfaction is accounted for by the occurrence of pleasurable or displeasurable behaviors. Satisfied, happy couples generally exchange a higher rate of pleasurable behaviors, and report a higher ratio of pleasant to unpleasant behaviors occurring in their home. It should also be noted that they found that poorly adjusted marriages underestimated the actual frequency of occurrence of positive behaviors. In interview, the therapist can assess what each member of the couple sees as the strengths of the relationship, and what behaviors they note operating which provide pleasure to them in the relationship. There are also some specific techniques for assessment of the occurrence of pleasurable and displeasurable behaviors which are described in the following section.

Finally, important and practical issues need to be discussed, such as the financial status of the family, the current functioning of the children, the relationship of the parents to the children at this time, the sexual relationship, and the job status of the marital partners. Clearly, these important areas provide a backdrop for treatment above and beyond the specific areas of conflict just described.

Techniques for Assessment

There are three major techniques for assessing the marital relationship: interview, observation (including structured tasks or games, observer recording, and self-recording), and paper and pencil measures. Interviews have been discussed at length, and so are not described further in this section.

There are a diversity of observational procedures available to assess the marital relationship. It should be noted at the outset that the degree of importance placed on the need for direct observation of natural behaviors varies with the therapist's theoretical persuasion. For example, the psychoanalytically oriented therapist is most interested in the distortion of events which the couple reports, and the resistances which appear in the therapy hour. Therefore, what "really" happened is not as significant as the couple's response to events. The systems therapist and the behavioral therapist place much greater emphasis on the importance of knowing what "is," and believe that the gathering of such data is crucial to evaluating the marital and alcoholic marital relationship.

Several of the studies reviewed in this book have used methodologies for observation which could be applied in the clinical setting. The most elaborate observation systems are those used by Steinglass, Davis, and Berenson (1975), Paolino and McCrady (1976), and McCrady, Paolino, Longabaugh, and Rossi (submitted for publication), which involve observing couples living together in a structured treatment environment. To date, neither group has reported on systematic means to record and process the incredibly large amount of information gathered through these observations. An alternative possibility in observing marital relationships would be to have an observer in the living situation. Of course, in either of these ongoing observation procedures, the presence of the observer would undoubtedly change the marital interaction in unknown ways.

An alternative naturalistic observation procedure would be to have some form of taping equipment in the home, which would be turned on by the couple at specified times. Small samples of behavior obtained from the tapes could be more easily coded through such observation instruments as the Marital Interaction Coding Summary (MICS) (Hops, Wills, Patterson, & Weiss, 1971) or the recent marital communication and decision-making coding procedures developed by Thomas (1977). It should be noted that Miller and Hersen (1975) report use of such an assessment procedure in their case report, discussed in chapter 5.

A second type of observation involves placing the couple in a structured task situation, and videotaping their behavior. For example, providing them with a task of discussing the alcoholism with the goal of developing a solution, and coding the interactions through use of the MICS (Hops et al., 1971) or other coding procedures would provide rather structured information about marital decision making. Couples could also engage in marital tasks, such as the game tasks described by Gorad (1971) or Kennedy (1976). Several other structured games, such as the SIMFAM (Olson and Straus, 1972) could be used.

A third type of observation involves spouse recordings of their own or each other' behavior. The Spouse Observation Checklist (SOC) (Weiss, Hops, & Patterson, 1973) is designed for couples to record, from an exhaustive list, the daily frequency of occurrence of various spouse behaviors, which are labeled as pleasurable or displeasurable. This provides a "quasi-observational" (Jacobson & Martin, 1976, p. 547) record of daily behavior.

Self-report inventories have been used very little in the area of marital assessment for alcoholism. Drewery and Rae (1969) used a modification (Drewery, 1969) of the Edwards Personal Preference Schedule (EPPS) (Edwards, 1959) to assess perceptions of each partner of themselves, of their partner, and of their partner's perceptions of them. There have been numerous marital inventories not specifically designed for alcoholic marriages which could be used as assessment procedures. For example, Stuart and Stuart (1972) have developed a behaviorally oriented marital inventory which assesses satisfactions in the marriage, goals, decision making, typical daily schedules, and communication patterns using a self-report format. Various measures of marital satisfaction have also been used in other contexts, such as the Locke–Wallace Marital Adjustment Scale (MAS) (Locke & Wallace, 1959) or the Marriage Adjustment Inventory (Manson & Lerner, 1973). Finally, Tharp and Otis (1966) have developed a measure of functioning in marital roles and couple satisfaction with functioning in these roles. Since this is an issue of particular significance for alcoholic marriage couples, this is an instrument, not yet applied to alcoholic marriages, which might yield significant and intriguing information for the therapist as well as the observer.

THE DELIVERY OF TREATMENT

In discussing the implementation of treatment, the reader should recall that in a recent review of over 300 published papers on treatment outcome for alcoholics, Emrick (1975) concluded that any kind of treatment intervention strategy is more effective than no treatment at all. He found abstinence rates no different in treated and untreated groups, but found that significantly more treated alcoholics who continued to drink decreased their drinking markedly. Combined abstinence and improvement rates for treated alcoholics were about 60%. He did report, however, that he found no significant differences among treatment approaches. Very recent behavioral treatment programs, however, have routinely been reporting 70% or greater improvement rates (Hedberg & Campbell, 1974; Hunt & Azrin, 1973; Sobell & Sobell, 1976). Therefore, it appears that behavioral strategies may provide a more effective approach to treating alcoholics and alcoholic couples. The clinical observations and data provided by the other frameworks discussed in this book, however, extend the issues to be considered in treatment and enrich our understanding of the processes by which treatment interventions may work.

The first step in implementing treatment is deciding on the target of treatment. Psychoanalytic and systems therapists both regard the alcoholic drinking behavior as a manifestation of a more fundamental underlying disorder. That is, the psychoanalytically oriented therapist would regard the alcoholic's destructive drinking as a manifestation of an unconscious, intrapsychic conflict. Therapists basing their work on systems theory would regard this same drinking as reflecting a conflict in the system, either in role relationships, as a response to the threat of disruption of the homeostasis of the system, or as an integral aspect of the system, necessary to maintain its functioning. Sociological theory does not specifically address the meaning of the alcoholic's behavior. Behavioral therapists do not regard the drinking as symptomatic of other conflicts, but do consider that the drinking behavior must be understood within the context of the antecedent conditions which elicit the drinking, and the reinforcers which maintain the drinking. Therefore, a psychoanalytically oriented therapist or a systems therapist would focus their treatment primarily on underlying conflicts, without necessarily focusing specifically on the drinking behavior itself. Behavior therapists would focus on both the drinking behavior and the factors which appear to maintain it.

As discussed in chapter 5, behavior therapy considers problem drinking in terms of identifiable antecedents to the drinking, the consequences of the drinking which maintain it, organismic variables, the nature of the drinking response itself, and the contingency relationship between the responses and consequences. This section discusses the modification of antecedent conditions which may elicit drinking, primarily through problem-solving techniques, modification of the consequences of drinking and sobriety through contracting and increasing the overall rewardingness of the relationship, and consideration of cognitive issues in treatment.

Modification of Antecedents through Problem Solving

Skills training involving social skills training and problem-solving techniques can be used with alcoholic couples to enable them to modify certain antecedent conditions to drinking, most notably the problematic situations within the marriage. Additionally, teaching such a couple problem-solving techniques gives them a skill to use to deal with drinking, as another problematic behavior.

A variety of communicational and problem-solving skills have been identified by researchers involved in behavioral couples treatment (Hops et al., 1971; Jacobson, in press a,b; Jacobson & Martin, 1976; Miller & Hersen, 1975; Peterson & Frederiksen, 1976; Weiss et al., 1973):

1. Communication in conflicted relationships is often seen as being characterized by coercive attempts at generating change, which involve coercive and negative verbal communications. For example, in conflicted marriages, couples frequently will use put-downs, attempt to humiliate each other, or turn off the other one nonverbally through not looking, turning away, or interrupting.
2. Troubled couples are notorious for spending excessive amounts of time talking about a problem or its cause, rather than attempting to generate solutions. For example, Miller and Hersen (1975) suggested that alcoholic couples spend a great deal of time discussing the alcoholism, how it has affected the relationship, how it has hurt their marriage in the past, how annoyed the alcoholic husband has been by his wife's nagging, and so on. Relatively little time is given to attempting to generate positive solutions to the alcoholic problem.
3. Additionally, alcoholic marriage couples may spend a great deal of time attempting to assign responsibility for the drinking, with spouses often asking "Am I to blame for his drinking?" or groups of alcoholic men bemoaning together how their wives "drove them to drink."
4. Another ineffective behavior in problem-solving frequently identified is that of sidetracking, in which couples will bring up a variety of issues which are only tangentially related to the problem which they are actually trying to resolve. This often results from using vague, generalized statements, such as "the problem is that he drinks," rather than pinpointing a specific behavior which leads to specific unpleasant consequences.

With such unpleasant interactions, in which couples blame each other, put each other down, turn each other off, and compete for dominance of the discussion, it is not surprising that they are unable to generate any kind of constructive solutions to problems, and it is in fact not surprising that they will often terminate communications, which may lead to the alcoholic's fleeing the scene and beginning to drink.

There are a variety of more productive problem-solving skills which can actually be taught to couples. First, "pinpointing" (Weiss et al., 1973) is a skill which couples can be taught to be able to delineate specific, observable behaviors which they would like to see the other person change. For example, with pinpointing, an alcoholic husband might change a statement, "She's a bitch," to a more specific statement, "When I come home later than I say that I will for dinner and she smells alcohol on my breath, she begins to tell me in a loud voice, over and over, all the rotten things she thinks about my drinking and how it is hurting her." Teaching a couple to specifically pinpoint behaviors which they do not like helps them to learn to define specific, changeable problems, rather than apparent personality characteristics, which they frequently see as immutable and untouchable.

In addition to helping couples describe problems more specifically through pinpointing, there are a variety of techniques to help them to be certain that they are defining the same problem. One technique that can be used is to have a listening partner restate or paraphrase what the person presenting the problem is saying, and then to ask whether they are correct in their rephrasing of the problem. Couples can learn to not try to generate solutions to problems before they have both agreed on the problem definition. It is difficult to solve a problem if they are not trying to talk about the same problem.

In discussing a problem, there are a variety of techniques which make it more likely that the couple will continue to problem solve. Helping them to make the interaction more positive, through increasing eye contact, smiling, physical contact, acknowledgment that the person is receiving the message, and expression of positive feelings all make it less aversive to attempt to solve a problem which the couple has found difficult to deal with in the past. A therapist can actually instruct and coach a couple to use these skills as they interact.

Other specific skills to focus on in communication training include teaching couples to avoid many of the aversive behaviors described previously, helping them to avoid sidetracking onto other issues, and helping them to engage in effective problem solution generation. In negotiating solutions to a problem, each partner should learn to state their own position, and identify the difference between their position and the other partner's position (Peterson & Frederiksen, 1976). Each partner can then suggest alternatives, and together they can evaluate the alternatives and come to a final agreement.

There are three major techniques available for actually teaching couples the kinds of communication and problem-solving skills just described: feedback, modeling, and behavioral rehearsal. When giving a couple feedback about their interactional behavior, it is desirable for the therapist to first be able to identify successful problem-solving behaviors, and to praise the couple for using these desirable behaviors. Then, feedback should be precise, behaviorally specific, and presented as constructive criticism, in which the therapist offers a constructive alternative behavior other than the one in which the couple is engaging. Although many behavioral therapists have used video feedback, the experience of systems theorists in alcoholism (Steinglass, Weiner, & Mendelsohn, 1971) must raise a note of caution to the therapist attempting to use behavioral video feedback with alcoholic couples. If the systems hypothesis is correct that the alcoholic system is an unusually brittle one, with few adaptive means of dealing with threats to homeostasis, feedback needs to be carefully measured, and not directed at large segments of maladaptive behavior at any one point. This latter procedure would probably be quite likely to threaten the alcoholic system, and possibly result in the couple fleeing from treatment. Additionally, videotape feedback has the disadvantage of being delayed feedback, in that the couple must engage in the behavior, finish the problem-solving session, and then see themselves on videotape, all before they get any feedback about their behavior. As discussed in chapter 5, immediate reinforcement or punishment for any behavior is the most effective means of increasing or decreasing the likelihood of that behavior recurring, and therefore delayed videotape feedback may have less impact than immediate feedback as soon as the behavior has occurred.

There are at least three major potential problems with skills training for problem solving with alcoholic couples. These include the issues of affect versus logic, the definition of problems, and the emphasis on behavior as opposed to thoughts and feelings.

The behavioral approach essentially requires the couple to suspend their affective, reactive response system, asking them instead to be rational, self-reflective, computerlike problem solvers. This deemphasis of the "emotional" aspect of human experience is one of the weaknesses of the behavioral perspective. The deficiencies in the "logic" approach are highlighted by both systems theorists (as exemplified by Transactional Analysis) and psychoanalytic theorists. As is cogently described in Transactional Analysis (Appendix D), the Adult computer is only one aspect of any human's functioning, and in fact may not be the component of the person which is most involved in a certain problem. For example, it is difficult to imagine using problem-solving techniques to help a couple whose primary problems involve being unable to play together, laugh, or make uninhibited love, all through their Child. In behavioral treatment, there is no ready recognition of the role of the Child. A further limitation of the rational model is suggested by the psychoanalytic perspective, which has strongly emphasized that in order for interpretation of unconscious conflict to have an effective impact on the person, the response must be both cognitive and emotional and the insight must be "worked through," assimilated, and integrated. A person who understands the problem only on an intellectual level is unlikely to show much change in their behavior. Thus, in treating an alcoholic couple, the emotional aspects of behavior must be recognized and appreciated.

The second weakness of behavioral problem solving involves the definition of what is an acceptable and reasonable or unrealistic and unreasonable problem definition. From the behavioral point of view, any behavior which one spouse defines as dissatisfying is a problem with which the couple must deal. The disturbed personality hypothesis and decompensation hypothesis have made it quite clear, however, that the potential exists for problems to be based, not on the marital relationship, but on the early developmental histories of one or the other spouse. Many couples come to marriage with expectations about the behavior of their marital partner which are quite unrealistic to a marital relationship. For example, the alcoholic husband who expects that his wife will always love him and stay with him, no matter how grotesquely inappropriate his behavior is, because that is what his mother did, may perhaps unjustly request his wife to respond to his drunkenness with affection, acceptance, or other such behaviors which she is unwilling to engage in. Conversely, the wife who came to a marriage expecting her husband to always want to listen to her complaints (no matter what their nature), always provide her with physical affection, and always place her above his work, responsibilities, or friends, may be thoroughly surprised when she learns she is not the sole object of his attentions, as was true for her as a small child. A wife who, reflecting these irrational expectations, makes specific behavioral demands of her husband, is likely to be thoroughly disappointed and unhappy with the result, no matter how efficient they may become at generating solutions for each of her specific requests. That is, the specific request may not adequately deal with the unconscious wish. This is an example of when the therapist must consider the existence of unconscious mental processes which result in the inappropriate or exaggerated behavioral requests. At this point, the therapist might need to make a verbal or nonverbal interpretation with the purpose of directly making the patient aware of these unconscious mental processes. In other words, regardless of the perspective of human behavior which the therapist has adapted, he should, when clinically indicated, attempt to reveal the determinant order of unconscious thoughts, feelings, and mental processes. The technique for making these processes conscious is the technique of interpretation. As suggested previously, the interpretation should deal with both feelings and thoughts, and the therapist must always keep in mind that a given mental event has different thoughts and feelings associated with it for each person in each situation. In assessing the variables determining the untoward reaction, the therapist must always take into account developmental history, intrapsychic structure, genetic constitution, external environment, and the quality of interpersonal relationships, including that of the therapist–patient. The curative change which accompanies interpretation will not follow until the experiences which the interpretation makes conscious are repeatedly, consciously experienced in various situations, including the relationship to the therapist and the relationship to the spouse.

In addition to the weakness of the behavioral approach in focusing on couples as logical organisms, with no irrational wishes, problem solving emphasizes behavior change, rather than change in thoughts or feelings. Psychoanalytically oriented therapists and systems therapists (to a lesser degree) emphasize the superiority of discussing thoughts and feelings, rather than effecting behavior changes. The basic belief of the psychoanalytically oriented therapist is that verbal and emotional expressions serve as stimulants for additional thoughts, feelings, and insights. Once the patient has gained insight into his neurotic conflicts, and is freed from them, it is believed that he can most readily solve his own problems: "We do not deal with the happenings of the external world as such, but with the repercussions in the mind" (Anna Freud, 1960, as quoted by

Aarons, 1962, p. 522). Clearly the behavioral view suggests that couples do not have the inherent problem-solving capacities but rather are deficient in these skills, and need training to acquire them.

A possible way of integrating the behavioral techniques for teaching problem solving, with the psychoanalytic and systems notions of unconscious or out of awareness conflicts maintaining drinking and other problematic marital behaviors, would be through theme-centered problem solving. For example, Gorad, McCourt, and Cobb (1971) identified struggles for control as an essential struggle in the alcoholic marriage. The therapist might structure the problem-solving sessions with the conflict in mind, especially attempting to help the couple to generate solutions which result in each of them having control in certain areas. Additionally, specifically reinforcing the alcoholic's direct, responsibility-accepting communications and punishing somewhat the spouse's dominance of the problem-solving sessions, might result in the generation of behaviorally specific solutions which address the underlying conflicted aspects of the relationship. Or if the therapist identified affective expressiveness as a specific concomitant of the alcoholic's drinking which seemed to be a positive consequence that maintained the drinking, he might help the couple to define this as a problem area, perhaps through structured videotape feedback, and then to work with them on enabling them to be more affectively expressive during periods of sobriety.

Modification of Consequences

The second major area of intervention involves the manipulation of consequences in contingency relationships. Much of the behavioral view of marriage, not only of alcoholic marriages, describes marital discord as a function of a low rate of exchange of positive reinforcers, which results in each spouse becoming less and less attractive to the other, with the result that the overall relationship becomes less attractive. Concomitantly, the spouses engage in aversive techniques to attempt to change their partners, rather than focusing on positive control techniques.

Mr. and Mrs. Q. presented for treatment with an identified alcohol problem. Mrs. Q. stated that whenever Mr. Q. came home with the odor of alcohol on his breath, she would comment on his drinking, stating that it was getting to be a problem. She further stated "If I don't say anything, it gets out of hand, and he'll always drink the next day."

Clearly, Mrs. Q. felt that it was necessary for her to punish the results of the drinking behavior in order to avoid further drinking episodes. She was completely unaware that the punishment and nagging also served as antecedents to further drinking. This aversive, negative cycle is in marked contrast to the findings of Robinson and Price (1976) on couples who were satisfied with their marriage. Robinson and Price found that such couples exchanged a higher rate of pleasant behaviors with each other, and reported a higher ratio of pleasant to unpleasant behaviors as occurring in their home. Another indication of the low rate of exchange of positive reinforcers is the significant withdrawal of the spouse from her alcoholic mate, a decreased sharing of pleasurable activities, and a high frequency of arguments about drinking. These behaviors were detailed in the works of James and Goldman (1971) and Orford, Guthrie, Nicholls, Oppenheimer, Egert, and Hensman (1975) described in chapter 5.

The goal, therefore, in dealing with contingency relationships and consequences is to help the couple to increase the overall rewardingness of their relationship, to assure that positive consequences will result from desired behaviors, and that these positive consequences will not occur when undesired behaviors, such as drinking, occur.

There are two major vehicles for changing the overall rewardingness and contingent rewardingness of the relationship: increasing "pleases," and contracting. Weiss et al. (1973) and Stuart (1969) have described "love days," or "caring days." In these, the couple, in the therapist's office, attempt to identify a variety of small and specific behaviors in which their spouse could engage that would give them pleasure. These might include such minor actions as saying hello when the husband comes home at night, clearing the table, rinsing out a glass after having a drink of milk rather than leaving the glass on the counter, asking how the other's day was, giving a back rub, and so on. Each partner would then agree to engage in a large number of these caring behaviors, on a specific day during the week. These caring days should result in an increase in the overall rewardingness of the relationship, which would enable the couple to more willingly work on problematic aspects of the relationship, while making the overall relationship more fun. In an alcoholic marriage, such love days could initially be scheduled noncontingently, and then scheduled contingent on the alcoholic meeting a specified drinking goal for the day or week, and the spouse meeting a specified goal requested by the alcoholic partner for behavior change.

Another method of increasing the overall rewardingness of the relationship is through the Spouse Observation Checklist (SOC) (Weiss et al., 1973) mentioned earlier in this chapter. The SOC details innumerable spouse behaviors which might occur during the course of the day, and each partner is asked to rate at the end of the day the occurrence of these behaviors, and whether they were pleasing or displeasing. Couples can then exchange daily SOCs, and attempt to determine what aspects of their behavior were displeasing to the spouse, and therefore attempt to change some of these behaviors. Clearly, this assumes that the couple wishes to please each other. In an alcoholic marriage, as with many other marriages, when the spouses are angry, hurt, or do not "trust" each other because of repeated broken promises and disappointments, their desire to please the other is not always remarkably high. Further, as DPH theorists have clearly stated, it is possible that the wife of an alcoholic may indeed want to suffer, or may wish to see her husband suffer, and therefore would be unlikely either to identify changes which she would find pleasurable, or actually engage in behavior changes which her husband would find enjoyable.

An additional difficulty with alcoholic couples who have often withdrawn from interaction with each other is that they may have very few mutually reinforcing and mutually enjoyable interactive times. Therefore, a significant corollary of increasing the overall satisfaction in the marriage would be to help the couple to develop possible activities which they would find mutually enjoyable. Use of the Reinforcement Survey Schedule (Cautela & Kastenbaum, 1967) or the Pleasant Events Schedule (Lewinsohn & Graf, 1973; Lewinsohn & Libet, 1972; MacPhillamy & Lewinsohn, 1974) might enable couples to identify potential activities in which they could engage that they would both enjoy.

As described in chapter 5, in order for behavior changes to be maintained, behaviorists believe that there should be positive reinforcement for desired behaviors. An effective means of assuring that positive reinforcement will occur for desired behavior changes is behavioral contracting (Hops et al., 1971). In contracting, specific behavior changes are identified, and the partner requesting the behavior change then will provide a desirable positive reinforcement for the behavior change. Therefore, if an alcoholic decides not to drink, a contract could be negotiated in which the alcoholic, for each day which he does not drink, would have his wife sit down and have a pleasant conversation with him about the events of the day, in which she did not nag, question him about his drinking, or complain about past "transgressions." On days in which he did drink, she would not engage in these desired behaviors, but rather could either ignore the drinking behavior or could contract to engage in specific negative behaviors such as leaving the home, or not allowing him in the home. The many increases in desired and pleasurable interactions described herein (such as caring days) could be made contingent on the person's sobriety or specified drinking goal.

Couples sometime have a remarkable capacity for not carrying out behavioral contracts. One or the other of the couple often will not follow the contract, will say they forgot it, will state that they decided that they did not like it, or that they did not think that their partner would live up to it, and therefore will not honor the contract. The behaviorists would view this problem as an indication of inadequate generalization. That is, the couple might have learned specific problem-solving skills, or decided to engage in a specific behavior in one situation (the treatment setting) but the cues for engaging in this behavior outside of the session are inadequate. Behaviorally, the therapist can gradually decrease the frequency of the treatment sessions as treatment progresses, decrease his own degree of activity and directiveness, and be certain that he is teaching principles about problem solving or contracting, rather than merely solving problems with or for the couple. The systems theorist, however, would clearly see the same resistance in a different light, i.e., as an indication that the system has a strong need to maintain the status quo, and that unless the specific need of the system for certain roles is addressed, any behavioral change techniques will be ineffective. The psychoanalytically oriented therapist would see this as clear resistance, reflecting each spouse's need to maintain conflict in the relationship, to be dissatisfied in the relationship, or to experience hurt, rejection, and psychic pain. According to the psychoanalytically oriented therapist, until the source of these resistances is analyzed and interpreted, and the members of the couple are able to experience and appreciate this interpretation on an affective and integrative level, specific behavioral change procedures are likely to continue to be inadequate and ineffective.

Cognitive Issues in Treatment

The third major issue to consider in the treatment of alcoholic couples is the area of intervening organismic variables, especially cognitive factors. There are several areas of cognition to consider in treating couples, including irrational ideas, attribution of problems, and accompanying attribution of control for problems. We would like to suggest four irrational beliefs that alcoholic couples may hold. Although there is no empirical support at this time for this catalog of irrational ideas, we believe that consideration of these ideas is important in treatment, pending research findings that support or disprove our assumption.

Irrational Belief 1: "He could stop if he really wanted to." The alcoholic's version of this is, "I can stop any time." In both of these versions, the couple attribute intentionality to the alcoholic in terms of his drinking, seeing it as a freely willed decision, over which he has complete control. Acceptance of the belief may generate increased anger in the spouse because she believes that her husband is continuing to drink to spite her, or for some other personally directed reason. Such anger may result in verbal abuse, nagging, or other aversive behaviors in the spouse. The alcoholic's version of this belief may lead to his avoiding treatment.

Irrational Belief 2: "He must not really love us if he drinks so much," is also based on a belief in voluntary control and may lead to similar spouse behaviors as described in Belief 1.

Irrational Belief 3 is some version of, "If he (I) were really a man, he (I) could control it." There are variations of Irrational Belief 3, including "If I were really an adult, I could handle my liquor." These negative beliefs lead to put-downs on the part of the wife, and self-put-downs on the part of the alcoholic, both of which may lead to further drinking episodes.

Irrational Belief 4 is some variation of, "He's a sick man, so I have to take care of him," or, "How can I abandon my husband in a time of trouble?" The alcoholic version is "I have a disease, so how can you expect me to do anything about it?" This belief is a loose derivation from the view of alcoholism as a disease (this should be discriminated from the disease concept) in which behaviors are seen as sick, and *completely* out of the control of the drinker. This irrational belief results in the spouse protecting the alcoholic from experiencing any of the negative consequences of the drinking, or feeling the psychic pain associated with out of control drinking, and therefore helps to keep the person drinking. The alcoholic's version may lead him to avoid treatment, or not attempt any means to change his drinking pattern (such as telephoning a fellow AA member when he feels like drinking).

There are several major treatment strategies which can be used to deal with these so-called irrational beliefs. The psychoanalytically oriented therapist would work to understand the meaning of these statements for each individual's psychic balance, and understand how these beliefs protect or defend the person from examining his own unconscious conflicts, which are either involved in or exacerbated by the drinking. A systems therapist would be most interested in seeing how such beliefs are carried in the system, how they are maintained in the system if one member perhaps gives up the beliefs through involvement in AA, Al-Anon, or other form of treatment, and how his beliefs are necessary for the functioning of the system. Behaviorally, there are two treatment strategies which are aimed at modifying so-called irrational beliefs: rational–emotive therapy (Ellis, 1962) and self-instructional training (Mahoney, 1974).

In rational–emotive therapy, the therapist would first help the couple to see how their irrational thoughts generate and maintain subjective distress. For example, the therapist could point out that each time the spouse states that her husband is not really a man because his drinking is out of control, she begins to question her own adequacy as a wife, begins to feel depressed and anxious, and begins to nag him, which leads to increased drinking, and so on. Then, the therapist would help the couple to systematically observe their own irrational self-statements, and see the logical inconsistencies in their beliefs. In theory, when the individuals or couple recognize the irrationality of their belief, they should automatically alter them. There is, however, some research evidence, reviewed by Mahoney (1974), which does not support this assumption.

In self-instructional training, the therapist also helps the couple to discover how their irrational beliefs contribute to their subjective distress. He would then help the couple to observe and systematically discriminate their own beliefs, and develop possible alternative beliefs or statements which they could practice both within the therapy session and at home. Modification of these negative self-statements would occur in a gradual fashion, with each member of the couple providing self-reinforcement and reinforcement to the other for improvements in these negative self-statements.

Another technique for helping a person or couple to change beliefs is "thought priming" (Mahoney, 1974, p. 240). In this technique the couple or individual members of the couple would identify a certain belief which they did not like to hold. They would then, with the help of the therapist, attempt to generate alternative beliefs or alternative statements, write these down, and read them at frequent intervals. Although this procedure appears mechanical, there are clinical reports (Mahoney, 1974) suggesting that an individual may suddenly discover himself believing these originally artificial self-statements.

The second area of cognition to consider involves the attribution of problems. In examining the attribution of problems, Mahoney (1974) has stated, "If our obesity, smoking or depression are seen as caused by heredity, addiction or a disease, we may be much less likely to instigate an active self-improvement enterprise" (p. 213). This is similar to Irrational Belief No. 3. This raises questions for the disease concept of alcoholism, which McNamara (1960) had raised previously. That is, if a person or a couple believes that one member of the couple has a disease that is beyond his or her control, it is likely that he or she may feel much more distressed, which may lead to increased nagging or drinking, and which also might lead him or her to be more likely to deny or minimize the significance or seriousness of the symptoms. Another aspect of the attribution is, "I drink because I'm an alcoholic," or, "He drinks because he is an alcoholic." There are two results to these beliefs: (1) they decrease the likelihood that the person is going to attempt to identify situational or internal factors associated with drinking or to identify stimuli maintaining the drinking, and (2) they most likely will generate depression or anxiety because the person feels hopeless, which further exacerbates drinking. Although the disease concept has been extremely influential in leading to more humane treatment for alcoholism, obtaining insurance coverage for treatment for alcoholism, and helping alcoholics to accept the seriousness and long-term nature of their problems, it may have antitherapeutic effects as well.

The means for changing attribution of problems are rather rudimentary at this time. One way of changing beliefs about control is to program small, significant success experiences early on in therapy. For example, helping the couple to have several caring days, or to negotiate a treatment contract which they can implement successfully will lead them to begin to believe that they do have control over behavior change in their relationship, and that their problems are not solely a result of heredity or immutable personality characteristics. Also, doing a careful behavioral analysis of a drinking episode with a couple, showing how it was related to antecedents, cognitions, and consequences may lead the couple to understand the drinking better and therefore to begin to attribute the drinking to environmental and relationship events.

THE THERAPEUTIC RELATIONSHIP

A final important area in treatment not yet addressed, and not specifically involved in any one therapeutic technique, is made up of the issues related to the therapeutic relationship. The relationship of any therapist to a couple is a rather unique one which must be considered. First, that relationship is a triangle if there is one therapist. This means that there is always a possibility that there will be two against one in the treatment session. This appears to be a special danger in the treatment of alcoholic couples. Although an alcoholic may come to treatment professing a desire to deal with his drinking behavior, this is frequently a conflicted desire. If the therapist is fully allied with the goal of a person to control or stop his drinking (usually the conscious wish of the spouse), this may result in an alliance between the spouse and the therapist against the alcoholic to "get him" to stop drinking. The therapist needs to develop early on a collaborative set with the couple, in which each have clearly specified goals, and a clearly specified positive stake in treatment. The therapist would then define himself as a neutral consultant to the relationship. Psychodynamically there are also very important positive aspects of the triangle situation. The triangle in therapy may remind each spouse of the original triangular Oedipal situation of the child with the parents, which gives the spouse the opportunity to see how he/she has projected the parental image onto his/her own spouse. A corollary of this is the therapist's assumption of a reality stance with the couple, in which he is clear about his own role in the treatment, and clear about what he will and will not do. In Bowen's terms (Bowen, 1971) the therapist defines his own self to the family, clearly differentiating himself from the couple. This forces them to examine their own level of differentiation, and helps in the "step-by-step process of externalizing and separating out their fantasy, feeling, thinking systems. It is a process of knowing one's own self and also the self of the other" (Bowen, 1971, p. 186).

Although the degree of activity of the therapist, the specific content of his interventions, in terms of interpretation, modeling, feedback, etc., varies with the therapeutic approach, these more general issues of the relationship between the therapist and couple must be considered in every therapeutic relationship regardless of the theoretical orientation of the therapist.

CONCLUSION

As described at the beginning of this chapter, we have attempted to provide some ideas for the practicing therapist about the treatment of the alcoholic marriage, deriving these ideas from the various perspectives reviewed in this book. Our intent has been to raise a series of possibilities for the therapist, and to suggest some practical intervention strategies. If this chapter and this book have enabled the practicing therapist to think more clearly and objectively about couples afflicted with the problems of alcohol abuse, and have provided some hunches, hints, hypotheses, or hopes for successful treatment, then we have accomplished our purpose. Whatever the therapist, researcher, or theoretician's ultimate theoretical adherence, if our book has helped that person to approach the alcoholic and his spouse with greater knowledge, understanding, compassion, empathy, and optimism for the ultimate successful treatment of the couple, then we are satisfied that our efforts in writing this book have been justified.

REFERENCES

Aarons, Z. A. Indications for analysis and problems of analyzability. *Psychoanalytic Quarterly,* 1962, *31,* 514–531.

Al-Anon Family Group Headquarters, Inc. *The dilemma of the alcoholic marriage.* Cornwall, N.Y.: Cornwall Press, 1971.

Blum, R. Psychoanalytic views of alcoholism. *Quarterly Journal of Studies on Alcohol,* 1966, *27,* 259–299.

Bowen, M. The use of family theory in clinical practice. In J. Haley (Ed.), *Changing families. A family therapy reader.* New York: Grune & Stratton, 1971.

Cautela, J. R., & Kastenbaum, R. A. Reinforcement survey schedule for use in therapy, training, and research. *Psychological Reports,* 1967, *20,* 1115–1130.

Chafetz, M. E. *Second special report to the U.S. Congress on alcohol and health.* Department of Health, Education, & Welfare, 1974.

Drewery, J. An interpersonal perception technique. *British Journal of Medical Psychology,* 1969, *42,* 171–181.

Drewery, J., & Rae, J. B. A group comparison of alcoholic and non-alcoholic marriages using the Interpersonal Perception Technique. *British Journal of Psychiatry,* 1969, *115,* 287–300.

Edwards, A. *Edwards Personal Preference Schedule (manual).* New York: Psychological Corp., 1959.

Ellis, A. *Reason and emotion in psychotherapy.* New York: Stuart, 1962.

Emrick, C. D. A review of psychologically oriented treatment of alcoholism. II. The relative effectiveness of different treatment approaches and the effectiveness of treatment versus no treatment. *Journal of Studies on Alcohol,* 1975, *36,* 88–108.

Gorad, S. L. Communicational styles and interaction of alcoholics and their wives. *Family Process,* 1971, *10,* 475–489.

Gorad, S. L., McCourt, W. F., & Cobb, J. C. A communications approach to alcoholism. *Quarterly Journal of Studies on Alcohol,* 1971, *32,* 651–668.

Hedberg, A. G., & Campbell, L. A comparison of four behavioral treatments of alcoholism. *Journal of Behavior Therapy and Experimental Psychiatry,* 1974, *5,* 251–256.

Hops, H., Wills, T. A., Patterson, G. R., & Weiss, R. L. *Marital interaction coding system.* University of Oregon, Technical Report 8, December 1971.

Hunt, G. M., & Azrin, N. H. A community-reinforcement approach to alcoholism. *Behavior Research and Therapy,* 1973, *11,* 91–104.

Jacobson, N. E. A behavioral approach to relationship discord. I. Problem solving skills. *International Journal of Family Counseling,* in press (a).

Jacobson, N. E. Problem-solving and contingency contracting in the treatment of marital discord. *Journal of Consulting and Clinical Psychology,* in press (b).

Jacobson, N. E., & Martin, B. Behavioral marriage therapy: Current status. *Psychological Bulletin,* 1976, *83,* 540–556.

James, J. E., & Goldman, M. Behavior trends of wives of alcoholics. *Quarterly Journal of Studies on Alcohol,* 1971, *32,* 373–381.

Jellinek, E. M. Phases of alcohol addiction. *Quarterly Journal of Studies on Alcohol,* 1951, *12,* 673–684.

Johnson, V. E. *I'll quit tomorrow.* New York: Harper, 1973.

Kennedy, D. L. Behavior of alcoholics and spouses in a simulation game situation. *Journal of Nervous and Mental Disease,* 1976, *162,* 23–34.

Lewinsohn, P. M., & Graf, M. Pleasant activities and depression. *Journal of Consulting and Clinical Psychology,* 1973, *41,* 261–268.

Lewinsohn, P. M., & Libet, J. Pleasant events, activity schedules, and depressions. *Journal of Abnormal Psychology,* 1972, *79,* 291–295.

Locke, H. J., & Wallace, K. M. Short-term marital adjustment and prediction tests: Their reliability and validity. *Journal of Marriage and Family Living,* 1959, *21,* 251–255.

MacPhillamy, D. J., & Lewinsohn, P. M. Depression as a function of levels of desired and obtained pleasure. *Journal of Abnormal Psychology,* 1974, *83,* 651–657.

Mahoney, M. J. *Cognition and behavior modification.* Cambridge, Mass.: Ballinger, 1974.

Manson, M. P., & Lerner, A. *The Marriage Adjustment Inventory manual.* Los Angeles, Calif.: Western Psychological Services, 1973.

Maxwell, R. *The booze battle.* New York: Praeger, 1976.

McCrady, B. S., Paolino, T. J., Longabaugh, R. L., & Rossi, J. *Effects on treatment outcome of joint admission and spouse involvement in treatment of hospitalized alcoholics.* Submitted for publication.

McNamara, J. H. The disease conception of alcoholism: Its therapeutic value for the alcoholic and his wife. *Social Casework,* 1960, *41,* 460–465.

Miller, P. M. *Behavioral treatment of alcoholism.* Oxford: Pergamon, 1976.

Miller, P. M., & Hersen, M. Modification of marital interaction patterns between an alcoholic and his wife (unpublished manuscript).

Olson, D. H., & Straus, M. A. A diagnostic tool for marital and family therapy: The SIMFAM technique. *The Family Coordinator,* 1972, *21,* 251–258.

Orford, J., Guthrie, S., Nicholls, P., Oppenheimer, E., Egert, S., & Hensman, C. Self-reported coping behavior of wives of alcoholics and its association with drinking outcome. *Journal of Studies on Alcohol,* 1975, *36,* 1254–1267.

Paolino, T. J., & McCrady, B. S. Joint admission as a treatment modality for problem drinkers: A case report. *American Journal of Psychiatry,* 1976, *133,* 222–224.

Peterson, G. L., & Frederiksen, L. W. *Developing behavioral competencies in distressed marital couples.* Paper presented at the Tenth Annual Meeting of the Association for the Advancement of Behavior Therapy, New York, December 1976.

Robinson, E. A., & Price, M. G. *Behavioral and self-report correlates of marital satisfaction.* Paper presented at the Tenth Meeting of the Association for the Advancement of Behavior Therapy, New York, December 1976.

Sobell, M. B., & Sobell, L. C. Second year treatment outcome of alcoholics treated by individualized behavior therapy: Results. *Behavior Research and Therapy,* 1976, *14,* 195–216.

Steinglass, P., Davis, D. I., & Berenson, D. *In-hospital treatment of alcoholic couples.* Paper presented at the American Psychiatric Association 128th Annual Meeting, Anaheim, California, May 5, 1975.

Steinglass, P., Weiner, S., & Mendelson, J. H. A systems approach to alcoholics. A model and its clinical application. *Archives of General Psychiatry,* 1971, *24,* 401–408.

Stuart, R. B. Operant interpersonal treatment for marital discord. *Journal of Consulting and Clinical Psychology,* 1969, *33,* 675–682.

Stuart, R. B., & Stuart, R. *Marital pre-counseling inventory.* Champaign, Ill.: Research Press, 1972.

Tharp, R. G., & Otis, G. D. Toward a theory for therapeutic intervention in families. *Journal of Consulting Psychology,* 1966, *30,* 426–434.

Thomas, E. J. *Marital communication and decision making. Analysis, assessment, and change.* New York: Free Press, 1977.

Weiss, R. L., Hops, H., & Patterson, G. R. A framework for conceptualizing marital conflict, a technology for altering it, some data for evaluating it. In L. A. Hamerlynck, L. C. Handy, & E. J. Mash (Eds.), *Behavior change: Methodology, concepts and practice.* Champaign, Ill.: Research Press, 1973.

Appendices

Appendix A

Statistics

The statistics on alcoholic marriages are helpful in understanding the relevant facts and theories. Marriage and divorce rates for alcoholics and what they reveal are often discussed by both lay people and professionals. The material in this appendix gives the reader some idea of the source of the generalizations made about the divorce rates for alcoholics.

Reports on marriage and divorce statistics add to the knowledge about the various theories of the alcoholic marriage. For example, if a significant number of wives divorce their alcoholic husbands, this fact weakens the validity of any hypothesis which says that these women *need* to be married to alcoholics. Or if the onset of alcoholism tends to follow the date of marriage, the validity of the DPH and DH is weakened. Also if alcoholics tend to marry as often as other people do, research on the alcoholic marriage is of much greater value than it would be if alcoholics tended not to marry.

In this appendix we review statistical data in the following three areas:

1. The percentage of alcoholics who never marry as compared to the general population.
2. The percentage of all alcoholics who do marry but then separate or divorce as compared to the general population. (Many people never formally separate or divorce yet their marriage is nonsatisfying and emotionally divorced. In this appendix, however, the group of disruptive marriages which do not separate is not considered.)
3. The chronological relationship between the date of marriage and excessive drinking.

In order to appreciate the following discussion, the reader must bear in mind that marital statistics for an alcoholic population are of little value unless they are compared to a control population that accounts for the important variable of age. This has been done for all studies included here. Furthermore it must be remembered that we are comparing the alcoholic population to a control population *at that point in time.* For example, the Towle (1974) study uses the U.S. Bureau of Census, which reports that 20% of the people in that age range have "never married" at that point in time. This is not the same thing as saying "20% of people in that age range have never married and will never marry." In fact, reliable research (Hicks & Platt, 1970; Jacobson, 1959) shows that over 94% of Americans marry at least once in their lifetime.

WHAT PERCENTAGE OF ALCOHOLICS HAVE NEVER MARRIED?

Before 1950, it was generally assumed that the "typical" alcoholic had a personality that precluded marriage. Heron (1912) studied 865 women alcoholics and 166 male[1] alcoholics committed to inebriate reformatories in and around London from 1906 to 1909 and compared the results of this study to the general population of England and Wales and the borough of Skoreditch. Heron found that 34% of the women and 68% of the men were never married. Heron's major contribution to the literature is that he was the first investigator to use control groups and to correct for the age factor regarding alcoholic marriage statistics. For example, of 281 female alcoholics between the ages of 25 and 35, Heron found that 42% were never married. He then compared this to a general population of 9,349 women in the same area and age range and found among the comparison group that 24% were never married.

The first major report on the frequency of marriage among problem drinkers in the United States was that of Bacon (1944), who studied 1,196 males arrested for drunkenness in Connecticut cities. Bacon found that 53% of these arrested inebriates were never married, compared to 20% of the general population.

In 1944, Malzberg (1947) studied 675 first admissions for alcoholic psychoses to all mental hospitals in New York State and showed that 31% never married. When Malzberg (1949) studied 402 *nonpsychotic* first admissions for alcoholism to New York mental hospitals, he noted that only 20% of the nonpsychotic alcoholics had never married, a figure which was less than that of the general population.

---

[1]The obvious preponderance of female alcoholics in the Inebriate Reformatories is explained by Heron (1912) as follows:

Various reasons have been assigned to account for this striking preponderance of females, such as the deficiency in institutional accommodations for men, the reluctance on the part of magistrates to commit men, and the difference between the effects of alcoholic excess upon men and women. (p. 4)

It is of interest to compare Malzberg's findings with those of Rosenblatt, Gross, and Chartoff (1969), who studied 567 men admitted for alcoholism to the Downstate Medical Center in New York City. The marital status of 5% of these men was not recorded but for the remaining sample, 33% were never married. Rosenblatt does not identify his sample as psychotic or nonpsychotic, and, as Malzberg has shown, the reasons that these men never married probably include medical and sociocultural confounding variables, such as the presence or absence of psychoses.

Up until 1950, most of the research on alcoholics was done by studying patients in public institutions. With the development of outpatient clinics for alcoholics, a new population was available for study. In 1951, Straus and Bacon studied 2,023 male patients from nine such clinics in five states and reported that these alcoholics married as often as urban males of comparable age. There are some methodological problems with this study. For example, Straus and Bacon did not indicate the differences between the nine clinic populations studied (Schneyer, 1954).

Most studies after 1950 continued to show that at least middle- and upper-class male alcoholics married no less frequently than the general population did. Wellman, Maxwell, and O'Halloren (1957) examined 830 male alcoholics admitted to a private psychiatric hospital and found that only 8% had never married, a percentage which was below that expected for the general population. Wellman's report also has methodological problems, however. For example, there is a strong selection factor in that patient populations of private hospitals of that time usually had a higher socioeconomic status than the general population (Wolf, 1958).

Paolino[2] studied 119 people between the ages of 35 and 65 who were admitted to a private psychiatric hospital with the primary diagnosis of alcoholism and found that 11% were never married. These results are below those expected for the general population and are consistent with Wellman's findings.

Towle (1974) reported his findings from combined men and women populations served by different types of alcoholic treatment programs funded by the National Institute on Alcohol Abuse and Alcoholism. Towle studied 13,621 clients from 45 different comprehensive alcoholism treatment centers (ATC), 2,613 clients in "driving while intoxicated" (DWI) clinics, 496 clients of industrial alcoholism centers, and 2,239 clients of "public inebriate" programs. He reports that 17% ATC, 20% DWI, 13% "industrial," and 33% "inebriate" patients had never married. Towle's figures can be compared with 1970 census bureau statistics which show that after correcting for the age factor, 20% of the people in the general population had never married.

---

[2]Paolino, T. J. *Some marital statistics on hospitalized alcoholics.* Unpublished manuscript.

Table A-1 A Comparison of Those Who Never Married at the Time of the Study in the Alcoholic and General Population

Study by author	Size of sample (N)	Characteristics of sample	Percent never married in sample	Characteristics of comparison population corrected for age	Percent never married in comparison population corrected for age
Heron, 1912	166	Male inmates of a London reformatory	68	General population of England, Wales, and a borough in Scotland	24
	865	Female inmates of a London reformatory	34		
Bacon, 1944[a]	1,196	Arrested male inebriates in Conn.	53	General male population of Conn.—1940 Census	20
Malzberg, 1947[a]	675	First psychiatric hospitalization for psychotic alcoholics to N.Y. State psychiatric hospital	31	General male and female populations of N.Y.—1940 Census	28 M / 22 F
Malzberg, 1949[a]	402	First admissions of non-psychotic alcoholics to N.Y. State psychiatric hospitals	20	General male and female populations of N.Y.—1940 Census	28 M / 22 F
Straus & Bacon, 1951[a]	2,023	Male outpatients from nine alcoholic clinics in five states	17	General male population of Conn.—1940 Census	21

Study	Sample size	Sample description	%	Comparison population	%
Wellman et al., 1957[a]	830	Male patients of a Seattle private psychiatric hospital	8	General male population in the West—1950 Census	12
Rosenblatt et al., 1969[b]	567	Male patients treated in Downstate Medical Center, New York City	33	General male population of N.Y.—1960 Census	14
Rimmer, 1972	112	Male patients at a private psychiatric hospital	18	General male population U.S.—1970 Census	20
	61	Female patients at a private psychiatric hospital	3	General female population U.S.—1970 Census	21
Paolino, 1974[b]	119	Inpatients from a private psychiatric hospital in R.I.	11	General population of R.I.—1970 Census	11
Towle, 1974[a]	13,261	Patients from 45 ATC (84% male)	17	General male population, U.S.—1970 Census	20
Towle, 1974[a]	2,613	Patients from a DWI clinic (92% male)	20	General male population, U.S.—1970 Census	20
Towle, 1974[a]	496	Patients from industrial alcoholic centers (80% male)	13	General male population, U.S.—1970 Census	20
Towle, 1974[a]	2,239	Patients from "public inebriate programs" (97% male)	33	General male population, U.S.—1970 Census	20

[a] Studies corrected comparison population to fit ages of sample population.
[b] Corrected for age by authors of table.
Census data corrected for age, sex, and time periods provided the percentages for the comparison populations.

The alcoholic-marriage statistics studies in the United States have been done largely for alcoholic men; but most studies of women suggest that alcoholic women, at least in the middle and upper classes, are as likely to marry as women in the general population (Bacon, 1944; Lisansky, 1957; Rosenbaum, 1958).

Rimmer, Reich, and Winokur (1972) offer evidence that contradicts the bulk of research regarding sexual distinctions. In this study of 112 men and 61 women admitted to a psychiatric hospital with the primary diagnosis of alcoholism, Rimmer et al. report that 18% of the men and only 3% of the women had never married, with no significant difference in age between the two groups. This sample is too small, and further evaluation of Towle's data will probably confirm the popular hypothesis of no sexual distinction regarding the frequency of marriage among alcoholics (see Table A.1).

PROPORTION OF ALCOHOLICS WHO HAVE MARRIED BUT ARE SEPARATED OR DIVORCED AT THE TIME OF THE STUDY

Heron (1912) was also the first to include separations as well as legal divorces in his statistical analysis of marriage among alcoholics. Heron studied 430 female alcoholics who had married, and he reported that 59% were separated or divorced at the time of the study as compared to 7% of the general population recorded in the 1901 Census of England.

Bacon (1944) was the first to conduct a large-scale investigation of the divorce and separation rates for alcoholics in the United States. He found by questioning the same 1,196 arrested male inebriates mentioned on page 174 that of those who did marry, 33% of them were either divorced or separated as opposed to 5% in the general population.

Malzberg (1944) (see page 174), in his study of first admissions for psychotic alcoholics to New York mental hospitals, showed the frequency of divorces and separations to be 15% of those who marry. Although this figure is three times that of the general population, it is not as high as most other reports. It is very interesting to note that when Malzberg (1949) studied 402 *nonpsychotic* alcoholics, he found no significant difference between them and the psychotic alcoholics in frequency of separation and divorce; thus, as mentioned previously, Malzberg's research (see page 174) indicates that hospitalized nonpsychotic alcoholics are more likely to be married than hospitalized psychotic alcoholics, whereas the two groups do not differ in frequency of separation and divorce.

When Straus and Bacon (1951) (see page 175) investigated 2,023 male alcholics being treated in outpatient clinics, they noted that 27% were divorced or separated as compared to 7% of the general population at that time.

In 1957, Wellman et al. found that of 830 alcoholic admissions to a private psychiatric hospital, 23% were separated or divorced. This is the same percentage found by Paolino's study of the 119 patients admitted to a private hospital during 1974 with the primary diagnosis of alcoholism (see page 175).

The 1969 Rosenblatt study of 567 men mentioned on page 175 reported that 29% were either divorced or separated.

Towle (1974) (see page 175) investigated the four patient populations just mentioned and reported that 41% ATC, 30% DWI, 27% "industrial," and 53% "inebriate" clients were separated or divorced as compared to the 1970 census bureau statistics of 4.6% in the general population (see Table A.2 for a summary of this section).

DIFFERENCES AMONG WOMEN ALCOHOLICS

There is a paucity of solid data regarding the marital statistics on alcoholic women, and the literature that does deal with this subject is conflicting. Some researchers report that the rate of separation and divorce among women alcoholics is similar to that of male alcoholics (Bacon, 1944; Lisansky, 1957, 1958; Rosenbaum, 1958). Other investigators report that divorce and separation rates are significantly higher for alcoholic women as compared to alcoholic men (Kinsey, 1966; Malzberg, 1947; Mann, 1958; Shuckit, 1972).

It is our opinion that those studies reporting a higher divorce and separation rate for alcoholic women are probably valid, as suggested by three factors:

1. Alcohol misuse is usually less acceptable to the nonalcoholic husband than to the nonalcoholic wife (Ablon, 1974; Corrigan, 1974; Curlee, 1970; Fox, 1956; Jackson, 1962; Lindbeck, 1972; Lisansky, 1957, 1958; Mann, 1958).
2. A husband is usually not financially dependent on a wife and thereby freer to leave the relationship.
3. In a search of the literature we could find no study which concluded that divorce and separation were *less* frequent among alcoholic women than alcoholic men.

Before the issues of sexual distinction can be clarified, more research is needed, especially those studies that assess the impact of changing attitudes toward the roles of women in society, their social and economic freedom, women drinking, and divorce in general.

COMMENTS ON ALCOHOLISM AND
MARITAL DISRUPTION

An elaborate discussion of the relationship between alcohol and broken homes is beyond the purpose of this book. In order to orient the reader, however, a few comments on this subject are in order.

Table A.2   A Comparison of Those Who Were Once Married and then Divorced or Separated in the Alcoholic and General Population

Study by author	Size of sample (N)	Characteristics of sample	Percent separated or divorced in sample	Characteristics of comparison population corrected for age	Percent separated or divorced in comparison population corrected for age
Heron, 1912	430	Female inmates of a London inebriate reformatory	59	General population in England in 1901	7
Bacon, 1944[a]	1,196	Arrested male inebriates in Conn.	33	General male population of Conn.—1940 Census	5
Malzberg, 1947[a]	675	First psychiatric hospitalization for psychotic alcoholics to N.Y. State psychiatric hospitals	15	General male and female populations of N.Y.—1940 Census	5
Malzberg, 1949[a]	402	First admissions of nonpsychotic alcoholics to N.Y. State psychiatric hospitals	14	General male and female populations of N.Y.—1940 Census	5
Straus & Bacon, 1951[a]	2,023	Male outpatients from nine alcoholic clinics in four states	27	General male population of Conn.—1940 Census	7

Study	N	Sample	%	Comparison population	%
Wellman et. al, 1957[a]	830	Male patients of a Seattle private psychiatric hospital	23	General male population in the West—1950 Census	6
Rosenblatt et al., 1969[b]	567	Male patients treated in Downstate Medical Center, New York City	29	General male population of N.Y.—1960 Census	4
Paolino, 1974[b]	119	Inpatients from a private psychiatric hospital in R.I.	23	General population of R.I.—1970 Census	5
Towle, 1974[a]	13,261	Patients from 45 ATC (84% male)	41	General male population, U.S.—1970 Census	4.6
Towle, 1974[a]	2,613	Patients from DWI clinic (92% male)	30	General male population, U.S.—1970 Census	4.6
Towle, 1974[a]	496	Patients from industrial alcoholic centers (80% male)	27	General male population, U.S.—1970 Census	4.6
Towle, 1974[a]	2,239	Patients from "public inebriate programs" (97% male)	53	General male population, U.S.—1970 Census	4.6

[a] Studies corrected comparison population to fit ages of sample population.

[b] Corrected for age by authors of table.

Census data corrected for age, sex, and time periods provided the percentages for the comparison populations.

Alcoholism is significantly more frequent among the divorced and separated (Cahalan, Cisin, & Crossley, 1969; Gerard & Saenger, 1966). There is strong evidence that marital disruption is more prevalent among alcoholic marriages than among a matched group of nonalcoholic psychiatric patients (Wolf, 1958). Alcohol misuse is certainly destructive to family cohesiveness. Kephart (1954) analyzed 1,434 divorces randomly selected out of one Philadelphia court and noted that drinking was the stated reason for divorce in 21% of the cases. Kephart also analyzed the court records of 60,000 men legally charged by their wives during the period 1915–1949 with desertion and nonsupport. According to the wives of these men, drunkenness was a causal factor in 25% of all 60,000 desertions of family. Chafetz (1974) reports that in 41% of the families of an alcoholic person, there is considerable marital instability.

To what degree alcoholism is a cause or effect of marital instability is a question to be answered by further research.

THE TIME RELATIONSHIP BETWEEN MARITAL STATUS AND DRINKING PATTERNS AMONG ALCOHOLICS

There are few reliable data in the literature on when people marry in relationship to the onset of their alcoholism. This paucity of research is unfortunate since such data would elucidate the strengths and weaknesses of certain theories on alcoholic marriage. For example, the disturbed personality hypothesis (see Chapter 2) loses validity if well-controlled research reports that significant numbers of mates marry *before* there appeared to be any sign of a drinking problem.

Lemert (1960) (see page 50) interviewed 116 middle-class families contacted through a variety of public institutions and organizations and found that 52% of the wives had married at a time when their husbands already had a serious alcohol problem. Lemert (1960) states:

> This [finding] alters quite dramatically the "ideal typical" picture of a happy marriage in which a drinking problem merges from social drinking or from minor infrequent incidents of drunkenness or associated embarrassment to the spouse. In other words, the data show that large, heretofore unsuspected, number [sic] of spouses of alcoholics had been confronted with their problems full-blown at the time of marriage. (p. 683)

Clifford (1960) studied 50 wives of alcoholics and reported that all the women were aware of their spouse's alcoholism before marrying.

Jackson (1954), however, did a 3-year study of 50 Al-Anon wives and reports findings that are in contrast to those of Clifford and Lemert:

At the time marriage was considered, the drinking of most of the men was within socially acceptable limits . . . the women had no conception of what alcoholism meant other than it involved more than the usual frequency of drinking. (Jackson, 1954, p. 568)

Some theorists argue that Jackson's findings are the results of studying Al-Anon wives who are probably less likely to marry men who are recognizable alcoholics than the wives in other studies. [Jackson herself acknowledges this methodological weakness (see Footnote 1 in Chapter 4).] Lemert's (1960) data partially support this logic. Lemert divided the 105 wives in his sample into five subsamples depending on the source from which he obtained the subjects. The five sources were (1) alcoholics committed to a state hospital, (2) divorce cases in which alcoholism was the main reason for divorce, (3) Al-Anon wives who volunteered for the study, (4) welfare families, and (5) families from the County Probation Department. Lemert calculated the percentage of cases in each subsample in which the problem drinking preceded the marriage, and he found that the committment subsample was the lowest at 39% compared to 48% in the Al-Anon subsample. The proportions in the welfare, divorce, and probation cases were 55, 63, and 71% respectively.

James and Goldman (1971) randomly selected 299 names from a family service agency that dealt exclusively with problems associated with alcohol misuse. More than half of these people had moved from the city and several others refused to answer any questions, thereby leaving 85 wives who represented "the more permanently settled and cooperative wives" (p. 374). Of these 85 wives, 72% married before their husbands became "excessive" drinkers and 94% before their husbands became "alcoholics." This study supports the hypothesis that the wives who tend to do the most to help themselves and their families and who tend to volunteer for clinical research studies also tend as a group to marry before their husbands become problem drinkers.

Married couples should be evaluated for multiple personality and sociocultural variables, as was done by Rae and Forbes (1966), Rae (1972), and Rosenblatt, Gross, Malenowski, Broman, and Lewis (1971). Rae and Forbes demonstrated that when a group of 26 wives were categorized into specific MMPI profiles, the "439" (Psychopathic Deviate–Hysteria–Mania) profile category had a statistically greater premarital knowledge of problem drinking in the alcoholic spouse than the "273" (Depression–Psychaesthenia–Hysteria) profile category. In expanding on these ideas, Rae (1972) administered the MMPI to 58 couples in which one member was an alcoholic. Rae categorized the couples by MMPI profiles and reported that to a statistically significant degree Pd–Pd couples marry after manifestations of alcoholism, whereas non-Pd–Pd couples marry before drinking has become a problem.

Rosenblatt et al. (1971) studied the records of 805 consecutive male admissions for alcoholism to a New York City public psychiatric hospital in 1966. Of the 805 patients, 54% were first admissions and 46% were readmissions. The first admissions group showed a statistically significant lower frequency of divorce and separated marriages ($p < .05$) compared to the multiple admissions group. The mean age of Rosenblatt et al.'s first admissions and readmissions groups were not significantly different. When the variables of marital status and race were combined with age level, however, there were very significant differences between the first admissions group and the readmission group. For example, among the multiple admissions group in the age range 25–34, 37% were separated, whereas for the first admissions group in this age range the respective percentage was 21%. By combining the statistics from the Rosenblatt et al. (1971) study just mentioned, it was shown that in the age ranges 25–34 and 35–44, there was a significantly smaller percentage of separated and divorced in the first admissions group compared to the multiple admissions group.

Future investigations with larger samples must be done to learn more about the relationship between the onset of alcoholism and the date of marriage. It is most likely that systematic and rigorous investigation will show that no sweeping generalizations can be made.

SUMMARY AND DISCUSSION

Early studies gave a pessimistic slant to research results so that alcoholics were conceptualized as a stereotyped, unsocialized, homeless, antisocial, and mentally ill group of people who had a high rate of never being married and an even higher rate of separation and divorce. By broadening the sample of alcoholics, later reports fully established that alcoholics marry at the same rate as the rest of the population although they have a significantly higher rate of separation and divorce. Multiple variables account for the high rate of marital disruption, and there is a paucity of well-controlled studies to clarify these issues. If we make the safe assumption that the nonalcoholic spouse is frequently instrumental in implementing a divorce, however, we can use these data to challenge the concept that wives tend to *need* to be married to alcoholics.

The literature is mixed as to whether or not the nonalcoholic wife tends to marry before or after the onset of the husband's alcoholism, and it appears that no valid generalizations can be made on this issue. The increasing number of couples living together before marriage is another aspect of this area that must be considered in researching the relationship between the onset of alcohol abuse and the date of marriage.

A task of future research is to delineate and understand the various psychological and sociocultural variables in the alcoholic marriage.

REFERENCES

Ablon, J. Al-Anon family groups. Impetus for change through the presentation of alternatives. *American Journal of Psychotherapy*, 1974, *28*, 30–45.

Bacon, S. D. Inebriety, social integration and marriage. *(Memoirs of the Section on Alcohol Studies*, Yale University, No. 2). New Haven: Hillhouse Press, 1945. Also in *Quarterly Journal of Studies on Alcohol*, 1944, *5*, 86–125, 303–339.

Cahalan, D., Cisin, I. H., & Crossley, H. M. *American drinking practices*. New Brunswick, N.Y.: Rutgers Center of Alcohol Studies, 1969.

Chafetz, M. Health, Education, & Welfare Report, *Second special report to U.S. Congress on Alcohol and Health,* June 1974.

Clifford, B. J. A study of the wives of rehabilitated and unrehabilitated alcoholics. *Social Casework*, 1960, *41*, 457–460.

Corrigan, E. M. Woman and problem drinking. Notes on beliefs and fact. *Addictive Disease: An International Journal*, 1974, *1*, 215–222.

Curlee, J. A comparison of male and female patients at an alcoholism treatment center. *Journal of Psychology*, 1970, *74*, 239–247.

Fox, R. The alcoholic spouse. In V. W. Eisenstein (Ed.), *Neurotic interaction in marriage* (chap. 15). New York: Basic Books, 1956.

Gerard, D. L., & Saenger, G. *Outpatient treatment of alcoholism: A study of outcome and its determinants.* Toronto, Canada: Univ. of Toronto Press, 1966.

Heron, D. *A second study of extreme alcoholism in adults.* Eugenics Laboratory Memoirs, No. 17, London, 1912.

Hicks, M. W., & Platt, N. Marital happiness and stability: A review of the research in the 1960s. *Journal of Marriage and Family*, 1970, *32*, 553–574.

Jackson, J. K. The adjustment of the family to the crisis of alcoholism. *Quarterly Journal of Studies on Alcohol*, 1954, *15*, 562–586.

Jackson, J. K. Alcoholism and the family. In D. J. Pittman & C. R. Snyder (Eds.), *Society, culture and drinking patterns.* New York: Wiley, 1962, pp. 472–492.

Jacobson, P. H. *American marriage and divorce.* New York: Holt, 1959.

James, J. E., & Goldman, M. Behavior trends of wives of alcoholics. *Quarterly Journal of Studies on Alcohol*, 1971 (CAAAL 13769), *32*, 373–381.

Kephart, W. M. Drinking and marital disruption: A research note. *Quarterly Journal of Studies on Alcohol*, 1954, *15*, 63–73.

Kinsey, B. A. *The female alcoholic: A social psychological study.* Springfield, Ill.: Thomas, 1966.

Lemert, E. M. The occurrence and sequence of events in the adjustment of families to alcoholism. *Quarterly Journal of Studies on Alcohol,* 1960, *21,* 679–697.

Lindbeck, V. L. The woman alcoholic: A review of the literature. *International Journal of Addictions,* 1972, *7,* 567–580.

Lisansky, E. S. Alcoholism in women: Social and psychological concomitants. I. Social history data. *Quarterly Journal of Studies on Alcohol,* 1957, *18,* 583–623.

Lisansky, E. S. The woman alcoholic. *Annals of the American Academy of Political and Social Science,* 1958, *315,* 73–81.

Malzberg, B. A study of first admissions with alcoholic psychoses in New York State, 1943–1944, *Quarterly Journal of Studies on Alcohol,* 1947, *8,* 274–295.

Malzberg, B. First admissions with alcoholic psychoses in New York State, year ended March 31, 1948. With a note on first admissions for alcoholism without psychoses. *Quarterly Journal of Studies on Alcohol,* 1949, *10,* 461–470.

Mann, M. *New primer on alcoholism.* New York: Holt, 1958.

Paolino, T. J. Unpublished manuscript. 1974.

Rae, J. B. The influence of the wives on the treatment outcomes of alcoholics: A follow-up study of two years. *British Journal of Psychiatry,* 1972, *120,* 601–613.

Rae, J. B., & Forbes, A. R. Clinical and psychometric characteristics of the wives of alcoholics. *British Journal of Psychiatry,* 1966, *112,* 197–200.

Rimmer, J., Reich, T., & Winokur, G. Alcoholism vs. diagnosis and clinical variation among alcoholics. *Quarterly Journal of Studies on Alcohol,* 1972, *33,* 658–666.

Rosenbaum, B. Married women alcoholics at the Washingtonian Hospital. *Quarterly Journal of Studies on Alcohol,* 1958, *19,* 79–89.

Rosenblatt, S. M., Gross, M. M., & Chartoff, S. Marital status and multiple psychiatric admissions for alcoholism. *Quarterly Journal of Studies on Alcohol,* 1969, *30,* 445–447.

Rosenblatt, S. M., Gross, M. M., Malenowski, B., Broman, M., & Lewis, E. Marital status and multiple psychiatric admissions for alcoholism: A cross validation. *Quarterly Journal of Studies on Alcohol,* 1971, *32,* 1092–1096.

Schneyer, S. The marital status of alcoholics: A note on an analysis of the marital status of 2,008 patients of nine clinics. *Quarterly Journal of Studies on Alcohol,* 1954, *15,* 325–329.

Schuckit, M. The alcoholic woman: A literature review. *Psychiatry in Medicine,* 1972, *3,* 37–43.

Straus, R., & Bacon, S. D. Alcoholism and social stability: A study of occupational integration in 2,023 male clinicians. *Quarterly Journal of Studies on Alcohol,* 1951, *12,* 231–260.

Towle, L. H. Alcoholism treatment outcome in different populations, *Proceedings from the Fourth Annual Alcohol Conference of the NIAAA,* April 1974.

Wellman, W. M., Maxwell, M. A., & O'Halloren, P. Private hospital alcoholic patients and the changing conception of the "typical" alcoholic. *Quarterly Journal of Studies on Alcohol,* 1957, *18,* 388–404.

Wolf, I. Alcoholism and marriage, *Quarterly Journal of Studies on Alcohol,* 1958, *19,* 511–513.

Appendix B

Defense Mechanisms

In this appendix, we have listed some of the defense mechanisms that are commonly discussed in the psychoanalytic literature. For each definition, we give a clinical example that might commonly be seen in an alcoholic marriage. The reader should bear in mind three points: (1) The application of these defense mechanisms to the alcoholic marriage was quite common among the DPH (and DH) adherents. (2) The proponents of the sociological, learning, and systems theory perspectives would not rely on the concept of defense mechanisms to describe the clinical material. (3) The definition of "defense mechanisms" (see page 26) is that of an *unconscious* ego process in an attempt to resolve intrapsychic conflicts.

As mentioned in chapter 2 an in-depth discussion of defense mechanisms and the underlying psychoanalytic principles is beyond the scope of this book. We refer those readers interested in pursuing these concepts further to the various descriptions in the psychoanalytic literature, such as Anna Freud (1936), Hendrick (1958), Laplanche and Pontalis (1967), Moore and Fine (1968), Sjöbäck (1973), and Vaillant (1971).

Conversion. Conversion is a defense mechanism in which intrapsychic conflicts are manifested in a symbolic skeletal motor or sensory expression.

For example, a spouse might experience a wish to act violently toward her alcoholic husband. The spouse fears this wish and so resolves the intrapsychic conflict by developing limb paralysis or blindness toward the husband.

Compensation. Compensation is a defense mechanism in which the person strives to make up for actual or imagined inadequacies.

A common example of compensation is athletic endeavors to make up for inferior academic achievements. Another example is the spouse who seeks professional success to make up for her "failure" as a wife.

Denial (disavowal, psychotic denial). Generally speaking, denial is the mental process by which a person unconsciously refuses to acknowledge or excludes from awareness unpleasant feelings or thoughts. As with all defense mechanisms, denial can be adaptive or maladaptive.

For example, we all adaptively deny the imminence of tragedy, sickness, and death. If, however, a loved one dies, it would be maladaptive to persistently refuse awareness of the sad fact.

Sometimes "denial" is used to refer to a more specific phenomenon of "psychotic denial." "Psychotic denial" is a primitive, immature, and pathological defense mechanism in which the ego avoids conscious awareness of elements of external reality that are, for various reasons, unacceptable or painful. Usually psychotic denial is accompanied by a persistence in acting out the fantasies accompanying the denial. For example, in the case of a wife who denies her husband's alcoholism, denial of psychotic proportions would mean that the wife would not only fail to recognize the alcoholism but proceeds to think, feel, and act as if the husband had no problem with alcoholism at all.

Distortion. Distortion is a primitive defense mechanism in which the person grossly falsifies and misrepresents external reality in order to satisfy intrapsychic conflicts (Vaillant, 1971). Examples of distortion are beliefs inconsistent with intellectual development, delusions of wish fulfillment, hallucinations, and feelings of grandiosity or total worthlessness.

An example of distortion in the alcoholic marriage might be a wife's *conviction* that despite years of alcohol abuse, "one of these days" the husband will stop his drinking on his own accord. Distortion is usually not very adaptively successful, a fault found in all the primitive defense mechanisms. Certain religious beliefs, however, serve as examples of the capacity for distortion to be successfully adaptive.

Distortion differs from projection in that in distortion, unacceptable thoughts or feelings are replaced by grossly reshaped conterparts, whereas in projection, the unacceptable thoughts or feelings might not be changed at all but the responsibility for them assigned to something or someone other than the self.

Incorporation. Incorporation is a primitive defense mechanism in which the person metaphorically swallows or otherwise ingests a psychic representation of an object. The object usually is a person or part of a person.

During the oral psychosexual stage, incorporation is a frequent instinctual aim and a means of establishing object relationships. For example, a common fantasy of the infant is that the mother's breast has been swallowed and is now a part of the consumer. It must be remembered that incorporation is not necessarily only associated with the mouth or the oral stage. Other psychosexual stages, erotogenic zones, and bodily processes might also be involved in the fantasy of taking an object into one's self. For example, incorporation can occur via rectum, skin, lungs, ears, or eyes. It is not uncommon to see psychoanalytic literature associating alcoholism itself with incorporation whereby the drinking is viewed as a repetitive behavior of incorporating the alcohol, a symbol of some childhood object such as the breast.

Displacement. In displacement the ego transfers a thought, feeling, or instinctual impulse from one object to a more acceptable object that is related to the original object by a series of associations. A common example of displacement is the anger that a spouse might show toward her children, following an argument with her alcoholic husband. Although displacement is especially noticeable in dreams and mental illness, the mechanism also occurs to some degree in all waking people and plays a role in a variety of psychic phenomena, such as jokes, phobias, and prejudices.

Freud attempted to differentiate between displacement and *projection* by proposing that in the former a person or object is the recipient of the affect, whereas in the latter the transferred feeling or thought is attributed to the substituted person or object. Also, Freud at times distinguished displacement from *conversion:* displacement was described as a phenomenon occurring between ideas and thus more common in obsessional neurotics, whereas in *conversion hysteria* the affect is disregarded and the psychic energy is displaced from an idea to the body (Laplanche & Pontalis, 1967, p. 122). At other times, however, Freud referred to displacement as a general feature of all mental functioning including all symptoms. By this perspective, all "objects" can be seen as a result of displacement from the original object of an infantile instinctual wish. Also, in this general sense of the word, all defense mechanisms can be a form of displacement. For example, *conversion* itself can be a displacement of psychic energy from an idea to the somatic realm.

Idealization. Idealization is a defense mechanism in which an admired characteristic or aspect of an object is overrated or overvalued, sometimes to the point of perfection.

An example of idealization in the alcoholic marriage might be the high esteem in which the spouse holds the alcoholic husband despite his abuse of her.

Identification. Identification is the defense mechanism in which real or imagined components of another person's personality become part of one's own thoughts through a process of assimilation and patterning. The *conscious* counterpart of identification is *"imitation."*

Identification is especially important during the child's developmental years, when, for example, the little boy's conflict of love–hate toward his father is partially resolved by identification with the father. As discussed on page 31, pro-DPH adherents frequently assert that the spouses of male alcoholics "identify" with their mothers and thus choose alcoholics as husbands.

Isolation.   Isolation is a defense mechanism in which a thought or feeling is separated from other associatively connected thoughts and feelings. Isolation manifests itself in any procedure that contributes to an interruption in the temporal succession of thoughts and feelings, such as a pause in thought or speech or a memory gap or a ritual.

An example of isolation might be a wife telling the therapist of an incident when the husband beat her but showing none of the fear that she felt during the actual experience.

Projection.   Projection is a defense mechanism in which the person either refuses to recognize or repudiates as a part of himself painful thoughts or feelings (including qualities or objects) and then attributes the unacceptable thoughts or feelings to another person or thing. Projection has many manifestations. Some examples are unsupportable suspicion as a way to avoid intimacy, excessive caution to external danger, "blind" prejudice, and unwarranted hatred (Vaillant, 1971).

An example of projection in the alcoholic marriage might be the alcoholic complaining of his wife's dependence when in fact it is he who lacks autonomy.

Rationalization.   Rationalization is a defense mechanism in which the person attempts to explain unconscious motivation of unacceptable thoughts or feelings by presenting logically consistent or ethically acceptable reasoning.

Rationalization is very common and occurs in all aspects of normal and abnormal thought and behavior. At times, it is difficult to distinguish a well-integrated rationalization from a simple truthful explanation of a motive or behavior. Other forms of rationalization, especially those of grossly aberrant behavior, are more easily noticeable. For example, the wife of an alcoholic who has a need to be married to someone who abuses her might rationalize her behavior by arguing that she loves the man.

Many psychoanalysts do not consider rationalization a defense mechanism since rationalization is aimed at concealing other defense mechanisms rather turning directly against the unwarranted thoughts or feelings. In other words, the defense mechanisms themselves are rationalized. Etiological beliefs, political persuasions, and religious convictions can be considered rationalizations of defense mechanisms whereby the superego allies itself with ego defense (LaPlanche & Pontalis 1967, p. 376).

Reaction formation. Reaction formation is a defense mechanism in which specific thoughts, feelings, or behavior are adopted that diametrically oppose their unacceptable counterparts. For example, a recovered alcoholic might become a zealot for abstinence in response to unconscious urges to drink. The probability of a reaction formation being labeled a "symptom" is determined by the degree of maladaptability or social aberrancy that is characteristic of the chosen reaction formation.

No matter how generalized and well integrated a reaction formation is, it is frequently possible to recognize the thought or feeling against which the person is reacting. For example, in an obsesseive compulsive personality disorder, it is not uncommon to observe abrupt outbursts that are quite inconsistent with the usually rigid moral personality. These inconsistent outbursts are what sometimes help us to become aware of the symptomatic defensive role played by the otherwise adaptive personality traits (Laplanche & Pontalis, 1967 p. 378).

Another revealing sign of the symptomatic nature of the personality trait is that the person may follow the defensive position to such an extreme that he satisfies the forbidden wish. For example, the recovered alcoholic who becomes the zealot for abstinence for all people gets so involved in censoring liquor that he has immersed himself in the very subject against which he reacts. Or the obsessive compulsive housewife who is so thorough in her housekeeping with a supposed reaction against dirt that she has totally immersed herself in dust and dirt.

Another way to recognize a reaction formation is to observe how it might be less likely to be generalized into well-integrated personality traits and more likely to be localized into specific behaviors and particular relationships. For example, the wife of an alcoholic might be very loving with a husband whom she unconsciously hates, but she probably would not react to this hate by showing generalized love and pity toward all men.

Repression. Repression has two psychoanalytic meanings: the strict definition and the generic usage. According to the strict definition, repression is a defense mechanism in which unacceptable ideas or feelings, especially those directly bound to an instinct, are unconsciously repelled from consciousness. The ego puts repression into action because the satisfaction of that particular wish or instinct is considered potentially more painful than the deprivation of its satisfaction. This specific application of the word "repression" occurs in a variety of normal and abnormal behaviors, especially hysterical neuroses, and manifests itself in a variety of ways from apparently unexplainable naiveté and minute memory lapses to a severe pathological lack of perception of internal (intrapsychic) events. The "forgetting" or repression is unusual in that clear symbolic mental activity frequently accompanies the memory loss, thus indicating that the repressed elements are not totally forgotten.

As for the generic application, the term repression is essentially synonymous with "defense." The generic usage implies that repression is an initial stage as well as the prototype of all defense mechanisms.

Repression is distinguishable from denial although the two mechanisms frequently occur together. Denial interferes with the perception and recognition of *internal* (intrapsychic) events, i.e., thoughts, feelings, and instincts. For example, if a wife were angry at her alcoholic husband for hitting her, but she denied this anger or forgot some important detail of the incident, then this would be repression. In contrast, if she denied the existence of her husband's violence potential or if he denied the existence of the wound inflicted by him, then this would be denial (psychotic denial, see page 189).

Sublimation. Sublimation is a defense mechanism in which sexual drives (especially the component instincts, such as oral and anal drives) are diverted from sexual aims to nonsexual aims that are more acceptable to the ego and the superego. By the use of sublimation, the person is able to achieve an indirect or reduced direct expression of instinct without the usual painful consequences. Thus, an instinct can be considered sublimated if its energies are deflected via a nonsexual aim toward a socially valued object.

There are innumerable possible manifestations of sublimation. A traditional example of sublimated activity is the satisfaction of aggressive instincts through pleasurable sports and hobbies. Another common example of sublimation is the function of a romantic and socially acceptable courtship as a way of attenuating the sexual and instinctual drives. An example of sublimation in the alcoholic marriage could be the wife experiencing sexual frustration and sublimating these needs through artistic and intellectual activities.

Sublimation differs from displacement and projection. In *projection*, the person denies the existence within himself of some unacceptable feeling or thought and attributes it to someone else. In *displacement*, the person acknowledges the uncomfortable feeling or thought as belonging to himself but then transposes it to an object in a manner that offers very little, if any, instinctual satisfaction. In *sublimation*, the person acknowledges the existence of the feelings and thoughts within himself and then redirects the feelings or thoughts toward an object so that there results a certain amount of instinctual expression and satisfaction.

Substitution. Symbolization is a defense mechanism in which an unacceptable or unattainable thought, feeling, or object is replaced by one that is more acceptable or less unattainable.

Actually, substitution occurs to some degree in most, if not all, defense mechanisms. It is easier to conceptualize substitution as a quality of defense mechanisms rather than a specific type, and some analysts think that substitution should be excluded from the category of defense mechanisms.

REFERENCES

Freud, A. (1936). *The ego and the mechanisms of defense.* New York: International Univ. Press, 1946.

Hendrick, I. *Facts and theories of psychoanalysis* (3rd ed.). New York: Alfred A. Knopf, 1958.

Laplanche, J., & Pontalis, J. B. *The language of psychoanalysis.* New York: Norton, 1967.

Moore, B. E., & Fine, B. D. *A glossary of psychoanalytic terms and concepts* (2nd ed.). New York: American Psychoanalytic Assoc. 1968, p. 31.

Sjöbäck, H. *The psychoanalytic theory of defensive processes.* New York: Halsted Press, 1973.

Vaillant, G. Theoretical hierarchy of adaptive ego mechanisms. *Archives of General Psychiatry,* 1971, *24,* 107–118.

Appendix C

Differentiation of Self

Murray Bowen has been an early and a major figure in articulating family systems theory concepts. His major concept is that of the "undifferentiated family ego mass" (Bowen, 1971, p. 171), which he defined as "a conglomerate emotional oneness that exists in all levels of intensity—from the family in which it is most intense to the family in which it is almost imperceptible" (Bowen, 1971, p. 171). A common example of the concept is when a spouse states that she knows "exactly" what her husband was thinking and "just why" he started drinking. Such certitude reflects a lack of clear, recognized boundaries between herself and her husband.

Each individual in a family can be characterized by his own level of differentiation. Bowen has broken differentiation roughly into four levels:

1. Lowest quarter: These persons are characterized by being dependent on the feelings of those around them. Much of their energy goes into maintaining the relationship system, obtaining "love," or feeling comfortable. They make no differentiation between feeling and intellect. The only use of the word "I" is in terms of desires and pains, as opposed to convictions and beliefs.

2. Second quarter: Persons at this level are characterized by less intense ego fusions and have a poorly defined self. The focus of these people is still primarily on feelings in that they are responsive to emotional harmony or disharmony around them and their feelings climb with approval and crash with disapproval. Their sense of their own success is based on approval rather than on the inherent value of work or relationships. They have some elemental awareness of opinions and beliefs, but these thoughts are usually dogmatic, compliant, or rebellious.

3. Persons in the third quarter have a high level of differentiation and a lower degree of ego fusion. They hold well-defined opinions and beliefs, but with great pressure for conformity they will compromise their principles and make decisions based on their feelings. Such a person would avoid stating an opinion that was quite different from his group, although he might maintain that different opinion privately. They have

more energy for goal-directed activity and less energy involved in keeping an equilibrium.

4. Persons in the highest group are never seen in clinical practice. They are principle-oriented, goal-directed, and sure of their beliefs and convictions but not dogmatic. They are not particularly affected by praise or criticism. They can respect the identity of another person and become involved without trying to change them. They assume responsibility for themselves but are at the same time aware of their dependence on other people. They are able to form intense relationships without a need for the other that impairs that person or themselves.

In a marriage, each member of the couple uses the mechanisms previously used in their family of origin to deal with each other. If emotional distance was the norm, it will be used again. If extreme fusion was the norm, this will likely be the mode for the new couple. There are several mechanisms used to control the intensity of such fusion, however, most notably marital conflict, dysfunction in one of the spouses, or transmission of the problem to one or more of the children.

The degree of differentiation of a family is largely determined by the differentiation of the parents, although some children may be of higher or lower degree of differentiation. Children who are allowed some distance from the family are most likely to establish a slightly higher degree of differentiation of self, whereas those most closely bound into the family are most likely to show a lower level of differentiation. Over generations, there can be a gradual drift downward or upward in the degree of differentiation of each succeeding generation.

REFERENCES

Bowen, M. The use of family theory in clinical practice. In J. Haley (Ed.), *Changing families: A family therapy reader.* New York: Grune & Stratton, 1971.

Appendix D

Transactional Analysis

Transactional Analysis (TA) is a theoretical system created to provide a language of concepts applicable to interactional events. Developed by Eric Berne, TA utilizes simple, familiar, and sometimes fanciful language to express its ideas. The emphasis of the system is on analyzing behavior to effect *change* rather than on understanding as an end in itself.

The *transaction* is the basic unit considered in TA. A transaction occurs when one person makes a response that indicates recognition of another's presence. The second person in turn makes some response to the initial occurrence. These two behaviors, one from each person, constitute the transaction.

There are four levels of analysis in TA: (1) structural analysis of an individual's thoughts, feelings, and behaviors; (2) transactional analysis of two persons interactions; (3) analysis of short-term ways in which people structure time; and (4) analysis of long-term means of structuring time, also known as life scripts. We examine each of these four levels of analysis in turn.

Each person is considered to exist at any moment in one of three ego states, the Parent, Adult, or Child. (The term ego as used here is similar to the psychoanalytic concept of the conscious self, as opposed to the Ego, a macrostructure of the mind.) When capitalized, the terms Parent, Adult, and Child refer to ego states, whereas lower case letters refer to real people. The three ego states are "coherent systems of thought and feeling manifested by corresponding patterns of behavior" (Berne, 1972, p. 11). The Parent ego state represents "a huge collection of recordings in the brain of unquestioned or imposed external events perceived by a person in his early years" (Harris, 1967, p. 18). When young, a child observes his parents' responses, feelings, dictums, and initially he accepts them unconditionally as truths. He is unable at this early stage to question, modify through reason, or modulate this information. As an adult, the parental messages still strongly affect individual behavior. For example, the parental directive, "Don't go into the street without looking both ways" stays with us throughout our lives. When a person is behaving from his Parent, he thinks, feels, and behaves just as his parents did when he was a child. Thus, when a father cautions his son not to go into the street, his Parent is operating. Similarly, when he instructs his wife to look where she is going when driving, his Parent is in control. Note the similarity to the role of the superego, discussed in chapter 2.

The Child ego state encompasses all the internal reactions that the child had in response to the parent's behavior. Thus, the Child is primarily emotional, representing both the warm, happy, positive feelings coming from happy times with his parents as well as the fear, anger, and feelings of worthlessness that come with discipline and reprimands. Creativity, exploration, curiosity, and sensory awareness are also in the Child's province. When the Child is in control, the person is responding on an emotional level. Thus, if the wife who was told to be careful while driving were to feel hurt or think herself a bad driver or become angry at her husband and pout, her Child would be in control. If she and her husband were running hand-in-hand through a meadow of spring flowers, laughing and happy, her Child would also be in charge.

The third ego state, the Adult, is believed to originate when a child finally is able to accomplish things that originate from his own thoughts, actions, or awareness rather than wholly in reponse to his parents. The Adult has been described as the computer, which gathers information, weighs data against past experience and present alternatives, examines the validity of Parent data relevant to the current problem, determines what Child feelings may safely be expressed, computes probabilities, and comes to a decision on the basis of all these data. Thus, if a person is presented with feedback that his drinking is getting to be a real problem, and he listens, examines how his drinking is interfering, and comes to a logical conclusion that he should stop drinking, get treatment, cut down, or that indeed there is no problem, then his Adult is in control.

Generally, TA represents a person as the total of her or his three ego states, Parent, Adult, and Child. Graphically represented, it looks like this:

The second level of analysis in TA, transactional analysis, examines transactions between two people. To analyze a transaction, one must assess from which ego state a message is being sent and to what ego state it is being directed. Additionally, the receiver's response must also be analyzed in regard to what ego state is in control, and to what ego state the response is directed. There are four types of transactions: complementary, crossed, ulterior, and duplex.

The simplest transaction to understand is a *complementary* transaction. In this transaction, communication from one person's ego state to another is reciprocated by a response directed to the sender's sending ego state. For example, if an alcoholic's wife says, "All you do is drink, you're ruining your life," she is communicating from her Parent to her husband's Child. If his response is from his Child to her Parent, as in, "Get off my back, all you do is nag at me," this is a complementary transaction (although not a complimentary one). Diagrammatically represented, it looks like this:

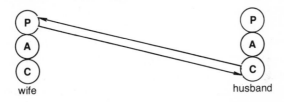

If, however, the husband responded, "I've been worried about my drinking lately, do you know where I could go to get some help?" he would be responding from his Adult to hers. Responding from a different ego state than that toward which the message was directed and directing a response to other than the sender's current ego state results in the second type of transaction, a *crossed* transaction:

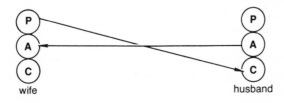

A third type of transaction is an *ulterior* one in which a transaction ostensibly is directed at one ego state but is actually designed to hook a response from another ego state. Beer commercials for lower calorie beers ostensibly appeal to an Adult desire to cut calories. The use of actors who act tough, stereotypically masculine, and somewhat intimidating, however, represents a covert appeal to the viewer's Child.

The fourth type of transaction, the *duplex* transaction, involves different communications on the psychological and social levels.

Persons exist on more than a transaction-to-transaction basis. According to TA, people use various strategies to structure their interpersonal time into predictable, repetitive patterns. The patterns may operate over short periods of time or over months, years, or a lifetime.

There are six ways to structure time short-term. In *withdrawal* there is no overt communication between two people. In *rituals,* two persons engage in formal or informal stylized interchanges, which are totally predictable. Wedding ceremonies represent a clear example of a ritual transaction. Informal rituals, however, operate in many drinking circles involving predictable greetings, "Hey, how're ya doing?" a stylized way of taking an order, "What'll it be?" and a predictable response, "The usual." Of course, the quotes are different for different groups, just as wedding ceremonies vary across religions. The important aspect is the predictable, stylized pattern involved.

A third way to structure time is through *activity* or work, in which the transactions are determined by the materials involved. *Pastimes* also represent repetitive interactions. Berne describes these as "socially programed by talking about acceptable subjects in acceptable ways" (Berne, 1972, p. 23). Discussions of last night's football game at the club or day-after discussions of a group of men who had celebrated at a stag party thus take a fairly predictable, accepted course, although the precise content is not predetermined in the same way that ritualistic interchanges are determined.

The fifth form of time structuring is the *game,* which is a set of repetitive, ulterior transactions that result in some form of psychological payoff to the participants. Games involve four necessary and sufficient features, the "con," the "hook," the "switch," and the "payoff." Examples of alcoholic games are described on pages 126–128. The final type of time structuring is *intimacy,* "a candid, game-free relationship, with mutual free giving and receiving and without exploitation" (Berne, 1972, p. 25). Intimacy clearly involves complementary transactions and is the most difficult to achieve of the ways to structure time.

Long-term time structures are referred to as *life scripts.* Scripts are life plans that arrange behavior over longer periods of time. Scripts may be directed toward failure, financial success, intimacy, conflict, and so on. It is Berne's contention that determining a person's script illuminates the meaning and purpose of much of his or her behavior.

REFERENCES

Berne, E. *What do you say after you say hello?* New York: Bantam Books, 1972.

Harris, P. A. *I'm okay–You're okay. A practical guide to Transactional Analysis.* New York: Harper, 1967.

Index

Page numbers in italics refer to figures. Page numbers followed by t refer to tables.